GULICK

PRAISE for SUSAN SILVER & *ORGANIZED TO BE THE BEST!*
(See also back cover comments)

- **Winner of the Benjamin Franklin Award, presented during the American Booksellers Association convention.**

- **Selected repeatedly by more than 10 book clubs!**

- **More than one-quarter million copies in print!**

A practical approach to improving organizational skills...a sound how-to, recommended.

> —*Booklist*, the literary review journal of the American Library Assn.

The title of the book says it all. *Organized to be the Best!* is the single best resource that I know of for anyone who wants to get more control of their time, computer, paperwork, work space or life in general. It's a state-of-the-art tool kit, resource guide, time management seminar and personal consultant all rolled into one.

> —**Michael LeBoeuf, Ph.D**, Author of *How to Win Customers and Keep Them For Life*, Metairie, Louisiana

Organized to be the Best! is a must read for today's busy career professional. This user-friendly guide is comprehensive in its content and engaging in its style. It is the bible of organization.

> —**Lee Gardenswartz, Ph.D.** and **Anita Rowe, Ph.D**, Co-authors, *What It Takes*, Los Angeles, California

This book has truly made it possible for me to increase my productivity by one and a half fold. My filing system is manageable and understandable for the first time in my life.

> —**Robert Simon, M.D.**, Chairman of the Board, International Medical Corps, and Professor and Chairman, Department of Emergency Medicine, Cook County Hospital, Chicago, Illinois

Your book was a delight to read and a tremendous help to me in setting up my home office. Your suggestions were most valuable in helping me decide upon an arrangement of furniture and resources. I was able to create an efficient filing system. I enjoy working in my office and feel I can accomplish much more because I have planned well for my needs.

> —**Ilana Hoffman**, Editor, *Portland Parent Newsmagazine*, Oregon

Worth a year in college.

> —**Fred DeLuca**, President and Founder, Subway Sandwiches and Salads

more...

Organized to be the Best! is an invaluable training tool that I used with participants in Personal Productivity Management training programs at the Jet Propulsion Laboratory. Each participant received a copy of the book, which served as both training material during the program and a take-away resource they used after the program. What's great about this book is that it shows such a wide variety of useful ideas and has something for everyone. It has both depth and breadth and does not have to be read sequentially.

—**Nancy Ferguson**, Former Training Specialist, Jet Propulsion
Laboratory, Pasadena, California

The impact of the time I spent with you continues to multiply. As you recommended, I set up a daily/monthly tickler file system to improve follow-up on the growing number of projects that I manage. I've trained myself to check it each day. It has really helped me stay on top of deadlines. Then working with my staff we created a tickler slip system we could all use. I am now delegating more confidently because I have an organized way of following up with people. I am saving time because I have the tools to move through my paperwork more quickly. Thanks for your ideas, coaching and advice!

—**Terry Preuit**, Training Director, Los Angeles, California

Finally...a book on organizational techniques that I can use to help coach my clients toward peak performance! Your straight forward, immediately applicable book fills a critical gap in my coaching library.

—**Lois P. Frankel**, Ph.D., Partner, The Frankel & Fox Group,
Consultants in Employee Development, Los Angeles, California

I've found your book to be really helpful, especially the time management and computer organization material. This ought to be standard issue for administrative people.

—**Alan C. Macdonald**, Vice President, Citibank, New York City

Susan Silver offers a wealth of practical advice and ideas from which even the most diligently organized of us can benefit.

—**Sanford C. Sigoloff**, President and CEO, Sigoloff & Associates, Inc.
Los Angeles, California

Organized to be the Best! is fantastic for getting organized! It's very easy to read and is *usable* as well as useful."

—**Patrick P. Grace**, President, Grace Logistics Services, Inc.

Organized to be the Best! will help anyone achieve his or her goals. I heartily recommend it.

—**Robert Kotler, M.D.**, FACS, Author, *The Consumer's Guide to Cosmetic Facial Surgery*, Los Angeles, California

Organized to be the Best! is one of the few books I keep referring back to for organizing ideas and product resources. It's an excellent resource book with numerous illustrations of office products and accessories and good suggestions on how to use them. It's also the only book of its kind to cover organizing of computer files. I've recommended it to over a thousand clients and students.

   –Harriet Schechter, Professional Organizer and Owner, The Miracle
      Worker Organizing Service, San Diego, California

Your book is great, fills a gap and is readily useful to organizer colleagues.

   –Paulette Ensign, President, Organizing Solutions
      Bedford Hills, New York

You have written a very useful and easily accessed guide for helping the public get organized, but also, for organizers or the organized public to continue to use as a reference for deciding which organizing tool to use.

   –Maxine Ordesky, President, Organized Designs
      Beverly Hills, California

As an attorney in a solo practice, I'm trying to make the office more efficient. The book was helpful for my legal assistant and me to organize our work and our office. It gets right down to the brass tacks.

   –Shirley A. Bass, Attorney at Law, Portland, Oregon

I was literally drowning in paperwork. Then I bought your book. It was the perfect solution. So far, I have put to use at least one suggestion from each of your chapters. Order is finally being created from chaos. And, I really love your practical approach to keeping your readers up to date on new office products via illustrations and diagrams. I can now just photocopy the appropriate picture and hand it to my assistant to order. Thank you for a terrific book.

   –Kori Lee Garner, Reference Librarian, University Library
      California State University, Fullerton, California

From advice on managing time, to assistance on creating efficient work space, *Organized to be the Best!* has it all. It showed me how to tame my chaotic schedule, clear the clutter from my home office and generally bring order to my life...the most helpful book on the subject that I've come across.

   –Elane Osborn, Novelist, *Skylark*, Reno, Nevada

I have read and used *Organized to be the Best!* in my work with clients, most of whom have Attention Deficit Disorder, through individual therapy and group therapy. Your suggestions are helpful and accommodate a range of learning styles quite nicely.

   –Mary-Jane Beach, M.Ed., LCSW, LMFT, Hyannis, Massachusetts

I have a long-standing prejudice that I understand my daily routines fairly well, and that help from consultants will not be too helpful. In relation to your book, this turns out not to be true. I read it a chapter at a time, over the last month, and I found it very helpful. What did I like? First, in time management, I liked the notion of A, B and C priorities. Second, keeping track of paperwork is a big problem for me because I have a multidimensional job and many interests. Two little things helped: 1) my desktop file rack is for *active working files* only and 2) taking five or ten minutes at the end of a day to put papers away makes it easier to be creative tomorrow.

  –**Peter Lev, Ph.D.**, Professor, Towson State University, Maryland

What a pleasure to tell you how much I enjoyed reading *Organized to be the Best!* I'm very excited about the useful information it contains; it has given me the inspiration to actually put your ideas into use, *right now!*

  –**Eadye Martinson**, Executive Secretary, Everett, Washington

Two hours with Susan changed my life. I turned a wasted room into a wonderful working environment. I had thought I should be able to do it myself. Wrong! Her guidance was what I needed.

  –**Sharon Bloom, Ph.D.**, Psychotherapist, Los Angeles, California

We all felt the opportunities presented by you for organizing our daily life in the office were without equal. Thank you for increasing our office's efficiency, positively! Your sessions were a catalyst to which our entire staff responded so enthusiastically that we are still buzzing over your presentation, discussions and the projects you inspired. And I have a new "bible"—your book!

  –**Robert Aronoff**, Former Controller, Weight Watchers of Southern California

It's obvious there's much work and love put into *Organized to be the Best!* It's a motivating book and the resources are excellent!

  –**Elaine Wilkes**, President, Show & Tell Multimedia, Los Angeles

Susan has a remarkable talent for identifying habits and work conditions which are unnecessary complications and prevent you from becoming more productive. She has a first-rate ability for selecting the tools or ideas that are best suited to your style and needs. Add to this the fact that she is a delight to work with and you have an invaluable consultant who can make a real difference in your productivity.

  –**Waltona Manion**, Public Relations Professional, San Diego, Calif.

Thank you for your book. Even the title is an inspiration to get started. In addition to providing a wealth of information, it is also well written and enjoyable to read. And when I go to an office supply store I can now point to the organizer I want to buy; I just bring your book along and point to the illustrations.

    —**Patricia L. Stewart**, AT&T Marketing Manager, New Jersey

...brilliant—definitely the best I've ever read—and I've read a lot. I liked that the focus initially was on goal determination rather than just purely getting organized. You named names, lots of resources to easily find and purchase products mentioned in the book. There's a lot of focus on computer applications; I'm impressed with how computer literate you are.

    —**Margaret H. Briggs**, Ph.D., Speech-Language Therapist, Pasadena, California

Organized to be the Best! is concisely comprehensive, giving insight into the overall organizational plan while focusing in on its components—an excellent guide through the organizational maze!

    —**Meryl Perloff**, ASID, Meryl Perloff Interiors, San Luis Obispo, California

Your book covered 90 percent of my work day—it would probably apply to my whole company.

    —**Jenny Prevatte**, Director of Computer Operations, Associated Brokers, Inc., Charlotte, North Carolina

I bought your book on a Saturday, finished reading it Sunday morning, went to the office Sunday afternoon to organize my desk and on Monday, I gave your quick self survey to all the employees at our Monday morning meeting and asked who wanted to read it. The vote was unanimous and I'm looking forward to organizing our whole company to be the best!

    —**Mark Taylor**, President, Evcor Systems Designers, Plymouth, Michigan

Your book gives lots of practical, easy-to-use suggestions in specific areas—you can just pick out what you need.

    —**Linda Watts**, Training Consultant, Tasmania, Australia

Thanks for writing this book! With multiple meetings every day, I am always at a loss for time. Your book has some great ideas that I'm implementing. Now I will get more out of every day!

    —**Mark Stevenson**, Special Agent, Northwestern Mutual Life, Bennington, Vermont

I have just finished your book and found it terrific! I believe that the basics in an office library are: 1) a good dictionary, 2) a good grammar book and 3) a copy of *Organized to be the Best!*

    —**Sharon Leahy**, Vice President, Tri-United Realty Development & Management Associates, Skokie, Illinois

Tremendously informative and useful...great to see Macintosh issues addressed in your book. I liked the details about suggested resources.
  —**Elsie M. Schaszberger**, Captain, USAF, NC

It's amazing! Your book worked! I work for an electrical utility in a small town in Northern Ontario, Canada. We inherited a young manager a couple of years ago and haven't seen the top of his desk since then. Last week I gave him your book opened at Chapter 4 and mentioned he might find some useful ideas. I saw results the next day. All his notes were in one pile and by the end of the week, his desk was completely cleared. Also, I gave him some correspondence and he filed it immediately! I quickly praised him and told him how impressed I was. (I was!!!) Thank you, thank you, thank you.
  —**Peggy Wikiruk**, Billing & Accounting Clerk, Ontario, Canada

Concise, easy to read and *so* appropriate for today's work environment.
  —**Dave Webb**, Supplier Standards Manager, Purchasing, Finning Ltd.,
  Vancouver, British Columbia, Canada

The list of nine questions for evaluating paperwork and the emphasis of evaluating paperwork versus one's life goals was extremely useful to me.
  —**James D. Brown**, Subcontract Administrator, BMY, York, Pennsylvania

Your book has everything and it's clear and concise. I think it's absolutely fabulous!
  —**Lesley Goranson**, Administrative Services Manager, SOFTBANK
  Expos, Foster City, California

I have just finished reading your excellent book and found it to be most helpful and will incorporate many of its suggestions in my day-to-day activities.
  —**Eli Goodman**, M.D., Internal Medicine, Elmira, New York

I have personally enjoyed and used your book and recommended it to people who have attended my seminars. I even decided to donate a copy to my local library. It seems to me to fill a gap by concentrating on organizing for work.
  —**Tommie M. Bryan**, President, The Organized Way, Somerset, New
  Jersey

Your book is definitely unique in its approach. I learned a lot from your abundance of pictorial examples and the specific naming of products and where to locate them. I don't recall ever seeing that done before. You did a great job on the book.
  —**Nancy Tawney**, Director of Development, Florentine Opera of
  Milwaukee

Organized
To Be The
Best!

New Timesaving Ways
To Simplify And Improve
How You Work

SUSAN SILVER

ADAMS-HALL PUBLISHING
Los Angeles

Requests for such permissions should be addressed to: Adams-Hall Publishing, PO Box 491002, Los Angeles, CA 90049

Library of Congress Cataloging-in-Publication Data

Silver, Susan
    Organized to be the best! : New timesaving ways to simplify and improve how you work / Susan Silver - 3rd edition
      p.   cm.
    Includes index.
    ISBN 0-944708-36-6 (softcover) / ISBN 0-944708-46-3 (cloth)
    1. Business records—Management—Data processing. 2. Information resources management. 3. Time management. I. Title.
HF5736.S54   1995   95-22391
650.1--dc20   CIP

Adams-Hall books are available at special, quantity discounts for bulk purchases for sales promotions, premiums, fund-raising or educational use. For details, contact: Special Sales Director, Adams-Hall Publishing, PO Box 491002, Los Angeles, CA 90049, 310/826-1851 or 800/888-4452

Printed in the United States of America   Printed on recycled paper
10 9 8 7 6   First printing 1995, Third Edition

Special thanks to Stuart Crump, Chris Farmer and Samantha Greenberg.

Distributed by Publishers Group West (800/788-3123)

CONTENTS

HOW TO BENEFIT
FROM THIS BOOK

This book is the answer for you if *any* of the following questions are true. Are you

- usually swamped with paperwork or inundated with information?
- struggling with too many priorities?
- feeling out of control or overwhelmed with your workload?
- working in a chaotic or cluttered environment?
- not using your personal computer as efficiently as possible?
- working with others without enough positive communication skills and teamwork?
- juggling multiple offices or traveling extensively?
- adjusting to downsizing?
- expanding your business?
- just looking for more ideas to help you grow professionally and personally in order to expand your opportunities?

WHY YOU NEED THIS BOOK NOW
MORE THAN EVER BEFORE

If you answered "yes" to even one question, this is the right book at the right time.

Even if you've read other similar books (including a prior edition of *Organized to be the Best!*), this is the time to make a commitment to yourself to develop your organizational quotient.

This is a time of great change and challenge in the work place and organizational skills are no longer a luxury or a whim–they're a necessity. They'll support you in your fast-paced, high-demand work place–whether it's located in an office building, a home office or a mobile office.

And talk about change! Did you know that more than 40 percent of the 1980 Fortune 500 companies no longer exist?

We're talking about survival in a world of instant communications, exploding technology and multiple priorities and deadlines, in a world where downsizing continues to be the norm (i.e., doing more with much less) and a world where you need to continually build your skills and marketability and keep your options open. Who knows–you may even end up working for yourself by choice or default–an option I've chosen and relished. By the way, I remember hearing an entrepreneur say that one of the biggest mistakes you can make is to think you work for someone else–which is to say you better take charge of your own career and destiny.

You may also be (or will be soon) one of the 43 million Americans working at home. Even with all the available technology at your fingertips, you'll still be struggling most likely with a lack of time and space.

Additionally you may find you were "college trained, not office trained" as a seminar participant of mine put it so well.

In any case, good solid organizational tools, habits and systems can greatly help to expand your marketability, your options and your satisfaction.

THE POSITIVELY ORGANIZED!
PROGRAM FOR ACTION

This book is different from others because it is *interactive.* This book is as close as possible to having a personal consultation with me right now. Together we will use the Positively Organized! Program for Action. Tried and tested over the years, this is a proven program designed for professionals who already possess strong determination and clear goals. I always use it in my consulting/coaching work as well as my training programs. The Positively Organized! Program recognizes the level of success you have already achieved and keeps on building and refining. It also gives you immediate access to *solutions*—specific tips, techniques and tools you can use.

In the Positively Organized! Program, we're a team—you're the player and I'm the coach. As a coach I require your full attention and commitment and I, in turn, will help you see what could be working better for you. I will point out the best strategies around so that you won't have to waste your precious time and energy reinventing the organization wheel.

Take what you *read* and translate it into *action.* You'll be able to create a simple plan of action for tackling your desk, paperwork, projects, filing cabinets or storage areas.

Or maybe you and a colleague will read this book and together you'll create a joint action plan to improve a communication system, implement a fail-safe method for follow-up or create an office paperwork procedure that simplifies how you work.

WHAT'S IN IT FOR YOU

This book will help you do what you've always wanted to do. You'll reduce your stress, find extra hours in the day for the most important activities in your life and achieve more of your goals. You'll accelerate your performance, productivity and your own personal sense of achievement.

If your share this information with others, you have a chance to improve quality, service and teamwork where you work.

You'll also discover handy desk accessories and helpful office products, including many for your personal computer.

And you'll learn that more important than having the right equipment and tools is having the right *habits* to use the tools. You'll create your *own* personal organization system—because there's *no one right way to get organized.* We're all different and this book recognizes and appreciates those differences.

Even if you have the previous editions of this book, you'll discover all kinds of new products and ideas in this edition because there's no one right way to write a book either. Just as I encourage all of my clients to continue striving to be the best they can be, so, too, I work at making each succeeding edition the best it can be. And it appears to be working; you're reading a nationally award-winning book with more than one-quarter million copies in print that's been selected by more than ten book clubs and continues to receive praise from readers just like you. No wonder it's called the Bible of Organization!

Just follow the advice of leadership expert Danny Cox when approaching a learning opportunity such as this book: "If you get one good idea that improves your effectiveness you've paid for your investment many times over." It's my goal that you'll get *many* good ideas but the real trick is to *apply* those ideas.

HOW TO SAVE TIME
WHEN READING THIS BOOK

This book is easy to use and will save you time because it has been specially designed for you, the busy professional. Special features make this book instantly accessible and usable. There is a complete table of contents and a useful index for easy reference. Also, there are brief "Quick Scan" summaries at the beginning of each chapter, distinct subheads in the chapters to help you read more quickly and plentiful resource guides at the end of Chapters 1 through 13.

And what's more, **you don't have to read the whole book!** Outside of Chapters 1, 2 and 14 (which are "required reading"), read only those chapters that apply to you.

The "Quick Survey" in Chapter 1 will let you see immediately where to fine tune and where to do a complete overhaul. After the survey, go to the detailed table of contents and mark those chapters that relate most directly to the items you marked that need improvement. The "Quick Scan" summary at the beginning of a chapter will help confirm whether you should read the chapter.

Whichever chapters you select, *be sure to read Chapter 14* to actually put the ideas from this book into action.

As you're looking at the table of contents (and perhaps comparing this third edition to a previous one), you'll notice that the earlier chapters are aimed more toward the individual and deal with some of the more traditional organization issues—e.g., time management, desk and paper management, work space setup and files (chapters 1 through 7). You'll see two chapters specifically on working more effectively with others (chapters 10 and 11) but you'll find workgroup solutions in many other chapters as well. Computers and technology, including the information superhighway, are emphasized in most of the later chapters (8, 9, 11, 12 and 13), but once again, you'll see some computer products or solutions in almost every chapter.

Allow me to pass on a couple of consumer bits of information as you read this book. Be aware that product prices are generally a manufacturer's suggested list or retail price; "street prices" can often be considerably less if you shop around. Also, if you think I should have included a product that isn't here, please write me using the easy form on page 357. There is also the possibility that I omitted products for which I tried repeatedly and futilely to obtain up-to-date information from either the product's manufacturer, distributor or public relations firm; I'm concerned that if they're too disorganized or uninterested in getting free publicity and hence additional customers, then most likely they aren't going to provide decent customer service for you either. The research phase of this third edition has confirmed that my professional services are needed now more than ever! There is also the possibility that a software product was excluded at the last minute because a review for the latest version was not up to par.

The products in chapter resource guides are in alphabetical order within each section.

A note about trademarks: assume that product or service names used in this book are trademarks or registered trademarks or service marks of the featured companies and are the property of those companies.

So grab a pen, pencil or highlighter or some Post-it tape flags for selecting key chapters and indicating key points. On your mark, get set, get organized—to be the best you can be!

1

HOW TO BE
POSITIVELY
ORGANIZED!

Quick Scan: This chapter is "required reading" because it helps pinpoint where you are now and where you'd like to be with your organizational skills. Through the Quick Survey, you'll assess your organizational strengths and weaknesses. Next, you'll identify your goals and values. Finally, you'll reassess your survey results in light of your goals.

Take a deep breath and relax. *Positively Organized!* does *not* mean being *compulsively* or *perfectly organized*. It's being **only as organized as you need to be**.

Your own style and degree of organization will depend on a number of factors—your level of activity, whether you have any support staff, the image you want to project, if you deal face to face with the public and how you like to work. It's up to you just how much organization you need.

It's *not* just having your papers in order; much more important is whether your priorities are in order. It's a question of *balance* between the details and the big picture, the micro and the macro.

There's no one right way to "get organized." As you'll soon see in this book, there are many different organization tools and habits you can use. In fact, I define an organization system as the combination of appropriate *tools* and *habits* to get a job done or to reach a goal.

There are also different organization styles that reflect both the choice of tools and habits, as well as how they are used. Styles often develop because of "brain dominance." Brain research indicates that most of us develop a dominant right or left hemisphere of the brain upon which we depend. If you are more "left-brained," you will tend to like more order, structure and routine; "right-brained" individuals prefer variety and flexibility. I believe it's possible to modify your natural "style" to a certain degree but it's important to become aware when you're going against the grain.

For example, a left-brained individual may prefer a clean desk and office where everything is put away. As a consultant I would help that person set up out-of-sight systems. But if a client comes to me stating an aversion to a "neat-as-a-pin" office, I would help design systems that are interesting, flexible and within eyesight and easy reach. As you're reading the book, be aware of your current style and perhaps your ideal style, as well as which products and ideas immediately appeal to you and which do not.

Be wary of *extremes*, however, for which this book will not be helpful. If your natural style (or that of someone with whom you work or live) is extremely rigid, compulsive to a fault and demanding of others, you could be suffering from Obsessive Compulsive Disorder (OCD). While there are many different manifestations of this disorder, one type includes arranging and rearranging rituals that are performed routinely and compulsively. If you think either you, a loved one or a co-worker suffers from OCD, contact the OC Foundation at 203/878-5669 for information and support.

This book will not be too helpful either for an extreme style that craves too much stimulation and variety. If it's difficult or impossible to stay focused for very short periods of time without getting distracted, Attention Deficit Disorder (ADD) may be a problem and professional counseling by someone specializing in ADD should be sought.

HOW ORGANIZED ARE YOU AT WORK?

As a consultant I usually begin working with clients by giving them a quick survey, which helps them determine their own organizational strengths and weaknesses. Here's one for you that ties in with the subject areas covered in this book.

Read and react quickly to each of the following items and check off the appropriate letter that describes how effectively you and/or your workgroup handle each item below—O for Outstanding, S for Satisfactory or N for Needs Improvement. If an item is not applicable to you, write N/A.

Figure 1-1. A QUICK SELF SURVEY

ORGANIZATION AREA	Your Rating		
	O	S	N
1. Your system for planning, prioritizing and accomplishing work and achieving your goals. [Chapters 1, 2, 3, 9, 11, 14]...			
2. Your paperwork. [Chapters 4, 5, 6, 7, 9]			
3. Dealing with interruptions. [Chapter 3]			
4. Your ability to easily access needed information. [Chapters 2, 4, 7, 8, 9, 11, 12, 13]			
5. Your telephone time. [Chapters 6, 10, 11, 12]			
6. Managing papers and possessions. [Chapters 4, 5, 7]			
7. Your follow-ups. [Chapters 2, 3, 4, 9]			
8. Your reading load. [Chapter 4]			
9. Your filing system. [Chapters 4, 7]			
10. Your desk and work space. [Chapters 4-6]			
11. Your personal computer organization. [Chapters 8, 9, 11-13]...			
12. Making habit changes in how you do things. [Chapter 14]			
13. Your attention to quality and/or service. [Chapters 2, 9-11]			
14. Juggling multiple projects and priorities. [Chapters 2, 3, 9, 11]			
15. Instant communications (fax, voice & e-mail). [Chapter 11]....			
16. Work flow. [Chapters 4, 9-12]			
17. Records management. [Chapter 7, 9, 11]			
18. Your portable, on-the-go, traveling office. [Chapters 2, 12]			
19. Communications and teamwork [Chapters 10, 11, 12]			

HOW TO SELECT THE AREAS
MOST IMPORTANT TO YOU

Look at the "Ns" you've checked. Decide which three Ns are most important to you right now. Star these three items. Keep them in mind as you decide which chapters to read.

Take a moment now to reflect on what it would mean to you, your business, your career and your life to improve your top three starred items. Think about the *benefits* that you would experience. Take 60 seconds to jot down as many benefits that come to mind on a sheet of paper or in a notebook or right in this book if it belongs to you. Star the most important benefit to you.

BENEFITS ARE THE KEY

Just why is visualizing and listing benefits so crucial? A benefit is the reason why you do something. It's the motivation behind an action or activity and it should be connected to at least one of your major goals. You'll need a *compelling* benefit to justify spending the time and effort required to organize anything. *If there's no real payoff to getting more organized, you won't.*

Organization gets put on the back burner because it doesn't *appear* to be a top priority. Your benefit has to be strong enough to make organization a top priority and to counteract all the reasons and excuses that justify this "back burner syndrome."

Make organization a top priority. Take it off the back burner and make time for it *every day*. Get into the organization habit. It will give you the professional edge, not to mention more control and less stress.

Once you've identified at least one top benefit, keep it uppermost in your mind. Second, keep reminding yourself about the benefit while you're reading this book and when you're applying what you read. You (and perhaps your work group) are very much like athletes in training who need to remind themselves constantly about what they want to achieve and why. You need to do the same.

TARGETING CHALLENGING, ACHIEVABLE GOALS

Your benefits will come into focus more clearly once you've identified your current goals. Organization is a tool to help you achieve your goals.

As Yogi Berra once said, "If you don't know where you're going, you'll end up some place else." This is the first secret to being organized—Positively Organized! All the organizational tools and techniques in the world and this book are useless if you don't know where you're headed, that is, what you want to accomplish at work and in your life.

Start with an up-to-date list of goals. Not having this list is like taking a trip without a map. Goals give you focus, purpose and direction. Goals can help you *attain* something you don't yet have or better *maintain* something you already do. Don't underestimate the power of combining these two types of goals; "maintenance" goals can keep you nurtured and anchored in the present, instilling a sense of gratitude while "attain" goals let you yearn and strive for an even better future.

Effective goals are simple, clear-cut and direct. They should also reflect both professional and personal values—what's most important and meaningful to you. My chiropractor, Dr. Mha Atma Singh Khalsa, stated it well in his newsletter, "Discover and clarify your mission in life—your overriding purpose."

Radio talk-show host Dennis Prager suggested his listeners ask themselves the following question after each day of work: "Are you proud of what you did today?"

Write down your goals on paper periodically during the year (this means more than once!). Make appointments with yourself to plan your goals on paper. Twice a year may be sufficient—in January and then again in July. Others prefer quarterly goals.

HOW TO WRITE DOWN YOUR GOALS

Use the Goals Work Sheet in Figure 1-2 to identify the "what," "why" and "how" of each goal.

Begin by listing "what" you want to attain or maintain and the extent or degree of accomplishment. In describing your goal, ask yourself what you want to **do, be** or **have**. Be as specific as you can. Write your goal in the present tense for a maintenance goal and in the future if it's not a regular part of your life right now. (Or you may prefer to write all goals in the present tense, making them double as positive affirmations of what you want.) Here are three "do, be, have" examples of personal and professional goals:

> **Do:** I exercise three times a week; I play volleyball on Sunday, tennis on Tuesday and racquetball on Thursday.
>
> **Be:** I am a peaceful person who greets problems as challenges and opportunities. (Here's an affirmation style goal, no doubt!)
>
> **Have:** I will have a job in my chosen field that is financially and personally satisfying by this time next year.

Answer "why" by listing any benefits and results you expect from accomplishing your goal. The "why" should also state the *value* this goal has for you in your life as a whole. If you choose goals that conflict with your life values, you'll be setting yourself up for sabotage and failure. Let's suppose, for example, one of your goals is to get a promotion within the next few years and to do so will require that you put in many more hours at work. But one of your values is to lead a balanced life that includes plenty of time spent with your family. You could have a conflict on your hands.

Your goals need to be in harmony with your most important life values. Taking the "do" goal listed above, here are some benefits or results to be derived: feeling fit; increased energy and vitality; getting those endorphins flowing; decreased stress; feeling more relaxed (exercise is one of the four natural tranquilizers—laughter, music and sex being the other three); having more fun; a better social life; and balancing a hectic lifestyle.

Answer "how" by listing specific ways you plan to achieve your goals—any strategies, action steps or tasks, in addition to the amount of time required (per day, week, month or year). Assigning deadlines—or "lifelines" as one person I know prefers to call them—will make your "hows" much more specific and helpful. Some specific "hows" for the "do" goal could include: calling to make reservations; confirming tennis and racquetball times with partner;

writing down activities and times in a calendar; and putting out sports clothes the night before by the door.

Now take five to ten minutes to complete the Goals Work Sheet in Figure 1-2 to quickly jot down three or more of your goals, including the "what," the "why" and the "how" for each one in Figure 1-2 below.

Figure 1-2. GOALS WORK SHEET

Date:_____

WHAT is your goal?	WHY do you want this goal?	HOW will you proceed?

THE POWER OF THE PEN

Putting your goals in writing helps affirm your *commitment*. Your chances of achieving your goals are much greater when you write them down. It makes your goals more real. It also helps plant them into your subconscious. One professional woman I know writes down her goals each year in January, seals them in an envelope, opens the envelope at the end of the year and discovers she has accomplished almost all of them.

AIM HIGH

Second, who says you have to accomplish them all? There's a saying that goes like this, "If you accomplish everything you planned, then you haven't planned well enough." You *should* plan a little more than you may actually do; practice aiming high because you'll probably accomplish more than if you lower your expectations and make them "realistic."

TECHNIQUES TO ENSURE SUCCESS

So aim high and use these eight ways to increase your chances of reaching your goals:

1. Put your goals in writing.
2. Take some action on your goals every day or at least every week.
3. Share them with one other person (and listen to theirs). But only share them with other people who also set goals of their own and reach them. Those are the kind of people who will be most supportive.
4. Read them daily before you do your planning and before you go to sleep.
5. Every week write down and accomplish smaller goals that relate to your long-term goals. List these weekly goals where you will see them every day.
6. Review and revise your goals at least twice a year, always making sure they reflect your deepest values.
7. Let them *inspire,* not haunt you.
8. Include both professional and *personal* goals to increase the balance of your life. Make sure, too, that your goals harmonize with those of your career, position or company; if they don't, you could experience some conflict in your life.

Now review your survey on page 8. Find your starred items and notice the chapter references. See which chapter numbers come up most often. Now go to the table of contents and select the most important chapters for you to read. Keep in mind, too, that you should make Chapter 2 and Chapter 14 part of your "required reading" no matter which "elective" chapters you choose to read.

Now look at your goals on page 12 and note which chapters will best help you reach your goals. And, remember, the idea isn't just to be organized. It's to become organized to be the best! That means the best *you* can be."

RESOURCE GUIDE

Here are some products to help you learn more about goal setting.

Create the Life You Want! is a SCAN/PLAN Success Guidebook that teaches you how to organize your life around what matters to you, to set goals and to create or achieve what you want using the SCAN/PLAN system of index cards. $14.95. **800/SCANPLAN** or 310/829-2888. SCAN/PLAN, Inc., PO Box 1662, Santa Monica, CA 90406

ManagePro for Windows is a software program that has received much praise to help you manage the goals for your organization as well as the individuals in your workgroup. **Windows and Network.** Single user, $199; volume pricing is available. **800/282-6867** or 510/654-4600. Avantos Performance Systems Inc., 5900 Hollis St., Ste. A, Emeryville, CA 94608

The Psychology of Achievement by Brian Tracy is a six-cassette program that distills the key ingredients of high achievement. Brian Tracy presents proven, practical methods and techniques that high achievers regularly use in their lives and careers. Available from Brian Tracy Learning Systems, 462 Stevens Avenue, Suite 202, Solana Beach, CA 92075-2065, 800/542-4252 or 619/481-2977. $60

What It Takes: Good News From 100 of America's Top Professional and Business Women by Lee Gardenswartz and Anita Rowe (New York: Doubleday, 1987). An inspiring work, this book shows how women at the top arrange their lives to achieve their goals and how you can assess your own aptitude for success. Hardback, $16.95. Available by calling 310/823-2466 or writing 12658 W. Washington Blvd., Ste. 105, Los Angeles, California 90066.

2

TIME MANAGEMENT:
WHAT YOU REALLY
NEED TO KNOW

Quick Scan: The second of three "required reading" chapters, this one gives you the secrets to getting the most important things done in your life. Learn the art of planning and prioritizing and why time management is the foundation for good organization. See a wide variety of quality time management tools and why it's important to be using the right one(s) for you.

Every problem with organization is in some way a problem with time. If your time isn't well organized, chances are your papers, projects and priorities won't be either.

Time management is the foundation of good organization. Its purpose is to help you do the most important things in your life.

Many people think the purpose of time management is to get as much done as possible. Not so. Let me repeat: **it's getting the most important things done.**

Do you *often* have days when it feels as if you have accomplished nothing? If so, you aren't taking advantage of time management.

You're not doing the most important tasks and activities.

Have you considered what "most important" means? Is it something that has an urgent deadline? Is it something your boss wants? Is it something *you* want that relates to one of your goals?

It can mean all of these. But watch out if you're only making *other people's demands* the most important things you do. To be your best, make time every day to accomplish something that *you* consider important.

Activities you deem important come out of the values and goals you identified in Chapter 1. (If you haven't read that "required" chapter please do so now.) Without clear-cut goals, your time management decisions will be made in a vacuum or else they will be all externally determined by outside circumstances and people. You won't be in charge. So take charge and start choosing activities that contribute to your long-term goals.

Time management is the great simplifier, putting things in focus and perspective. Time management is an awareness of time coupled with the ability to choose and control purposeful activities related to your goals. It's the basis for decision making.

Time management is making choices about activities that have meaning to you. These choices should balance short-term and long-term, urgent and less urgent, internal and external activities. Time management helps you control what you can, when you can.

Time management is also using the right tools and habits to improve *how* you do something. Effective time management tools and habits can improve the quality and quantity of your work, help you make better decisions and increase your performance.

HOW TO PLAN AND PRIORITIZE

Planning and prioritizing are two essential habits that are the bread and butter of time management. Use them to balance long-term and short-term goals and activities.

Why take the *time* to plan and prioritize? Research indicates that for every hour of planning, you save three or four hours. Effective planning and prioritizing ("P and P" for short) will help you get the most important things done each day, week, month and year.

You've already started with long-term P and P in Chapter 1. Long-term goal setting is a real time-saver because it's a handy yardstick against which you can measure all your day-to-day P and P decisions.

LEARNING YOUR ABCs AND NUMBERS

To master P and P, begin by learning to identify your "ABC" priorities. Author Edwin Bliss, in his wonderful book *Getting Things Done*, differentiates between these three priorities. He says A priorities are "important and urgent," as in crisis management. B priorities are "important but not urgent," as in long-term goals. You should try to spend most of your time on As and Bs. C priorities are "urgent but not important." Try to spend as little time on Cs as possible.

You're probably pretty good at handling As, which fall in the "fighting fires" category, but how many Bs do you work on each day? **Make time every day to work on your important-but-not-urgent B priorities and goals.** A good source for these priorities are the goals you listed on your Goals Work Sheet in Chapter 1.

Another way to describe A, B and C priorities is to substitute these three words: "must," "should" and "could." In other words, an A priority is something you *must* do, a B priority is something you *should* do and a C priority is something you *could* do.

And here's a trick using numbers that I learned from colleague Marjorie Hansen Shaevitz when she and I appeared on the same college program. Using a scale from 1 to 10, she suggests asking yourself these two questions if you're indecisive about whether to do an activity:

1. How much do I really want to do this activity (against the backdrop of everything else that is going on)?
2. How important is this activity?

ADD D, D AND D TO YOUR P AND P

To get the most important things done each day, add three other ingredients to your planning and prioritizing: **discipline, dedication,** and **desire.**

There is no substitute for a daily dose of **discipline.** Build planning into *every* work day and give it as much importance as if you were going away on a two-week vacation. (Did you ever notice how good you get at planning and prioritizing the day before you go away?)

Build a specific time slot into your daily schedule to work on top projects or priorities–and stick to it. For example, authors set aside certain hours of the day to write.

No matter what else happens, keeping that commitment to yourself will make you feel good about the day and your accomplishments. Nothing beats out single-mindedness of purpose when it comes to getting the most important things done.

What we're talking about is real **dedication** to your most important priorities. Start out the morning by asking yourself, "What are the most important items for me to handle today that would allow me to call this a successful day?"

And take time to acknowledge your accomplishments each day. Pat yourself on the back. This is a good way to spark your **desire**, which in turn will fuel your dedication and discipline. Keep relating your activities to your goals, which should also feed your desire.

SIX WAYS TO MAXIMIZE YOUR P AND P WHEN YOU MAKE YOUR TO-DO LIST

Now that you've learned the ABCs of planning and prioritizing, you're ready to use them plus these six ways to improve your **to-do list**–a daily or weekly list of activities that reflects your goals and priorities and helps you see the most important things you need to accomplish:

1. **Plan tomorrow, today, and put your plan in writing.** Take five or ten minutes today to write tomorrow's to-do list so you can start tomorrow fresh. (If you're an early riser, set aside some quiet time at home or at work to plan before the day really gets going.) Planning and prioritizing on paper (or computer) lets you *see* what you need to accomplish and when.

2. **Revise your plan–stay flexible and use common sense!** Check today's list several times throughout the day and if necessary, rearrange, postpone and yes, even *procrastinate on purpose.* "Planned procrastination"–consciously choosing to put off–is what prioritizing is all about. Remember your to-do list is a guide and *no one gets everything done.* Use common sense as

you plan out your priorities. If something comes up during the day that bumps another item in importance, so be it. Write in pencil so you can easily erase and move items on your list. Weigh the value of doing an item at a particular point in time. For example, it may be better to call Joe Blow at 1:00 p.m. today, even though Joe is only a "B" priority, because you're sure to reach him at 1:00; otherwise you'll be playing telephone tag with him for the next two weeks—which would be a major time waster.

Make at least one, screened-time appointment with yourself each day. Give yourself at least one hour of "screened, prime time" every day to work on top priority work. "Screened time" is quiet, uninterrupted time allowing you to concentrate and "prime time" is the time of the day when you're most effective. You can screen your time by doing any of the following: coming in an hour early, staying an hour later, having your calls screened by a secretary or colleague (and offering to do the same for them), working in another location (at home or a quiet, inaccessible office), closing your door, activating your voice mail system or your answering machine and writing in a one-hour appointment with yourself on your calendar.

Consolidate activities and avoid "laundry listing." If you're tired of making long, laundry lists of unrelated to-do's, then shorten your lists and group like items together. Have one section of your to-do list for scheduled appointments. Try grouping activities by category (such as "calls" and "correspondence"). Use priority groupings where you first list your top A priorities of the day—limit the number to three or four—and then list your B priorities.

Make time every day to work on B priorities. These are the priorities that most closely tie in with your goals. But most people tend to put Bs on the back burner, selecting only the more pressing, fire-fighting A priorities.

Write down several key goals, activities or projects for the week. Select no more than four and write them some place where you'll see them every day as you do your daily planning.

HOW TO CHOOSE
THE BEST TIME MANAGEMENT TOOLS

There is no one best time management tool. There are, however, the best tools for *you* at this point in your life and career to help you plan, prioritize and get the most important things done.

One thing is certain. The more complex and demanding your life and career become, the more you need time management tools that can help you keep track of the complex demands on your time.

Select the least number of tools. The simpler, the better. But don't force yourself to use a tool that you've outgrown or that no longer meets your needs.

You'll see a wide variety of tools in this book, many of which can be used alone or with other tools. Some tools, such as a notebook organizer or computerized time management program, contain many tools already built in.

What's so great about today's time management tools and systems is that you have great flexibility to put together the components *you* need. Remember, too, not to feel guilty if you don't want to use all of the components. Use only what you need.

In this section we'll look at seven main types of time management tools: 1) calendars, 2) to-do lists, 3) master lists, 4) tickler systems, 5) planners/organizers, 6) computerized time management and personal information management (PIM) programs and 7) personal handheld electronic organizers. Be thinking about the following criteria as you evaluate these time management tools for yourself:

Size–what's the right one for you?
Portability–how portable does it have to be?
Accessibility–how easy is it to find information?
Features and adaptability–how important are they to you, as well as others with whom you work?
Looks, image and appeal–what is appropriate for your position and lifestyle?

Consider, too, your own personal style. Are you a person who likes to see the big picture, prefers a more detailed look at life or likes a combination of both? Are graphics and design just as important to you as function? Do you prefer simple or complex planning? These are some questions to ponder as you select time management tools. In most cases, go with your gut reaction; if you don't like a tool at first, chances are you won't down the line either. But if you're the kind of person who takes time to warm up to new ways of doing things, then give it a shot.

CALENDARS

The most basic planning and scheduling tool is the calendar, which can track future dates, events, meetings and appointments over a long range of time—at least a year out at a time.

Everyone needs a calendar but not everyone is using the right calendar or using it correctly. Calendars come in all shapes, sizes and configurations and often by many a name: date books, diaries, appointment books, desk calendars, desk pad calendars and wall calendars. Calendars are often part of other planning tools such as notebook organizers or computer time management programs, which will be discussed shortly.

Don't underestimate the importance of your calendar selection. Since this is an item you use daily, you should give your selection some thought. Don't be afraid to change to a different one, even in mid-year. Ask yourself these five questions:

1. Do you have more than one calendar?
2. Is your calendar either too small or too big?
3. Is it easy to miss seeing important dates (because they're hard to spot, there isn't enough room or your calendar is too cluttered)?
4. Are you afraid of losing your calendar?
5. Is it troublesome to carry it with you when you're away from the office?

If you have one or more "yes" responses, consider reevaluating your choice of calendar according to these criteria:

- You should not have more than one calendar unless you have a staff person and/or a foolproof routine to maintain the additional one. (Keep personal and professional items on the same calendar.)
- Select a calendar whose size and style are adequate for your work and appointment load. Don't force yourself to use a

calendar you've outgrown even if it is the middle of the year; switch to another one.

- Maintain a reliable backup system. What would happen if you lost your calendar? Do you have photocopies of the most important pages? If it's computerized, do you have backups?
- Your calendar should be accessible to you, both in and out of the office.
- Your calendar should have the right "look" for your profession and it should appeal to you in terms of appearance and ease of use.

If you're trying to cram too much information into your calendar or appointment book, consider a larger format or a different time management tool, such as a planner or an organizer. A calendar is for mapping out long-range plans; it's not generally the ideal tool for detailed, daily planning. If you're continually using many slips of paper to make notes to yourself because your calendar simply isn't big enough, you're ready for a change.

Allow me to comment on the desk pad calendar. I'm not fond of this calendar because it's so big, it's not portable, it adds to desktop clutter, it often becomes a big doodling pad, there's no place to conveniently store past month sheets and it's not the most professional looking tool you can get. (Other than that, I love it!)

And for you calendar trivia buffs, see if you know any of the following: the earliest-known calendar had 12 months of 30 days each and was a lunar calendar invented by the ancient Egyptians; the Babylonians were thought to be the first to observe a seven-day week; and the word "calendar" comes from the Latin word "calendarium," which means "interest register" or "account book."

TO-DO LISTS

Most people should use some kind of to-do list for daily or weekly planning at work and/or in their personal life.

If your work is very routine or very physical, it's possible you wouldn't need this tool. If you're a teller, a baker or a mechanic you probably wouldn't need this on the job. But if you're a manager or supervisor with administrative responsibilities besides hands-on work, it might be helpful to write them down on a to-do list. And if you have a busy personal life, a to-do list is essential.

A good to-do list should have two basic sections—a place for scheduled activities and a place for your nonscheduled activities. Scheduled activities include appointments as well as blocks of time you set aside to do specific types of work, e.g., projects, paperwork and planning. Nonscheduled activities are items on your to-do list that aren't scheduled to be done at any particular time of day. Choose forms in stationery stores and catalogs that provide these two important sections. You can buy these commercial to-do list forms separately or as part of a time management system or organizer. Figure 2-1 shows the Personal Resource System two-page-per-day planning forms with scheduled and nonscheduled spaces.

It's important to see both your scheduled and nonscheduled activities at the same time and have them next to one another. Whenever possible or feasible, make your nonscheduled tasks into scheduled ones because they're more likely to get done when you've attached a time frame or deadline. When you set time aside to accomplish a task, you're more likely to do it than if it's just an unscheduled item on a to-do list. If you've set aside time to do tasks and you have trouble gauging time, use an electronic countdown timer from an electronics store such as Radio Shack to help you stick to your schedule.

If you get tired of transferring today's uncompleted to-do's to the next day's list, consider using a two-page-per-week format (Figure 2-2). You'll have a little less space to write, but you won't have to keep rewriting to-do's. You can also see your entire week, including any items that are incomplete. (A computer time management program or personal information manager (PIM) can also eliminate the need to rewrite and transfer uncompleted to-do's, as you'll soon see.)

MASTER LISTS AND OTHER BIG PICTURE PLANNING TOOLS

If you have a large number of projects, activities and tasks (as compared to meetings and appointments, which go on a calendar), it may be helpful to group these items in special places other than calendars or daily to-do lists.

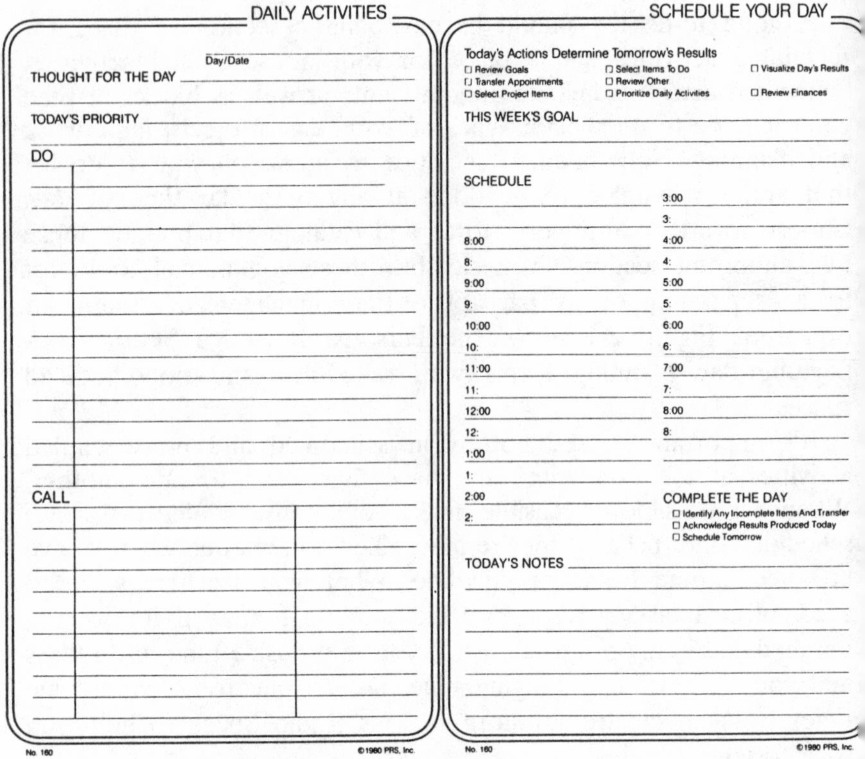
DAILY ACTIVITIES

Day/Date

THOUGHT FOR THE DAY

TODAY'S PRIORITY

DO

CALL

No. 160 ©1980 PRS, Inc.

SCHEDULE YOUR DAY

Today's Actions Determine Tomorrow's Results

☐ Review Goals ☐ Select Items To Do ☐ Visualize Day's Results
☐ Transfer Appointments ☐ Review Other
☐ Select Project Items ☐ Prioritize Daily Activities ☐ Review Finances

THIS WEEK'S GOAL

SCHEDULE

8:00
8:
9:00
9:
10:00
10:
11:00
11:
12:00
12:
1:00
1:
2:00
2:
3:00
3:
4:00
4:
5:00
5:
6:00
6:
7:00
7:
8:00
8:

COMPLETE THE DAY
☐ Identify Any Incomplete Items And Transfer
☐ Acknowledge Results Produced Today
☐ Schedule Tomorrow

TODAY'S NOTES

No. 160 ©1980 PRS, Inc.

Figure 2-1. The Personal Resource System daily planning forms have sections for scheduled and nonscheduled activities, letting you group certain tasks together. There are also places to record information related to goals, projects and results. These forms come in dated and nondated styles.

A **master list** is useful for listing activities that will occur over a period of time, from one week to several months. A master list serves three functions. First, it consolidates ideas you've been storing in your head and on your desk into one source. Second, it gives you an overview and some perspective of the "big picture." Third, you can use it to select items to put on your daily list.

To make your master list more effective, categorize and prioritize it. Some people simply flag the most important items with a red star. You may want to combine a red star with a start date or a due date.

Others prefer to have separate lists. Some of my clients create two lists, one for personal and another for professional. Some create a separate list for each project, case or type of work. Usually the

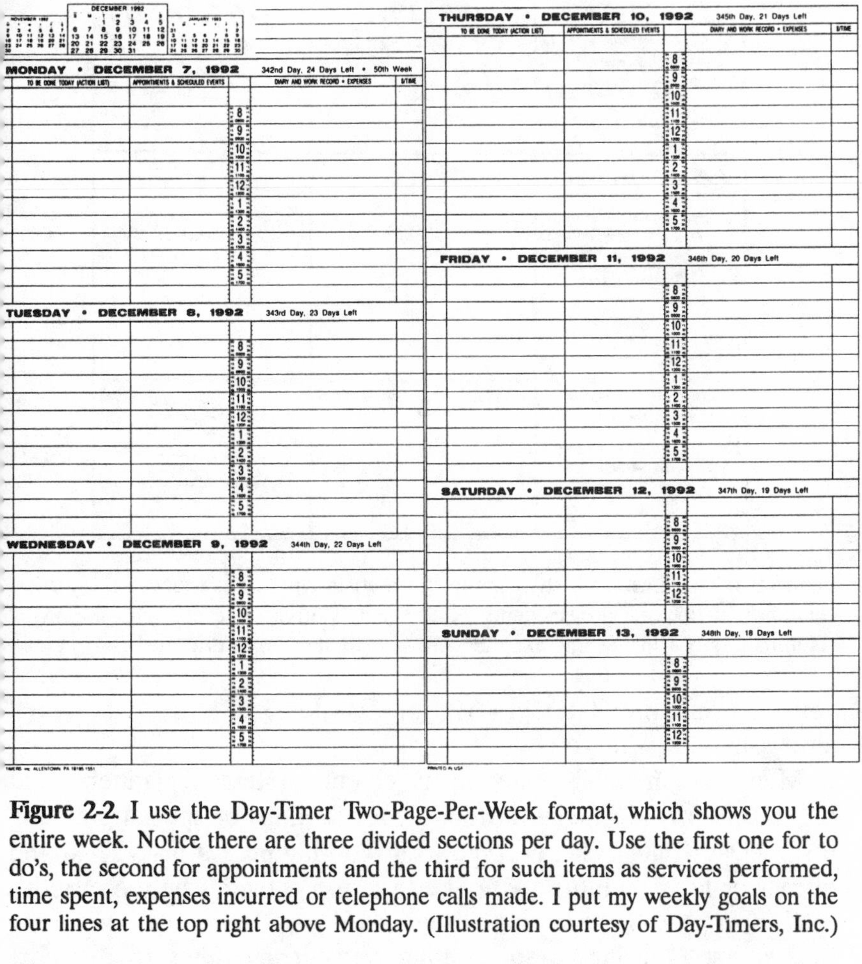

Figure 2-2. I use the Day-Timer Two-Page-Per-Week format, which shows you the entire week. Notice there are three divided sections per day. Use the first one for to do's, the second for appointments and the third for such items as services performed, time spent, expenses incurred or telephone calls made. I put my weekly goals on the four lines at the top right above Monday. (Illustration courtesy of Day-Timers, Inc.)

fewer lists the better, but the trick is to remember to *use* them. The more lists you have, the easier it is to forget to use one of them.

Whenever possible, put your master list on *one* sheet of paper. See Figure 2-3 for an example of a simple master list in chart form that groups activities by type and priority. List your activities on the chart in pencil (to write really small and get more items on a page, use a mechanical lead pencil with 0.5mm lead). Writing in pencil lets you erase and rewrite items when your priorities change. Remember to include some kind of deadline or time frame because almost nothing gets done without one. If you carry an organizer, hole punch

ACTION	CALLS	CORRESP.
A 1. Expense report w/10-16 2. Market summary w/10-16 3. Presentation for 10-19 sr. mg mt. 4. _____ 5. _____	1. Joe 293-1121 10-13 2. Chris 10-17 3. _____ 4. _____	1. Budget memo to staff w/ 10-16 2. _____ 3. _____

B 1. Annual sales mtg. -
   theme, location, etc.
2. Job search for temporary
   office mgr. going on leave
3. Set aside time to
   read trade journals -
   1 hour per week
4. _____
5. _____
6. _____
7. _____
8. _____
	1. _____
	2. _____
	3. _____
	4. _____
		1. _____
		2. _____
		3. _____
		4. _____
		5. _____

P 1. Paint bathroom
2. Plan surprise b/d
   party
3. Community dinner
   for homeless
	1. Make plans for weekend
	   - call friends
		1. Thank you - Aunt Louise
		   for b/d present
		2. B/d card to Mom
		3. _____
		4. _____
		5. _____

Figure 2-3. This master list chart groups three main types of activities in the vertical columns—"Action" or project items, "Calls" and "Correspondence." The horizontal columns group activities into "A," "B" and "P" (for Personal) priorities.

your list and file it under "M" for "Master List"; that way you'll always have it with you.

Many commercial time management systems, planners and organizers provide their own master list sections or special planning forms. Day-Timer systems come with **monthly master lists**. This kind of master list is helpful if you like to group activities by the month.

If most of your items extend beyond a month, however, you may find yourself having to spend time transferring items to the next month's list. You may prefer Personal Resource Systems' open-ended time frame "Items to Do" form, which lets you list one item per line and has you put any notes about a particular item number on the back, thereby keeping the notes convenient but not cluttered. This form becomes a concise master list that isn't cluttered with any extraneous written notes or reminders.

If you work on projects with many detailed steps, use a **project sheet** or **project planner** in addition to or instead of a master list. Make a simple list for each project or buy project planning forms that are commercially prepared (see Day Runner, Day-Timers and

Personal Resource Systems listed in the chapter Resource Guide). See also Chapter 9 for some other examples of project forms.

Memogenda is a thin, spiral bound book that is a great combination master list and project planner. You can keep an up-to-date listing of all the things you have to do in one convenient, compact, lightweight source. It's available from Norwood Products in Nashville, 615/833-4101.

If you work with others on joint projects, you may prefer large **wall charts** or **visual control boards** that display activities or specific project tasks for many people to see at one time. Different varieties include "write-on-wipe-off" boards and magnetic boards with movable strips and cards. If portability is not a factor, these boards can be just the thing. See also Chapter 9 for more information on charts.

TICKLER SYSTEMS

Almost all of us need to have our memories reminded or "tickled." A **tickler system** is a reminder system that tickles your memory. (The term "tickler" originally referred to a special feather that was used to tickle churchgoers who nodded off during a sermon.)

A calendar and a to-do list are the simplest tickler systems just about everyone uses. But you need more than these tools if you have many, many reminders or follow-ups that are too numerous or tedious to write down in the ways we've discussed up to now.

TICKLER CARD SYSTEMS

A **tickler card system** is useful if you regularly follow up with certain people over a period of time or have particular tasks to do on a project on certain days. A tickler card system typically consists of plain or colored index cards, monthly and 1-31 index guides and an index file box. (See Figure 2-4 on the next page.)

A tickler card system is particularly useful for sales follow-up. You could use it for a prospect who isn't ready to buy your product or service today but could be ready over the next several months. You'd first prepare a prospect card with the person's name, address and phone number. Then you'd place the card behind a numbered tab (if you're calling within the next 31 days) or behind the tab for the month in which you plan to make the call. Each time you call or write you make a notation on the card and indicate your next

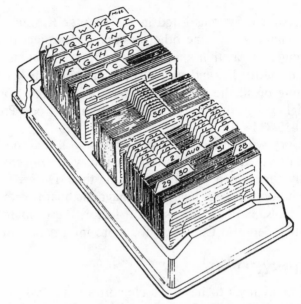

Figure 2-4. Here's a tickler card system with 1-31, January to December and A-Z divider tabs. Inactive cards can be filed behind the alphabetical tabs.

follow-up action. The card keeps moving through the system until you decide to remove it and/or transfer the information into a computer or paper file.

Let's look more closely at how it works. You'll want to select the right size index cards—they come in different sizes—3 by 5, 4 by 6 and 5 by 8 inches. Decide what kind of data and how much you plan to write on each card.

Here's what you can write on each card. Begin with the name of the organization or the name of the individual, whichever name you're most likely to think of first. Then write the address and phone number and the key contacts and titles. Make a point of listing names of secretaries, receptionists or other staff members to whom you speak, too.

Write in an "action date" on the far left of the card for an action taken, e.g, actually talking to a key individual, as well as entering the date when leaving a message in their absence. The day you send out correspondence is an action date, too.

Keep a very brief summary of ongoing activity. For every attempted contact, write a date on the line at the far left. You may then want to use your own codes and abbreviations. I use "TT," which means "*T*elephone *T*o," and signifies I initiated the call. If I have to leave a message after I called, TT is followed by "LM," which indicates I "*L*eft *M*essage." LM will be followed by the name of individual in parentheses with whom I spoke. "Fol" plus a specific date and often a time indicates the next phone call *Fol*lowup or appointment. I also use "LMM" when I have *L*eft *M*essage on *M*achine and "FT," when I have *F*axed *T*o someone—you get the idea.

When someone I've called isn't available, particularly someone I don't know well, I ask the receptionist or secretary to take down my name and company and indicate *I'll* call back, preferably at a specific time. I ask the receptionist or secretary what time would be best to call back. Then I jot down "IWCB," (*I W*ill *C*all *B*ack) on my card. This lets me put my name before a new contact or prospect without making any demands on the person. It's also good marketing to give my name repeated exposure and hence some familiarity. No call is ever wasted. It's a good way to make cold calls warmer.

For more detailed information, you could keep a **prospect notebook** that contains correspondence and notes that are stapled together, hole punched and filed behind alphabetical tab dividers. (Or use an A-Z style desk file or sorter to avoid hole punching.) There they remain until the prospect becomes a client, whereupon the material goes into a client file folder. The prospect notebook is the longhand version of your marketing activity; the index card tickler system is the shorthand. And if prospects should call *you* before the next follow-up date, you can quickly find the latest prospect information alphabetically in the prospect notebook.

TICKLER SLIP SYSTEM

If you have a very busy office in which you're responsible for many details and delegations, you may consider purchasing a **tickler slip system** such as the All-state Tickler Record System (800/222-0510 or 201/272-0800), SYCOM's Memory Box (800/356-8141) and Safeguard's General Reminder/Assignment System (800/523-2422), which all come with at least three-part NCR (No Carbon Required) forms.

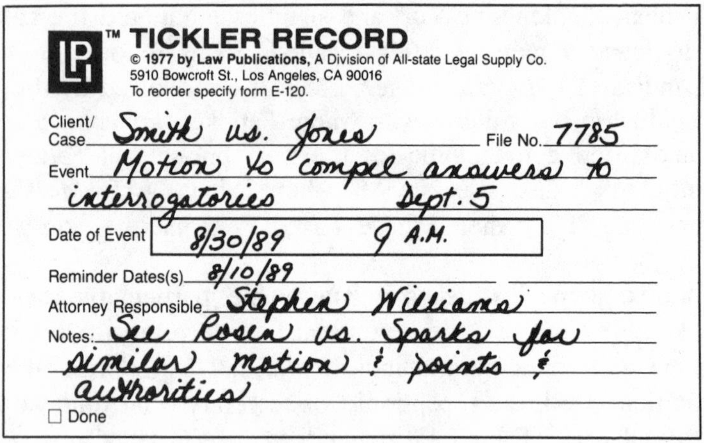

TICKLER RECORD
© 1977 by Law Publications, A Division of All-state Legal Supply Co.
5910 Bowcroft St., Los Angeles, CA 90016
To reorder specify form E-120.

Client/
Case _Smith us. Jones_____ File No. _7785_

Event _Motion to compel answers to_
interrogatories   Dept. 5

Date of Event | _8/30/89_   _9 A.M._ |

Reminder Dates(s)_ _8/10/89_____

Attorney Responsible _Stephen Williams_

Notes: _See Rosen vs. Sparks for_
similar motion & points &
authorities

☐ Done

Figure 2-5. The All-state International Tickler Record System slip is available through the All-state Legal catalog

The **tickler slip system** works in much the same way as the card system except you use preprinted NCR (no carbon required) forms. Because you can make several copies of the original form, this system is particularly useful for activities such as delegations that involve other people. For example, if a co-worker has agreed to complete a report for you, you would jot down the co-worker's name and number, the report name and the due date on the slip. You could keep the original and give the copy to the co-worker. You'd file your slip behind the due date (or a few days before) in your tickler slip system file box and your co-worker would do the same. Ideally, the party most responsible for the activity (in this case your co-worker) would complete the report and give you a copy with the tickler slip attached. If the co-worker does not follow through, your system is a backup that makes sure nothing "slips" through the cracks. But when both parties are using the system, greater accountability and responsibility is usually the result.

Although designed for attorneys, the Tickler Record System also works great for other busy professionals with many deadlines. The three-part, NCR color-coded tickler forms are versatile. Don't let the legal terms throw you; let them stand for the kinds of work *you* do. A "case" could just as easily be a project or assignment and "attorney responsible" could be a staff member or colleague. See Figure 2-5 for a sample form.

DESK FILES OR SORTERS AND ACCORDION FILES

The tickler system that we use in our office is called a **desk file** or **sorter.** The desk file opens like a book and has an expandable binding on the spine. Our model has both 1-31 *and* January to December tabs. I use it every day for follow-ups and action items that are connected to some paperwork, such as a letter or notes. (I also use it for birthday cards to be mailed.) I keep the desk file conveniently located on a corner of my desk. I recommend the 1-31/monthly combo desk file tickler to almost every client. (See Figure 2-6.)

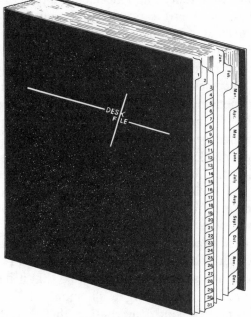

Figure 2-6. Combination 1-31 and January-December desk file by Smead

The **accordion file** is similar to the desk file except it is enclosed on three sides and usually has a flap that folds over. I find it less convenient than the desk file/sorter. And if it's less convenient, you'll be less likely to use it. If, however, your tickler needs to be portable, the accordion file could be a wise choice.

FILE FOLDER TICKLER SYSTEMS

Some people prefer a **file folder tickler system** that has file folders labeled both January to December and 1-31. A file folder tickler system can sit inside a desk drawer or in an upright rack or caddy on a nearby credenza, return or table.

There are many uses for such a system. One communications consultant I know uses a ruled sheet of paper in the front of each monthly folder to list follow-up calls for the month. He keeps corresponding notes for the calls inside an alphabetical notebook.

A file folder tickler system is also a great way to get reminder papers off your desk and into a chronological system. These are papers that require action on or by specific dates. They may include papers such as conference announcements, letters, memos, notes and even birthday or anniversary cards. If you like visual, tangible reminders, instead of a note jotted down in your calendar or planner, this system could be ideal for you.

Suppose you have some notes you'll need to use at a meeting on the ninth. Get those notes off your desk (or out of a generic, overflowing "pending file") and put them behind the "9" tab. A file folder tickler system is also handy for birthday cards filed on the day to be mailed or behind the appropriate month.

A file folder tickler system is very similar to the desk file/sorter and accordion file in that it also has file folders labeled January to December and/or 1-31 and it, too, is designed to handle paper triggered actions. You can have more flexibility for the names of your tabs, however, e.g., you could use weekly tabs. This system can sit inside a desk drawer or in an upright rack or caddy on a nearby credenza, return or table. Again, it's not quite as convenient as the desk file/sorter and some people are afraid that if it's out of sight in a file drawer that they'll forget all about it. Once it's a habit, however, and part of your daily routine, that shouldn't be problem.

For convenience, you can buy preprinted file guides or Pendaflex hanging folder label inserts in 1-31, A-Z and January-December styles. Pendaflex also makes Follow-up Tabs that run lengthwise across a hanging folder and have space for the file name plus two sliding signals that can be moved to indicate the month and the day of the month. Smead makes a Chan-L-Slide Follow-Up Folder that allows you to easily change deadline or follow-up dates across the top of the folder.

```
Today's date _____


                    FOLLOW-UP REMINDER

Re:          _____   FOLLOW-UP DATES

Client:      _____       _____

Client #     _____       _____

Subject:     _____       _____

Individual making request  _____ _ _____


Remarks:     _____
             _____       _____
             _____       _____
             _____       _____
             _____       _____
             _____       _____
             _____       _____
```

Figure 2-7. Custom office tickler form used in an accounting office

CUSTOMIZING YOUR OWN TICKLER SYSTEM

Consider designing your own tickler system. One accounting firm created the simple tickler form shown in Figure 2-7 for use in its office file folder tickler system. Staff members complete the form, keep a copy and put the original in a centralized file folder tickler system arranged by the days of the month and the months of the year. One person in charge of the system makes sure that follow-through occurs.

When Terry Preuit was manager of Management Development at a restaurant chain, she worked with her staff to create their own customized tickler slip system. Their slip, which measures 8½ by 5½ inches, is a combination memo/assignment slip in four parts (see Figure 2-8). The sender keeps two copies, one to file by project (so all correspondence and due dates for the project are in one place) and one to file by date (as a standard tickler reminder). The receiver gets one copy. The department's program coordinator gets one copy that keeps her up to date on the status of all major assignments, helps her field questions when the rest of the staff are unavailable

```
                    MANAGEMENT DEVELOPMENT MEMO

    DATE: _____        DUE DATE:_____

    TO:        _____

    FROM:      _____

    PROJECT:   _____

    INSTRUCTIONS/MESSAGE:

    ☐ See me to discuss details            ☐ Handle/then brief me afterwards
    ☐ Prepare response then we'll discuss  ☐ Handle/update at next meeting

    _____

    _____

    _____

    _____

    _____

    _____

    _____

    _____

    ☐ Done/Date:_____      ☐ See Back/Attached

    ORIGINAL - RECEIVER   CANARY-SENDER/DATE FILE   PINK-SENDER/PROJECT FILE   GOLD-LAURA
```

Figure 2-8. Custom tickler slip designed by Terry Preuit and staff

and in general, cuts down on "telephone tag."

If you handle reoccurring tasks, projects or reports each month, consider using the tickler card system developed by administrative assistant Judy Nowak. Judy uses two sets of 1-31 cards for two months in a row. When she completes a task on a card as it comes up chronologically, she immediately files the card behind the appropriate number for the next month when the task will come up again. In this way she "files as she goes" and doesn't have to file a whole group of cards at the beginning of the next month. She's all set to go.

Nowak also makes sure she never misses a deadline because she has a reminder card that she files a few days before the actual card comes up in her system. She moves both the reminder card and the task card to the next month's 1-31 set when the task is complete.

COMPUTERIZED AND ELECTRONIC TICKLERS

Automatic calendar and reminder tickler functions are now part of many software programs and electronic organizers.

Some of these programs and devices even have alarms that ring to remind you of appointments and deadlines. Some will remind your *computer* when to do things; for example, you can set the alarm clock so the computer dials a phone number at a certain time. Some programs have a "pre-reminder" capability that lets you place a pre-reminder two to five days before your final deadline. The pre-reminder stays on your calendar. Computer analyst and writer Lawrence Magid jokingly calls programs with alarms and reminders "nudgeware."

You can find tickler reminder and alarm features in many time management programs, personal information managers (PIMs) and electronic organizers. These programs and devices are discussed later in this chapter. Some contact management software programs also contain these features (see Chapter 9 or the index).

PLANNERS AND ORGANIZERS

Planners and organizers are becoming more and more versatile and packed with many different features and have great portability.

WHAT TO LOOK FOR IN A PLANNER

When you need more than a calendar or appointment book but less than a full blown organizer, a planner may be the perfect solution. And in fact, every organizer should include a good planner as its main feature.

A good planner combines both long- and short-range planning. For long-range planning, you should be able to see the major events of the year and/or each month of the year. For short-range planning, you should have planning pages that present either the entire week (which is my preference) or separate pages for each day.

Your planner should have enough writing space. If you're adding notes all over the place, you could either be short on space or the format isn't working for you.

Decide whether you want a dated or undated planner. With the latter you have to spend more time writing in the dates, but you also won't waste any sections of your planner if you should purchase it after the year has begun. With loose-leaf planners that isn't a problem, unless dated sheets are prepackaged by year or quarter.

If your planner comes with a telephone directory, try to find one with sections for *each* letter of the alphabet rather than two letters combined so you can use the sections not only as phone/address pages but also as subject dividers for resource information. For example, on my "R" page, I keep names that start with that letter and behind that address page I keep pages of information that start with the letter "R," such as "Restaurant" pages, listing my favorite restaurants. (See Figure 2-9).

The size of your planner may pose some problems. You may want it to be small and compact enough to carry with you yet large enough to carry standard size papers. A tradeoff may be necessary. Choose the most important size considerations. Lean toward the *size you will use* and select a planner that has the most important features to you.

DO YOU REALLY NEED AN ORGANIZER?

Usually housed in plush ring binders, organizers help professionals manage both time and information. Organizers incorporate a variety of planning and scheduling tools, including calendars; daily to-do sheets; weekly, monthly and yearly projections; master lists; and schedules for special projects and activities.

Other features usually include a phone directory, sections for "fingertip information" referred to frequently, record keeping tools, special forms, compartments for credit cards and cash (Figure 2-10), pen and pencil holders and combination calculator/rulers. The Day-Timer combination ruler/calculator is an accessory for your organizer that's hole-punched, includes inches and centimeters and is solar-powered. Organizers are portable "Swiss army desks" equipped with all the essentials professionals need close at hand. You need never be at a loss for important resource or scheduling information—particularly vital if you're out of your office frequently.

A variety of styles and sizes adapt to many different professional needs. Some are small enough to fit in a coat or shirt pocket; others fit in a briefcase or purse; still others are self-contained mini-briefcases or combination organizer/purses that can be carried on the shoulder with a strap. Many come in leather and make for professional accessories that are functional as well as attractive.

I'm particularly excited about the combination organizer/purse with a shoulder strap that has been evolving over the last several years.

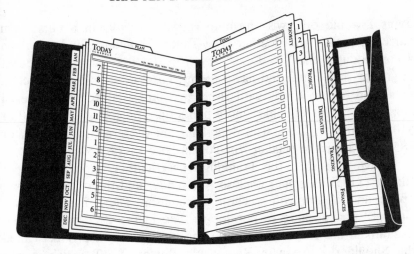

Figure 2-9. The Day Runner PRO Business System organizer is a flexible organizer for managing people and projects. The PRO features either a 5½ by 8½ or 8½ by 11 page size in a 7-ring loose-leaf format and can be customized with over 30 PRO refills. I like the one-letter-per-page dividers that work great as subject dividers.

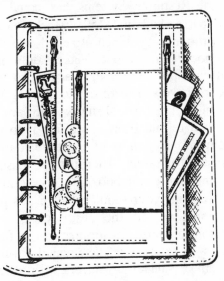

Figure 2-10. The "Carry-All" Multi-Zippered Holder is a Day-Timer organizer accessory I've used for years. (Illustration courtesy of Day-Timers, Inc., Allentown, PA 18195-1551)

I've used this style organizer for many years and appreciate that it's portable enough to carry my organizer and large enough to carry items I would otherwise have to carry separately in a purse. I'm currently using the leather Day-Timer Shoulder Binder, which accommodates the "Jr. Desk" size (5½ by 8½ inches) loose-leaf organizer that I use, and has a roomy, gusseted outside zip pocket. Inside are seven handy card slots, five utility pockets, a zippered compartment for valuables and a pen loop. The cost is either $90 or $105 for the Jr. Desk size, depending on the grade of leather, or $85 or $98 for the smaller "Sr. Pocket" size (3¾ by 6¾ inches).

I have also used the Franklin Quest leather Shoulder Zipper Binder ($165). A zipper encloses the binder and the outside pocket opens and closes with a clasp mechanism. There is an interior zippered pocket and two pen loops. (See Figure 2-11 on page 43).

Franklin has recently come out with an innovative product called the Shoulder Purse with Removable Binder ($200) which is two products—a binder organizer housed in a roomy leather purse. If you want to go to a meeting and not take your purse, just simply detach it and take just your binder.

Finally, Personal Resource Systems has come out with their leather Classic Purse and Case ($150), which features removable shoulder straps, a roomy 6-by-9-inch attached outside clutch purse, a second outside pocket on the back and inside a zippered leather pouch with eight card pockets on the back. Also inside are three pen loops and four pockets. The three rings are 1½ inches.

In the interest of health, I would suggest with any shoulder purse or organizer that you refrain from a) stuffing it to the gills and b) carrying it on your shoulder most of the time. I use the shoulder strap for convenience (or safety) when it's not feasible to hold the organizer in my arms like a notebook. It's not good for your spine to have anything weighing your shoulder down. It's probably a good idea to switch shoulders, but the best idea is to refrain from constantly carrying an organizer or a purse in this fashion. Another option, of course, is to select a smaller, scaled-down organizer; the above companies make smaller organizers with attractive shoulder style purses or wallets.

What I also like about organizers are the handy accessories and forms you can select to customize your system. I keep the Tri-Point Pen/Pencil ($30 or $32) from Day-Timers in my organizer and use it every day. This high quality, versatile writing instrument has two fine-point pens in black and red ink and a 0.5mm pencil. I always write my calendar and to-do items in pencil, take notes in black ink and use the red to highlight or mark special notations. (A Quad-Point Pen/Pencil ($40 or $44) is also available with an additional blue ink pen.) The Pentel Colored Automatic Pencil ($9.95) with eight brightly colored pencils in one holder available from Personal Resource Systems (PRS) works great for Mind Mapping (see Chapter 9) and color-coding.

PRS also has Page Reinforcing Strips (12 for $2.95) that strengthen those pages you use frequently. For pages you use constantly, Day-Timers has durable plastic "Tabbed Sheet Holders" (8 clear tabbed, punched pockets, 24 index sheets and 80 colored tab tablets for $6). Both PRS and Day-Timers, as well as Day Runner carry plastic, punched diskette holders.

Both PRS and Day-Timers offer a wide variety of loose-leaf forms. They each offer colored ruled sheets, great for color-coding note taking by project or category type (e.g., correspondence and telephone calls). And now Day-Timers has colored sheets that are "short-trimmed" so they won't hide the date at the top and are also "double-punched." The latter is great for taking notes on the other side of paper—have you noticed those rings always get in the way? Double-punched papers let you easily open the rings and turn the paper over so that you can write just as easily on the back as the front! Day-Timers even has a special "Double-Punched Narrow Hot list" with a salmon, green or blue border that's great to use as a traveling master list that eliminates transferring of items, moves easily throughout your organizer and because it's narrow, keeps most of your organizer pages in view.

3M has developed some handy personal organizer accessories. Here are a few of my favorites: Scotch Magic Pre-cut Tape Strips No. 673TP1 (you no longer have to take a roll of tape with you), multi-colored Post-it Tape Flags in a thin pack dispenser (No. 683-5CF or No. 673LP1) or a thin pack combo of Tape Flags with Post-it Notes (No. 673TG1) and a thin pack with Post-it-Fax Notes (No. 673LP6).

The organizer is my personal time management favorite but it's not for everyone (nor is any tool for that matter). If you're at your desk most of the day and don't move around from office to office or meeting to meeting, you may not need the portability and compactness of the organizer. Some people don't need to have that much information at their fingertips and find notebook organizers bulky and cumbersome. Some see organizers as too "trendy" for their taste.

Others ask, "What would you do if you lost it?" Here are three measures to prevent the dire consequences of such a disaster. First, always photocopy any critical material and store it in a safe location. Second, use a computerized time management program or PIM (see the Resource Guide). With this option, you would print out your hard copies (which you can use in your organizer) and make regular computer data backups. Third, write the following statement on a business card that you laminate and attach to the inside front cover of your organizer: "REWARD: $150 for returning this lost book."

COMPUTERIZED TIME MANAGEMENT PROGRAMS AND PIMS

There are many advantages of using a computerized time management program or PIM (personal information manager). First, it combines most of the other tools we've discussed in this chapter (calendar, to-do list, master list, tickler system and planner/organizer) in one system. Second, it's easy and quick to input and *retrieve* information. Third, because many of these programs allow you to print out information onto paper forms that will fit right into your paper-based personal organizer, you have the best of both computer and paper worlds. Fourth, with most such programs, you have the flexibility to store and arrange random bits of information such as notes, ideas, plans and activities in free-form style, linked loosely by categories that you create. Fifth, it's also easy to make backup copies for added protection.

The only down side is if you're away from your computer much or most of the time (and you're not using a laptop or electronic personal organizer) and you make lots of handwritten notes on your printed-out version, it will be tedious to have to input all these notes into the program when you return to your office. And more than likely, you won't bother to do it and so you're defeating the purpose of using a computer program.

The term "personal information manager" was first coined by Lotus Development Corp., who used it in conjunction with their former "Agenda" program. Lotus founder, Mitch Kapor, developed Agenda because he was looking for a better way to organize himself.

PIMs have evolved to include both free-form and structured information. Time management programs have tended to be more structured in nature. In general, you'll probably want to look for a PIM that can manage your calendar, to do's, phone and address database, projects and ideas.

If you have a computer that you use all the time in your office and/or a laptop that you use on the go, it makes sense to buy a PIM. Such a program usually comes with many different time management features, including calendar/scheduling, to-do list and tickler functions, as well as information management functions.

An especially nice feature of a computerized program is that you can quickly search for information in a variety of ways. Let's suppose you want to find every contact you've had with a particular customer. You can search that customer by name and within seconds find the information you need.

I'm excited about seeing all the new software being developed at long last for use with specific brand-name paper-based organizers. If you've found a paper-based system that you like, such as a Day-Timer, Day Runner or Personal Resource System, the transition to its software should be fairly easy. Try to determine in advance just how seamless that transition is; often the computer screens do not look like your paper-based systems, although the printout will. See if there is a "print preview" mode, so you can see in advance what the printout will look like so you don't end up wasting paper and time. Find out if there are any independent reviews on new software (I'll be mentioning whether products have been reviewed and/or received any awards).

The Resource Guide is loaded with some of the best PIMs and time management software solutions available.

ELECTRONIC ORGANIZERS

This is a growing product line that has great appeal to those of us who like portability combined with gadgetry plus some of the calendaring, tickler and personal information features found in time management programs, PIMs and personal paper-based organizers. Some of them can exchange information directly with your computer and perform telecommunications functions, such as e-mail.

Some people like to use an electronic organizer along with one or more of the other time management tools. One PIM manufacturer I spoke with, uses his own PIM in the office and takes along a Sharp Wizard electronic organizer on the road.

Look for these features: a QWERTY keyboard with well-spaced, raised keys that beep or click when pressed; a large space bar at the bottom; dedicated function keys; a backspace key that erases as it backs up; a large, clear display that tilts and has a contrast-adjustment control; personal computer/telecommunications links and memory cards. (See also Chapter 12.)

RESOURCE GUIDE

Time management is an ongoing challenge and adventure. There are no magic wands but hopefully this listing will open your eyes to the many exciting solutions that are available.

TIME MANAGEMENT TOOLS AND SYSTEMS

Practically every time I turn around, I see a new time management tool or system. The following are among the best I've seen. See also Chapter 9 for additional ideas.

CALENDARS, PLANNERS AND ORGANIZERS

Day-Focus System is a life management system and personal organizer designed to help you clearly focus upon your goals, personally and professionally, in order to accomplish the most important things in your life and create more balance; well-designed system and forms; training tape available; two sizes: 4¼ by 6¾, $54.95 to $94.95 and 5½ by 8½, $64.95 to $139.95. 800/662-5300 or 714/366-2939, Day-Focus, Inc., 934 Calle Negocio, Ste. E, San Clemente, CA 92673

Day Runner personal organizers and planners are available nationally in department and stationery stores in an affordable, versatile range of styles, sizes, features and accessories. **Day Runner Planner for Windows** is their newest organizing software designed especially for paper-based system users and can be used with their specially-designed pre-formatted and pre-punched computer paper refills. $120

800/635-5544 or 714/680-3500, Day Runner, Inc., 2750 West Moore Avenue, Fullerton, CA 92633

Day-Timers, Inc. planners and work organizers come in probably the widest variety of different sizes, formats, supplies and accessories. Check out their new software (see the PIMs section later in this chapter). Free catalog. 800/225-5005 or 610/266-9313, Day-Timers, Inc., PO Box 27000, Lehigh Valley, PA 18003-9859

Filofax small planners incorporate date book, project, expense and phone/address information in compact, attractive, leather binders. Available in department and stationery stores. 800/345-6798 or 203/846-6520 (to get names of stores in your area that carry Filofax) Filofax Inc., 101 Merritt, 7 Corp. Pk., 5th Fl., Norwalk, CT 06851

The **Franklin Day Planner** is a full-featured organizer system. The Franklin catalog offers a nice selection of high quality binders (including one with a shoulder strap and outside purse pocket as shown in Figure 2-11) as well as special forms and training materials. 800/654-1776 or 801/975-1776, Franklin Quest Co., 2200 West Parkway Blvd., Salt Lake City, UT 84119

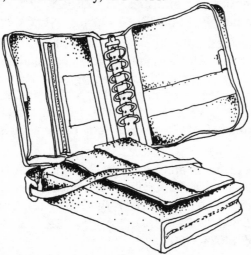

Figure 2-11. The Shoulder Binder by Franklin Quest is a convenient way for a woman to carry both her organizer and a few personal items in the outside purse pocket. It's available in black, burgundy, forest and navy.

Geodex Systems are binder-style organizers that are available in 12 different profession-specific styles, as well as more universal styles.

A new Life Management format has been added to all systems to help users identify a "Vision of Success," a personal "Purpose" and a "Life Plan" to help you balance your work, self and home (which includes family, friends and community). A wide selection of detailed forms are available. 800/833-3030 or 707/938-0001, Geodex International, Inc., PO Box 279, Sonoma, CA 95476

The **Personal Resource System** is a cleanly-designed, leather, zippered notebook organizer system that comes with an instruction booklet and an audio tape. It now comes in three sizes, 3¾ by 6¾, 5½ by 8½ or 8½ by 11 inches. For more in-depth training, there is the "Second Edition Beyond Time Management" cassette tape series and workbook. **PRS for Windows** is their new software and comes with a sample of special hole-punched, perforated laser printing paper ($149). 800/255-9018 or 619/259-6001, Personal Resource Systems, Inc., PO Box 2529, Del Mar, CA 92014

Planner Pad (Figure 2-12) is a concise weekly planner available in three different sizes that has sections for things-to-do, appointments, expenses and space for your own categories. It helps you think in terms of categories and priorities. $19.95 to $24.95. 402/592-0676, Planner Pads, Inc., PO Box 27187, Omaha, NE 68127-0187

Pocket-it Organizers offer the practicality of 8½ by 11-inch sheets with the convenience of a small pocket-sized planner; they fold to the size of a 3-by-5 inch card for carrying in a slim wallet and then unfold for filing in a three-ring binder; $59.95 to $99.95. Pocket-it Software, **DOS**, $59.95. 800/955-0800 or 619/558-8287, Success Organizer Systems, Inc., 6215 Ferris Square, Ste. 220, San Diego, CA 92121

QUO VADIS planners are readily available in stationery stores and allow you to plan by the week. I particularly like their **Prenote**, **Trinote** (see Figure 2-13) and **RAF Businessnote** planners. 800/535-5656 or 716/648-2602, QUO VADIS, 120 Elmview Avenue, Hamburg, NY 14075-3770

SCAN/PLAN The Creative Organizer instant information systems use unique transparent plastic pockets that hold index cards and remarkably let you read and write on both sides of the cards without removing them! For cards you do wish to move, they move very

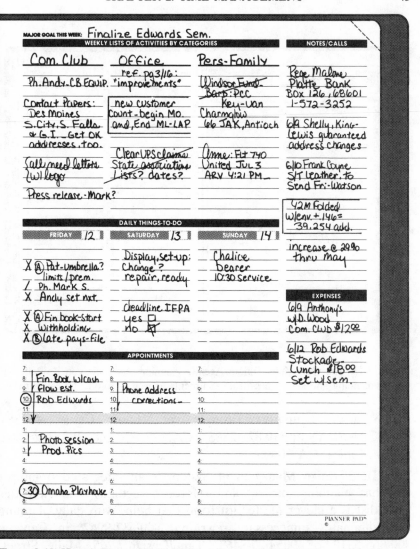

Figure 2-12. Here is Planner Pad's right-hand page (the left-hand page has Monday through Thursday). Planner pad is a combination appointment book, daily to-do list and weekly master list. Note the columns across the top that allow you to create your own categories of to-do's for the week.

easily. These versatile systems are great for managing time, projects and all kinds of information and come in a variety of different sized planners and accessories. You can use SCAN/PLAN with personal organizers or binders (see Figure 2-14). You can also use SCAN/

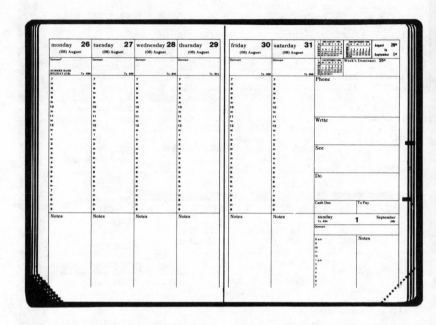

Figure 2-13. The Quo Vadis Trinote Agenda Planning Diary lets you do daily and weekly planning and keep track of appointments as well as to-do's by category.

PLAN with computers (using Avery Laser Cards #5388). **800/SCANPLAN** or 310/829-2888. SCAN/PLAN, Inc., PO Box 1662, Santa Monica, CA 90406

The **Time/Design Management System** is an integrated organizer that has planning, project and reference sections. The Activities Checklist is a clever master list form that helps with daily planning and eliminates unnecessary rewriting. 800/637-9942; in Canada: 800/665-5310 or 905/629-8463, Time/Design, 265 Main Street, Agawam, MA 01001

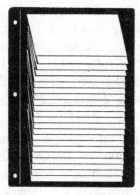

Figure 2-14. The "21 Scan Page" is a binder page that holds 21-42 3-by-5-inch index, Rolodex or computer printout cards. It fits into a 5½-by-8½-inch three ring binder or personal organizer.

ELECTRONIC ORGANIZERS, PALMTOPS, PDAs

Casio Executive B.O.S.S. (Business Organizer Scheduling System) has an appointment calendar, phone directory, memo function, birthday/anniversary reminder and business card library; it comes with 256K of memory (you can also add a 256K memory card) and weighs three pounds. $449.95. 800/634-1895 or 201/361-5400, Casio, Inc., 570 Mt. Pleasant Ave., Dover, NJ 07801

HP 200LX Palmtop Computer has complete time management software and is the only palmtop with built-in "Pocket Quicken," cc:Mail Mobile and datacomm that runs DOS-based software off the shelf. It implements PCMCIA version 2.0, which enables users to plug in a modem card or mass storage, and has infrared connectivity to PCs and printers. It weighs 11 ounces. $649. 800/443-1254, Hewlett Packard, 1000 NE Circle Blvd., Corvallis, OR 97330

Psion 3A was gadget product reviewer Andy Pargh's recent "all-around favorite" electronic organizer. Psion looks and operates like a real calendar with day, week or month views. It has built-in Microsoft Word, 512K memory that can expand to 8.5 megabytes ("MB"), several minutes of digital voice processing and weighs 9.9 ounces. The 512K version is $350-390; 1MB, $499; 2MB, $599. ($295 additional for optional send-only fax/modem). 800/547-7466 or 508/371-0310, Psion, Inc., 150 Baker Ave., Concord, MA 01742

Rolodex Pocket Organizer EL3200 is a 128K memory electronic organizer with scheduling functions, space for 2,000 names and numbers and a calculator. It has alarm, anniversary, notes and confidential file functions. Infra-red transfer lets you transfer contact files between other Rolodex units or with a PC using Rolodex's PC Link. It weighs 5 ounces. $169. 201/348-3939, Rolodex Corp., 245 Secaucus Rd., Secaucus, NJ 07094

Sharp Wizard personal information managers are loaded with features. Model **OZ-6500** applications include a calendar, a scheduler, three user files, two anniversary functions, to-do list, three telephone directories, notebook function, outline processor, word processing, calculator, home and world clocks and a secret function for sensitive information. Communications are possible with Windows, DOS or Macintosh computers using Sharp infrared technology. A fax-modem comes with the **OZ-6500FX** model. It weighs 8.6 ounces and has 512K of internal memory. It takes two AAA batteries for 65 hours of power or two months of normal use; a lithium battery is used as backup and lasts for approximately five years. $499.99; $599.99 for FX model. Consider also the **OZ-9500** and **OZ-9520** models with 256K and 512K memory respectively; they're loaded with features, can share data with personal computers and connect to e-mail and online services. $589 and $719. The newest model is the **OZ-5500**, which features financial tracking, project management, wireless communications and a built-in interactive setup program with templates. 800/BE-SHARP, The Wizard Division-Sharp Electronics Corporation, Sharp Plaza, Mahwah, NJ 07430.

Voice Organizer is a keypad-free, 3.5 ounce, palm-size voice recognition "office on the run" that is a combination appointment calendar, memo pad, tickler system and phone directory; it stores up to 400 phone numbers for 100 people, 99 voice reminders with time lags (and it beeps when they're due) and 99 voice memos; you can set your calendar a year in advance; locks with your own 4-digit security code. See Figure 2-15. $219.95 Phone: 818/905-0950, FAX: 818/905-0564, Voice Powered Technology, 15260 Ventura Blvd., #2200, Sherman Oaks, CA 91403

Figure 2-15. Model 5500 Voice Organizer can be hand held or can sit in recharger base unit as shown.

TIME MANAGEMENT SOFTWARE
AND PERSONAL INFORMATION MANAGERS (PIMs)

See information on page 206 for abbreviations and software consumer tips. See also Chapter 8 and the index for other products and especially Chapters 9 and 11 for more group scheduling, contact management and project management products.

AnyTime for Windows is a PIM that's easy to use, inexpensive and has a large selection of printouts. The program has a familiar, notebook-like interface that's intuitive, making the program easy to learn. $24.95 **Peanuts Family Organizer** is a new product that looks like fun for tracking family and personal schedules. **Win** $19.95. 800/822-3522 or 510/734-6767, Individual Software, 5870 Stoneridge Drive, Suite 1, Pleasanton, CA 94588

Day-Timer Organizer is award-winning software that combines the power of the PC with the ability to print pages that fit the different formats of your paper Day-Timer system, as well as other popular paper-based binder formats; accommodates the different Day-Timer formats using special computer forms; group scheduling on the network version. **Win, DOS, Net.** $139.95 for Win or DOS; call for information about the network version (up to 100 users). 800/225-5005 or 610/266-9313, Day-Timers, Inc., PO Box 27000, Lehigh Valley, PA 18003-9859

DeskTop Set Professional Organizer for Windows is an award-winning full-featured, powerful PIM that's easy to use; can download to Sharp Wizard, Casio BOSS and HP 95LX electronic organizers; extensive printing formats. **Win** $99. 800/438-6562 or 201/909-8600, Okna Corporation, PO Box 522, Lyndhurst, NJ 07071

ECCO Professional is an award-winning PIM that starts with calendar, phone book and task management and then adds customizable folders and powerful cross-referencing that give your fingertip access to every task, project, conversation or action item that has relevance in your daily life. Now with group scheduling, multi-user shared calendars, phone books, task outlines and file synchronization, ECCO Professional extends this productivity to the workgroup. It's for both stand-alone use and users on a network. **Win & Net.** $179. 800/457-4243 or 206/885-4272, NetManage-ECCO Division, 2340 130th Ave. NE, Bellevue, WA 98005-1754

In Control is an award-winning planner and organizer for the Macintosh that combines project outlining, scheduling and to-do list management and links automatically to database and contact managers including FastPace Instant Contact, FileMaker Pro, Dynodex, Now Contact and TouchBase Pro. It also helps you define, organize and prioritize your goals and plan a schedule to achieve them. $84.95. **In Control for Workgroups** lets you and your team collaborate on group projects, tasks and activities by sharing outlines, calendars and to-do lists over networks, right from your Mac or PowerBook. **Mac** Single unit: $149.95; ten pack: $949.95. 800/925-5615; Fax: 617/776-1626

Now Up-to-Date is an award-winning calendar and scheduling application for individuals within workgroups. Users can quickly and easily manage their own schedules as well as share and synchronize pertinent scheduling information with colleagues. **Mac** $69.95; bundled with Now Contact, contact management software, $99.95. 800/237-2078 or 503/274-2800, Now Software, Inc., 921 S.W. Washington St., Ste. 500, Portland, OR 97205-2823

Sidekick for Windows has received some excellent reviews and ratings as an example of "slimware software"—a small, fast product that delivers the most useful features in the easiest manner. **Win** $49.95. 800/370-8963 or 408/439-0942, Starfish Software, 1700 Green Hills Road, Scotts Valley, CA 95066

Touchbase & Datebook Pro Bundle combine a highly rated schedule and contact manager into a single, powerful, very easy-to-use system. The latest version has greater speed due to memory-based indexing. A project organizer allows users to schedule to-do items and tasks on their calendars related to a particular project. The TouchBase Menu feature lets you access contact information even when the application isn't open. **Mac** $49.95. 800/237-2078 or 503/274-2800, Now Software, Inc. (Portland, OR)

EXTRA TIME MANAGEMENT LEARNING OPPORTUNITIES

American Management Association provides educational forums worldwide where members and their colleagues learn superior, practical business skills and explore best practices of world-class organizations through interaction with each other and expert training practitioners. Look for three-hour satellite updates, six hour one-day seminars in your area, multi-day programs presented in major cities, national conferences, and customized on-site training. AMA's publishing program provides tools individuals can use to extend learning beyond the classroom in a process of life-long professional growth and development. **800/255-4141** or 913/451-2700. American Management Association, 11221 Roe Avenue, Leawood KS 66211

Day-Timer 4-Dimensional Time Management Public Seminars include Day-Timer products as part of their training materials. $99. 800/654-0346, Day-Timer Concepts, Inc., One Willow Lane, East Texas, PA

Managing Your Time and Priorities is a dynamic three-video cassette series with a participant workbook that will show you how to get control of your workday, stay organized, increase productivity and control stress. Train yourself or staff at the same time by purchasing extra workbooks. $189.95. **800/873-7545** or 913/362-3900, SkillPath Publications, 6900 Squibb Road, Ste. 300, Mission, KS 66201-2768

SkillPath Seminars present more than 8,000 seminars on 30 topics throughout North America and the Pacific Rim. The seminar leaders are a select group of trainers at the top of their profession—skilled teachers with a tremendous depth of knowledge in their respective topic areas. **800/873-7545** or 913/362-3900, SkillPath Seminars, 6900 Squibb Road, Ste. 300, Mission, KS 66201-2768

3

HOW TO HANDLE
TOO MUCH TO DO
IN TOO LITTLE TIME

Quick Scan: If you have an increasingly busy schedule in your professional and/or personal life, you'll discover time-tested tips on managing interruptions, telephone time, delegation, multiple priorities and the "rushing game." See how to better balance the "great juggling act," make room for your personal life and start using ten terrific time-savers.

Rarely, if ever, do people I meet have the luxury of working at a leisurely pace. There are always countless deadlines and shifting priorities, which all add up to mounting pressure.

The issue is not how much you have to do but rather how much you have to do that is really *important.* You learned how to sort the important from the less important in Chapter 1 and Chapter 2. You also learned how to organize work into categories and priorities so that you could *see* what you had to do.

The next step is to take a good hard look at *how* you work. See if there are better ways for you to get things done.

HOW TO CONTROL INTERRUPTIONS AT WORK

The most common complaint I hear is, "There are too many interruptions." The main question to ask yourself is, "How many of these interruptions can I control, minimize or influence in some way?"

In my training programs I will often use the following chart to have participants list all their typical interruptions:

Type of Interruption	I can control them...			How I could control or influence them
	Almost Always	Sometimes	Never	

First, jot down as many interruptions as you can imagine and be sure to include those from others as well as those you initiate *yourself.* How many times a day do you interrupt *yourself* to handle something now when it should be handled later, switch to something more pleasurable as an escape from the difficult task at hand or simply decide to do something easier?

Second, check whether each interruption is one you can control or influence "Almost always," "Sometimes" or "Never."

Third, for every interruption that enters your day, ask "Is this interruption *necessary*?" Some interruptions are part of your job. If you're a customer service representative or a receptionist, for example, telephone interruptions *are* your business. Even so, you can learn to maximize your telephone time so that you have more control. Write an "N" for Necessary next to each interruption that needs to be handled.

Fourth, using your imagination, jot down anything you *could* do to control or influence each interruption in some way. It may be an interruption is necessary but can be handled later. Perhaps you could prevent similar interruptions from occurring in the future.

One large company I'm consulting with has mail delivery three to four times a day. Each time the mail is delivered represents another possible interruption. How would *you* control these interruptions?

I'm sure you came up with a few ideas. (It's always easier to try solving someone else's problem by giving advice; in fact, whenever you get stuck on a problem, take it to someone else for some fresh ideas!) Here are a few of my ideas:

- Handle the mail once a day and don't look at it during other times.
- Take a minute to scan the mail each time it comes for anything critical but process it only during a regularly scheduled mail appointment with yourself.
- Have an assistant or secretary scan it for you based on pre-established criteria.
- Suggest the company reduce mail delivery to twice a day.

The idea is to start looking for ways to control and prevent interruptions. Analyze interruptions carefully. Don't just assume they are all necessary. Become proactive, not reactive, whenever possible. And always use common sense and good judgment, especially when dealing with interruptions and concerns of other people.

FIVE SECRETS TO TAME TELEPHONE TIME

Many consider the telephone both a drain on time and the single greatest source of disrupting interruptions. Actually, the telephone can be your greatest ally if you follow these five essential ingredients to make your telephone time work best for you.

ONE: TAKE CONTROL THROUGH PREPARATION AND PLANNING

The key to mastering the telephone is doing much of your telephone work in advance, making more outgoing calls and taking fewer incoming calls. Whenever possible, set up telephone appointments. Prioritize and consolidate all callbacks. Prepare for each outgoing call or telephone appointment by having all the necessary material in front of you and *writing down* in advance any key questions or areas to cover as well as a projected time limit for each call.

Planning the time you call can be critical in preventing telephone tag. The busiest time for business calls is usually Monday morning, between 9 and 11 a.m. Sometimes calling before 9 a.m. or after 5 p.m. is a good time to catch those hard-to-reach people.

TWO: WHAT YOU SAY GOES A LONG WAY WITH A PTA

Do you have a "Positive Telephone Attitude"? A PTA is essential for building rapport and good working relationships.

In particular, there is nothing like the power of praise when you're trying to accomplish your goals through the telephone. Acknowledge good telephone behavior by those who assist you, be they colleagues, contacts, prospects, receptionists or your own staff members.

I make a big point of thanking assistants or secretaries who have gone out of their way to take down a long message or connect me with someone who's been difficult to reach. I often will tell their boss. Fund raiser Suzanne Marx sends thank-you notes to secretaries and hotel operators as well.

A PTA also includes helpfulness and follow-through. A well-intentioned PTA becomes hollow indeed if what was promised isn't delivered.

THREE: USE CONCISE COMMUNICATION

Be specific when you communicate. Corporate communications consultant Dr. Allen Weiner of CDA in Sherman Oaks, California, teaches professionals "bottom line communicating," which is similar to Dragnet Sergeant Friday's, "Just the facts, ma'am." Nothing will speed up a call like getting to the point sooner.

Try these two proven techniques: first, set time limits up front (e.g., "I've got five minutes to talk") and second, outline your calls (e.g., "I'd like to discuss these two questions...").

Even your voice mail or telephone answering machine message should be as concise as possible. We get a lot of compliments on ours: "Thank you for calling Positively Organized! Please leave your name, number *and the best time to call you back*."

FOUR: TAKE NOTES AND TAKE ACTION

Take notes during the call if you think you may need to refer back to the call in the future. Don't rely on a good memory and don't be tempted by the thought, "I'll remember this call."

I use an 8½-by-11-inch sheet of paper (as compared to slips of paper that can get lost). Always date the entry, list the party, who initiated the call, any main points to be covered and list comments *as you go.* I like to number comments as well. Better yet, use your computer—you'll be able to search easily for notes later on.

Right after the call, highlight key points and take any necessary follow-up steps, such as transferring information to your calendar or listing the next action step in your tickler system. (For more information on tickler systems, see Chapter 2.)

FIVE: TRAIN YOUR TELEPHONE TEAM

If you're fortunate enough to have someone else in your office handling your telephone, you have an opportunity to boost your effectiveness, provided you *train* that person how to screen and prioritize calls, take messages and use all of the effective telephone habits listed here. For more telephone tips, see also "Value Your Voice Mail" in Chapter 11.

HOW TO DELEGATE YOUR WAY TO SUCCESS (EVEN IF YOU'RE NOT IN A POSITION TO DELEGATE)

Whether or not you're in a position to delegate, delegation is a tool to help you increase your work output and performance in the least amount of time—provided you know how to use it and you understand what delegation really means. For the delegator, it's giving people things you don't want to do, or often, things you *do.*

In fact, according to Ben Tyler, past Burlington Industries Transportation Division president, "It's giving up things you enjoy to someone else and recognizing that not only can they do it, but sadly, they can do it better." For the delegate, delegation is an opportunity to grow and develop and to shine.

Effective delegation requires four steps: 1) organize, 2) train, 3) entrust and 4) follow up and evaluate.

First, organize yourself. You need to see the whole picture in order to make delegation decisions. Think through the process. You'll also need a good personal organization system in order to follow up later. Top designer and entrepreneur Calvin Klein says he organizes himself first so he can delegate effectively to others.

Second, train your delegate. The amount of training and direction will vary according to the delegate's abilities and the nature of the assignment. Take time to clearly teach the delegate how to do something. Helping people be the best they can be is the highest and most productive level of delegation.

Third, entrust your delegate with the assignment. Resist the temptation of peeking over shoulders. By the way, the dictionary definition of the verb "delegate" is "to entrust to another."

Fourth, follow up, evaluate and *praise a job well done.* Of course, you can't do this step if you haven't mastered step number one. So we've come full circle, back to organization.

If you find it tough getting people to follow through and give you things on time, do what Kathy Meyer-Poppe did when she was a director at Revlon. She told her staff, "This is what I need and this is the date I need it by." Then she wrote it on her calendar and her staff knew she had done so. They also knew she would ask for it if it wasn't done. But usually she didn't have to ask. She said, "They knew it was truly important when I said, for example, 'I need this by next Friday'—that I'm not just blowing in the wind." She stayed flexible, too; if her request were unrealistic, her staff told her and together they selected a new goal and agreed on it. At times she suggested they reprioritize their work.

REVERSE DELEGATION

When Meyer-Poppe's staff came back to her to negotiate work assignments or deadlines, they were practicing a type of **reverse delegation.** This tool works best when you're organized and can clearly see the important things you have to do, how long they will take and how they relate to the goals of your delegator, your department and yourself.

This type of reverse delegation occurs when a person gives a delegated task back to the delegator. It requires great tact and diplomacy and communication skills. It also requires a thorough understanding of goals and objectives for the company or office and for the delegator. There has to be a real *benefit* for the delegator whenever you reverse delegate.

When I was the communications manager for an aerospace company, my boss wanted me to get involved in coordinating one of his new pet projects—the creation of a historical aviation museum. Since I had no interest in his project and saw no relation in it to either my job or career, I suggested that he involve someone else who was far more qualified than I. Coming up with the name of someone else was an easy task; the company historian worked right within our department and was a natural for this project. I didn't know it at the time, but I was practicing reverse delegation.

There's one other type of reverse delegation that you should always practice whenever you're given an assignment or project. Take each of the four steps of effective delegation—organize, train, entrust, and follow up/evaluate—and make sure *you* are doing them. Organize yourself, get any necessary training or information, get the trust or authority to do a job and finally, make sure *you* follow through on evaluating the job with your boss. This type of reverse delegation is a marvelous communication and self-marketing tool; it can show your boss just how well you work, not to mention how dependable and organized you are!

HOW TO JUGGLE MULTIPLE PRIORITIES

When you handle many different projects, priorities and deadlines, you're very much like a juggler from Vaudeville who would run around keeping a dozen plates spinning on sticks.

Sure, you can try to keep up this act all day, but you'll certainly burn out before too long. Unfortunately, this method is used by far too many people. To prevent burn out, here are four tips that can help. (The first three recap key ideas you learned in Chapter 2.)

First, **plan and prioritize on a daily basis** and if necessary, several times a day. Do your main planning for the day, *the day* *before.* Then stay flexible in order to reprioritize, if necessary, throughout the day.

Second, **use the right planning tools** that give you enough of an overview. I'm not talking about a flood of reminder notes scattered all over your desk. Such tools could include a wall chart that shows upcoming deadlines, a project or time management software program that lets you see priorities in a variety of ways or a master list.

Third, to prevent having to remember too many things in your head, **use an appropriate follow-up system.** A tickler system that you use every day, for example, can save a lot of wear and tear on your gray matter.

Fourth, **use effective communication tools, techniques and systems** with those people making demands on you. Get clarity from others in terms of the real, not imagined, urgency of each request. Have others use a special written form that indicates both the nature of the request and the time frame for its completion. Chapter 10 describes how to create such a form. A written request doesn't interrupt you and lets you plan and prioritize similar requests and time frames more easily.

If several people from the same department or office are making conflicting demands on your time, bring it up at a staff meeting for a brainstorming session. Often, people may not be aware of the severity of the problem. Involve them in a cooperative way, not through finger-pointing, but through an exchange of ideas that can solve a problem. (For more on problem solving, communication and teamwork, once again see Chapter 10.)

HOW TO AVOID RUSHING

If rushing makes you crazy, make a commitment to stop doing it whenever possible. As a famous Simon and Garfunkle song says, "Slow down, you move too fast."

I keep reading articles in the paper about life in the fast lane. The more we do in our lives, the faster we need to do it. One recent newspaper story reported that even some microwavable foods aren't fast enough; if a meal has a two-step cooking process, consumer dissatisfaction sets in, even if the total cooking time amounts to no more than five minutes.

Some rushing may be unavoidable. Beware though if it's a regular habit of yours. In most cases, advance planning can prevent most cases of rushing.

Be realistic about time by becoming more *aware* of time. Be honest with yourself about how long an activity will *really* take. Estimate the minimum amount of time and a maximum and then aim for an amount in the middle.

Things usually take longer than we think (the unexpected almost always comes up). And yet, Parkinson's Law says that work expands to fill the time available, which is to say that if you allow too much time to do something, you'll do it in that period of time. Sometimes the opposite is also true: work contracts to fill the time available; it's amazing how much you can get done quickly when you have to.

Follow your own time clock but speed it up and slow it down when necessary. If you practice setting your own realistic deadlines and time frames, and sticking to them, you will soon accomplish so much more and with less rushing.

My own mother used to rush all the time (and be late for almost everything) until she decided that the associated stress was just too much. She now allows more time to get ready for appointments and commitments and also does more advance planning. The combination results in less stress and greater respect from clients, friends and her daughter, the organizer.

TEN TERRIFIC TIME AND ENERGY SAVERS
FOR TERRIBLY BUSY PEOPLE

Here are ten things you may like to try to help you save time and energy and create more balance (they work for me):

1. Carry a planner all the time and write things down right away.
2. Consolidate similar activities, such as errands, telephone calls, correspondence or errands and do them together. You'll save time starting and stopping different kinds of activities.
3. Buy in bulk. Whether you're getting office supplies, gifts or cards, it's more efficient to buy for long-range needs than to frequently run out to buy individual items. Buy gifts in bulk (if you find a great item) or at least ahead of time; I always find

great gift items when I'm not looking for them but happen to see them while shopping.

4. Call to confirm appointments. Always call doctors to see if they're running on schedule before you go there.

5. Use voice mail/telephone answering machines for screening calls and preventing unnecessary interruptions. Ask callers to leave you the best time(s) to call them back. If you have a short message to leave someone, call at a time when you know their voice mail or answering machine is likely to be on, so you don't get involved in a lengthy, unnecessary conversation.

6. Sometimes do two things at once, such as listening to a self-improvement tape while commuting, or reading while waiting in line.

7. Never leave a room empty handed. Before leaving a room at home, ask yourself if there is something you can take with you that belongs where you're going.

8. Be creative, open-minded and look for better ways of doing things. Did you know you can buy stamps through the mail as well as by phone? (The latter operates 24 hours a day, takes credit cards and works by calling 1/800/STAMP-24.) Share ideas with your friends and colleagues. How do *they* organize their day and life?

9. Don't rush. There's a saying that the faster you go, the slower you are going to get there. It's the old tortoise and the hare story.

10. Make time for yourself every day ideally but certainly every week at the very least. Plan things you look forward to, that nourish you. They will revitalize you with energy to spare.

HOW TO FINISH YOUR WORK
AND STILL HAVE TIME FOR A PERSONAL LIFE

If your work hangs over you like a dark cloud and follows you wherever you go, it's time to stand back and gain some perspective.

I'm not concerned about an occasional heavy schedule or major deadline. But if you think about work all the time, take work home every night or suffer from insomnia over work-related problems, you need a break!

In fact, you need more than a break; you need **balance.** Granted, your need for balance will be different at various times in your life. But the first step is developing some awareness when you're losing your balance and then to take some realistic steps.

For some people, it's helpful to add more structure to your schedule. Establish a quitting time each day and stick to it! That's more difficult than it seems for the workaholics among us.

One company has started a "time management" program in which employees are urged not to stay late and are even pulled aside and told that it's the results that count, not the hours.

If you must work late once in a while, here are a couple of safety tips. If you need to sign in at the lobby: only write your first initial and your last name. Carry a cellular phone for emergencies.

If you must take work home, make an appointment with yourself. Decide to spend thirty minutes and thirty minutes only, for example, reviewing that report for tomorrow's staff meeting. (If necessary, use a timer.)

Make sure, too, you're not just playing a martyr role by taking on too much work or that you're giving in too much to your perfectionism ("no one else can do this as well as I"). Time management expert Mark Sanborn counters the myth that everything worth doing is worth doing well. He says, "Some things are worth doing well, some things are worth doing *very* well and some things are just worth doing."

Make an effort to talk openly with your boss or co-workers about your heavy work load. Don't just assume that there's no solution.

WHEN TOO MUCH IS JUST TOO MUCH

It does help to have a cooperative boss or co-worker. If you're working, however, with someone who's out to sabotage you or the company, or you truly do have too much to do and too little time, it may be best to look for a different working situation altogether. This is a last resort but consider it if you've tried the time management tools and techniques in this chapter (or book), all to no avail.

At every seminar I give there's at least one person in one of these "impossible situations," with an autocratic boss or a highly bureaucratic structure where no amount of organization could help.

Or maybe you're currently involved in a down-sizing effort, alternately called "right sizing" or just plain "capsizing," depending upon which boat you're in. One company I know has a downsizing "Cost Reduction Program," which the employees affectionately refer to by its acronym, CRP, (you have to pronounce it out loud for the full effect). If you're in any one of these "impossible" situations, it may be better to cut your losses and bail out. (On the other hand, some of these down-sized organizations can provide you with some new, exciting, empowered ways of working—see Chapter 10.)

Don't take job stress lightly. According to the Families & Work Institute in New York, job stress is more than three times more likely to spill over into the home than family problems are to crop up at work.

RESOURCE GUIDE

TIME/SELF-MANAGEMENT BOOKS AND TAPES

Time management is the process of making the most of your life in the time available. When fully understood, the concept of time management embraces self- and life-management. How you manage time outside of work has a direct relationship to time management at work and vice versa. The following books and tapes will help you make the most of *all* the time in your life, especially if you lead a busy life.

Creative Time-Plus offers three excellent tape cassette albums for busy people by home-organizing expert Ann Gambrell: "Quick Meals," "Paperwork, Paperwork" and "Clutter Control." $29.95 for each three-cassette album. Available from Creative Time-Plus, 2667 Monterey St., Torrance, CA 90503, 310/212-0917

Getting Organized: The Easy Way to Put Your Life in Order by Stephanie Winston (New York: Warner Books). Here's a great book to help you better manage personal areas of your life from financial planning to meal planning. Learn also to maximize storage space, organize your kitchen, run a household and even teach your child to organize. Paperback, $13.99

Getting Things Done by Edwin Bliss (New York: Scribner/Macmillan 1983). Literally the ABCs of time management, Bliss takes time management and organization topics such as "Deadlines," "Goals" and "Priorities," puts them in alphabetical order and succinctly provides practical and entertaining gems of wisdom. Paperback, $6.95

How to Create Balance at Work, at Home, in Your Life by Bee Epstein, Ph.D. is a dynamic, six-cassette program for working women. Epstein herself is a model of balance and success. This is a great program to enhance your life. Available from Adams-Hall Publishing, PO Box 491002, Los Angeles, CA 90049. $49

More Time for Sex: The Organizing Guide for Busy Couples by Harriet Schechter and Vicki T. Gibbs (New York: Dutton, 1995) is a fun-filled, yet practical guide to help couples reduce the unnecessary stress of managing and organizing their household logistics. $17.95

Newstrack Executive Tape Service is a twice-weekly tape cassette series that summarizes major newspaper and magazine articles related to business. $249 per year. 800/334-5771 or 703/548-3800. Encoders Inc., 1101 King St., Ste. 110, Alexandria, VA 22314

Nightingale-Conant business and motivational audiocassettes. An excellent selection of tape programs to get and keep you inspired to and from work. 800/323-5552

Peanuts Family Organizer is a software organizer designed for today's active family to help keep track of every family member's schedule and appointments, to do's and household activities. It also includes a Message Center for family messages, Peanuts comic strips and icons and personalized address books. **Win** $19.95. 800/822-3522 or 510/734-6767. Individual Software 5870 Stoneridge Drive, Suite 1 Pleasanton, CA 94588

Soundview Executive Book Summaries sends two or three eight-page summaries of business books and three one-page book reviews every month to subscribers. You can also buy back copies of summaries. 800/521-1227 or 802/453-4062

The Superwoman Syndrome by Marjorie Hansen Shaevitz (New York: Warner Books, 1985). This wonderful book is for women who want more balance and control in their life. Paperback. $3.95.

4

MASTERING
YOUR DESK
AND THE
PAPER JUNGLE

Quick Scan: If you're inundated with the "pile system" on your desk, if your work area is steadily shrinking into non-existence, if desktop clutter has got you down and under, this chapter's for you. Learn why your desk represents the single most important part of your office, how to make it work for you and what to do about paperwork.

Do you know where your desk is? This question is usually good for some chuckles at my seminars. The problem is most people can't even *find* their desk. It's under here somewhere...

You're not alone. You and 60 million other people in the U.S. have a desk of some kind. When I refer to a desk, I mean *any* piece of furniture that is used as your primary working surface. It may be a large executive model with many drawers in a traditional office or a simple work table at a computer work station.

Chances are good you spend many hours every day at your desk. Why not have it be the best looking, best functioning desk around?

THE MYTH OF THE MESSY DESK

No matter what you've seen on coffee cups, **a clean desk is the not the sign of an empty mind!** I know those coffee cup cliches will try to tell you otherwise. But don't be fooled. Most people think and act more clearly at a clean, well organized desk.

Don't fall prey to false notion that a messy desk means you're busy because you *look* busy. The reasoning is that if you *look* busy, you're productive. Take the advice of B. W. Luscher, Jr., from the U.S. Postal Service, who warns: "Don't confuse activity with productivity."

Far from indicating productivity, a messy desk signals a lack of dependability, control and focus, not to mention incomplete work, missed deadlines and lost information. One manager told me about an employee who had a ton of stuff on her desk. As the manager put it, "All those piles of paper told me she was in trouble."

While the woman was on vacation, the manager went in and saw a six-month-old check lying there with a bunch of invoices. He also discovered an important letter to 20 people that had never gone out. The letter was to announce a meeting the *manager* had planned. The manager found the 20 letters stuck in a drawer together with papers to be filed. All the letters had been typed and the envelopes addressed. All the employee had had to do was mail the letters! When the employee returned from vacation, she was devastated to learn of her mistake—she could have sworn she had mailed the letters months ago.

What was her problem? The manager says it was a combination of many things. She was very social, always wanting to know what was going on with other people and didn't take care of her own business. The manager observed, "You've got to worry first about what's on your own desk." He also said, "You've got to be a team player and let someone know if you're falling behind." In a nutshell, what she didn't have were the right organizational systems—the right tools and habits that signify a pro who is organized to be the best.

The fact is you are *not* more productive when you're working out of a cluttered desk. Besides feeling stress, you're continually distracted by all the different papers, piles and objects that keep pulling at you. It's easy to go into sensory overload as your eyes keep flitting from thing to thing and your mind keeps worrying whether you're working on the *right* task. No wonder you're exhausted at the end of each day!

Here's a rule of thumb: don't have more than one open paper file on your desk at any given time. You'll prevent papers from slipping into the wrong file.

Think of a clean desk as a little gift you give yourself.

THE PAPER EXPLOSION

Like most people, you're probably suffering from a paper explosion that never seems to let up. Despite computers, or rather because of them, we have more paper than ever before. The problem is two-fold: first, we produce paper documents faster and more easily now and second, most of us still crave hard copies because we like the feel of a paper document.

Here are some interesting statistics: a) The annual rate of paper consumption in the U.S. has nearly doubled, b) people regularly underestimate how much paper they use and c) Washington, D.C., the world's paper capital, consumes so much copier paper that if laid end to end it would reach the moon and back nine times over.

NOT A STORAGE LOCKER

Do not use your desktop for storage. It's a *work* surface, not a storage locker. Keep it clear, ready for action. Your desktop is *prime* work space and should contain only those items you use every day, such as your phone, calendar or planner and clock. Keep your desk as clean as possible.

But how clean is clean? That depends on a number of factors. First, consider who sees your desk. Colleagues? Clients? Customers? Patients? What kind of image do you want to create before these people? It's quite possible your desk should be spotless before the public but can be more of a workhorse before other staff members.

Incidentally, if you're concerned with image, consider this: research reveals that the cleanest desks belong to those individuals higher up in the organization. If you're on an upwardly mobile career path, have your desk look the part.

Second, consider what your level of aesthetics and function dictates. Start to become conscious of what *your* ideal level of order is and work toward it.

Some people really are more comfortable with clutter and claim they would dry up in an orderly, "sterile" environment. Neatness counts but neat isn't always organized or necessary. If you're one of those people who prefers "organized clutter," more power to you.

Most people, though, have simply never tried working in a clutter-free setting for more than a day or so. The expression "try it, you'll like it" certainly applies here.

HOW TO TURN YOUR DESK
INTO A SELF-CLEANING OVEN

Clients chuckle knowingly whenever I tell them, "Your desk is not a self-cleaning oven." They realize that they need to *do* something. Even with a self-cleaning oven, there are steps you need to take for it to work effectively: wipe up major spills, remove cookware and set the controls. So, too, there are steps to take with your desk to make it more automatic.

CLEAR A PATH

The first step is "clearing a path," as one of my clients described the process of thinning out the paper jungle and cleaning out the dead wood from her desktop and work area.

Think of yourself as an air traffic controller and your desktop as the runway. You're in charge. *You* determine which papers, piles, and projects can land on your desk—and stay there.

USE THE ACCESSIBILITY PRINCIPLE

I once had a client who sent me a snapshot of his terribly cluttered desk and office before we began working together. The caption read, "My office...where everything in the whole damn world is at my fingertips!"

Don't use your desk as one giant tickler system. You needn't be afraid that if papers and projects are out of sight, they'll be out of mind provided you do two things: 1) set up an appropriate **time management system** as described in Chapter 2 and 2) set up a **daily paperwork system**, which I'll describe soon.

Beware of the feeling that everything has to be accessible. How many of those things on your desktop do you actually use every day?

Every week? Every month? Every year? Make a list of the things you use every day. Of those things, which need to be sitting on your desktop? See if there isn't a better place, one that's accessible, but not on top of you.

Accessibility is the key word. Frequency of use should determine accessibility. How often are you using all of your items? Maybe you started out using an item every day in the past and at some point you stopped. But there the item remains. As a general rule, **the more often you use an item, the more accessible it should be.** Give your desk an Accessibility Survey. Sort the items on your desk into the following categories of usage: daily, several times a week, once a week, once a month, a few times a year and rarely or never.

Remember, frequency of use determines the proximity and accessibility an item should have. Keep close at hand only those things you're using every day or several times a week.

BEGIN TO SORT

The Accessibility Principle lets you see the big picture on your desk. Now you're ready to start sorting and grouping papers and other items on your desk, such as supplies and mementos, using another principle: **things that you use together or that require similar action, go together.**

As you sort through papers and other items, start grouping them in broad categories by asking yourself questions such as the following:

1. Do you see active paperwork or files you're using daily or several times a week? Put them on one area of your desk for now. Attach a self-adhesive, removable sticker to label this and the other temporary piles you will sort.
2. Do you see "reminder" papers with information that should be recorded elsewhere, such as your calendar, planner, phone book or computer? If you can do it quickly, transfer this information; if not, stack these papers together.
3. Are there any items of indecision that are sitting on your desk because you haven't decided when to handle them or what to do with them? These items make up what attorney Robert Span calls the "problem pile." Pull them together.

4. Do you see reference or resource items that somehow landed on your desk and remained? File them now if you can do it quickly or put them in an area or box for filing later.
5. Is there material to read—maybe magazines, books or reports? Separate personal from professional reading. When possible, tear out articles you wish to read and toss or recycle the rest of the publication.
6. Are there personal items related to a hobby or an interest that belong elsewhere?
7. Are there any supplies and equipment on your desk? Separate them by function and by frequency of use.

The trick is to start categorizing and prioritizing everything on your desk, focusing most of your attention on the active, action paperwork and projects and clearing away the clutter. See how many things you can remove from your desktop and store in other places. Even for items you use every day, don't clutter your primary work surface by putting them all on your desktop. They could still be very accessible in a drawer, on a credenza or on a table to the side. Remove any items you don't use.

SET UP A DAILY PAPERWORK SYSTEM

Now that you've cleared away some items and have begun to sort your desktop paperwork, you may be wondering, "Now where I am going to put this stuff?" When you don't know where to put papers, they inevitably end up staying on your desk or in the in-box on your desk. You may also be making extensive use of the "pile system," which has a way of spreading to every available horizontal surface in your work area.

Let's face it: most of us were never "paper trained." Setting up appropriate categories and containers in a **daily paperwork system** can help. The daily paperwork system doesn't take the place of your filing system, which is discussed in detail in Chapter 7. The daily paperwork system is for *active* paperwork that you process on a *daily* basis. It is a set of tools and habits to help you manage your mail, paperwork, projects and desk.

Begin by categorizing types of papers that come your way most often. Typical categories might include: "Action" (this week), "Financial," "Correspondence," "Calls," "Staff," "Reading," "Filing" and

"Pending." You might also include specific category names for *active* projects you're using on a *daily* basis. Using the initial groupings you've already created as a guide, make a list of basic category names you could use for your everyday paperwork.

If you're having trouble thinking of ones that fit your needs, try this simple exercise. Next time you process your mail and other paperwork, have some 3-by-5-inch index cards handy. Go through your paperwork, making decisions about what to keep and what to toss. (For many people this is the most difficult part. Be willing to get in the habit of freely tossing—more on this in Chapter 5). On an index card, jot down the major category for each type of paper you're keeping (e.g., "Reports," "Must do today"). A broad category name will often describe the general type of activity or level of urgency. Do this for a few days or for one day if you have a lot of mail and paperwork.

Go through the cards and **select the broadest, most general categories you'll use every day.** See if some of them can be combined. A category is a good one if you'll use it just about every day. Remember the purpose of these categories is for general sorting, not filing of paperwork.

Once you've decided on your basic categories, set up the tools of your daily paperwork system using existing file folders, boxes, caddies or organizers. Label these containers with your categories. Ideally, get as much off your desk as possible. Containers should be accessible but they shouldn't crowd your space.

Set up a trial paperwork system. Buy a package of assorted colored, "third-cut," manila folders at your local stationery store. See what you already have on hand in terms of boxes, trays and caddies. Don't invest in a lot of equipment; remember this is just a trial system. Some people, after getting all inspired about organization, rush out and buy too many accessories without first thinking through the system. I've walked into offices of some new clients only to find five name and address books or rotary files, ten letter trays and dozens of file folders—all of which had had "good intentions" but have since been abandoned. The supplies are not the system. They are *part* of the system. They are only the tools.

Start with a simple system. Select the smallest number of tools and label them with your category names. Arrange them in an easy-to-use, accessible location. A couple of pointers may be helpful.

First, use *vertical* systems whenever possible, as horizontal ones tend to promote the "pile system" of stacking papers. (See Figure 4-1 for examples of vertical, desktop active file organizers.) You may have noticed that the pile system has a way of spreading to every available horizontal surface in your work area. Piles add to confusion and a sense of work overload.

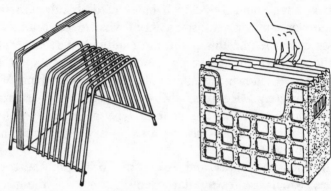

Figure 4-1. Colored manila folders for your daily paperwork system work great in a vertical wire rack (on the left). If you prefer a desktop file organizer that accommodates hanging file folders, consider the Oxford DecoFlex by Esselte Pendaflex, which comes with Pendaflex hanging folders.

Second, try the system out for two to three weeks, make refinements and *then* purchase any additional supplies you need.

Your daily paperwork system doesn't have to be visible; some of the best ones are "invisible." Use prime filing space in your desk or within an arm's-reach of your filing cabinet or credenza. If out of sight means out of mind, then perhaps a more visible system is indeed a good idea for you. But if you're the type of person who gets anxious just looking at paperwork, then design a more hidden, yet accessible, system and start using your time management tools to jot down things to do and remember.

Several tools may be particularly useful in your daily paperwork system. I use the **desk file/sorter tickler system** that is described in Chapter 2 to sort what would otherwise be miscellaneous follow-ups into an organized, chronological system. The Pendaflex Sort-Pal (Figure 4-2) is an expanding sorter file that organizes papers requiring specific routine actions, such as faxing, photocopying or signature. The Pendaflex Hanging Expandable File (Figure 4-3) fits inside your file drawer and has nine expandable filing sections that grow as your daily paperwork system grows.

Figure 4-2. The Pendaflex Sort-Pal is a great paper sorter to handle routine action items. It comes with six preprinted tabbed sections and includes blank labels to customize your own headings.

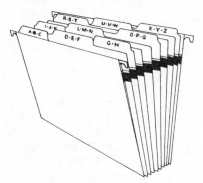

Figure 4-3. The Pendaflex Hanging Expandable File is a handy tool for your daily paperwork system and comes with blank, self-adhesive labels so you can make custom headings for your paperwork categories.

With regard to in-out boxes, consider a number of possibilities. First, consider whether you need them at all. If you're the type of person who either doesn't get much mail or paperwork or who's very decisive and organized and immediately takes action on papers that cross your desk, you might not need them at all. Or perhaps you could get by with just an out-box.

But most people are inundated with paper that doesn't require immediate action. You might consider having more than one box, tray or folder designated for different types of work or priorities and training any co-workers who give you work to pre-sort it into the appropriate container. It would be great if each person were to also use a priority slip indicating the level of urgency.

If such a system isn't feasible in your office, consider using the FIFO, First-In/First-Out, paper handling system (Figure 4-4) available through Daisy Wheel Ribbon Co., Inc. This paper handler replaces the traditional in-box. Simply place the transparent acrylic unit on your desk so that the v-shaped opening leans toward you. Place papers upright so the print faces you and place additional papers, publications, files and so forth behind. This system allows you automatically to see and remove your paperwork in the order it was received. If you choose not to handle a particular piece of paper, simply place it behind the existing papers, marking it with the date or simply a check mark and it will work its way forward to be handled in a timely manner.

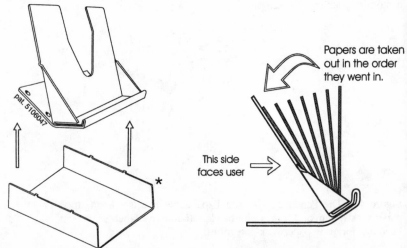

Figure 4-4. Innovative FIFO in-box; optional out-box sits underneath.

Ideally, you would not let the paper cycle through more than once. And of course, try to handle as many papers as possible the first time through the system. But we all have those "C" priority papers that would be nice to handle but simply aren't urgent enough for right now. The durable FIFO paper handler is $23, holds about

500 sheets of paper and can be used alone or with an optional out-box ($19) that fits underneath. You can purchase the set of two for $39. Contact: Daisy Wheel Ribbon Co., Inc., 3325 East Shelby St., Ontario, CA 91764, 800/266-5585 or 909/989-5585.

SURVEY YOUR WORK SURFACE

Now that you've cleared a path and set up a daily paperwork system, look at your desktop. **Do you have enough work surface?** Many people put up with a desk that is too small to begin with and becomes smaller and smaller as the paper jungle takes over. Now that you've cleared a path, try out your desktop for several days. See if you now have enough space to work.

Most people need at least two work surfaces in their office (not counting a return or table for typewriter or computer). The second surface should be accessible, placed within an easy swivel of your chair–behind you or at your side.

Don't use the extra work surface as a storage depot or junk table. This surface should only hold things that you use daily or several times a week. This surface is great for holding active, working file folders that sit vertically in upright caddies. You might use this surface for your stapler, tape and other supplies as well as reference materials, in-out boxes, mementos and index card files. Part or all of this second surface could be designated as a telephone station. A nearby table top, a credenza or even a two-drawer filing cabinet can work great as secondary work surfaces. If you prefer that spotless, executive, clean desk look, put items *inside* your furniture.

MAKE APPOINTMENTS WITH YOURSELF

Setting up the *tools* of a daily paperwork system is only half the story; setting up *regular routines and habits* is the other half. Any organizational system, by the way, consists of two components–tools and habits. I often use this simple equation in my seminars:

a system = tools + habits

The trick to making your daily paperwork system work is simply, to work the system! Here are some habits and routines that can help you work the system–circle any that you could use:

- Schedule appointments with yourself to process paperwork. One training manager I coached schedules "personal administrative time" every week to work in her office. This time has become a "safety net" that allows her to stay in control of paperwork and priorities. She meets with her secretary every Monday to block out her self appointments on their respective calendars. They both try to protect these appointments.
- Open and sort your mail every day you're in the office.
- If possible, have someone else open and sort your mail.
- Make a decision about each paper that crosses your desk the first time it crosses your desk. For the papers you're keeping, decide if they can be handled *now* or *later*. If a paper will take only a minute or two, do it now. If you're deferring papers for a later time, resist sticking them back in the pile or the in-box. Decide *when* you'll be handling each one and *where* each should go in terms of its function and meaning to you–i.e., where's the first place you're likely to look for the item and retrieve it for action?
- Keep it clean! At the very least, clean your desk and work area before you go. Or try the CAYGO habit–Clean As You GO–to prevent paper buildup during the day. And if filing is a real chore use FAYGO–File As You GO or do as Bill Butler from BCG International does–clean a file a day.
- Use time management tools such as your calendar, master list or organizer to record key information from papers that you can then toss.
- Consolidate information. Use notebooks, charts, forms, tickler systems and a good deskside filing system. (And read chapters 2, 7 and 9.)

CATCHING UP WITH READING

Make separate reading appointments with yourself to keep up with professional reading. If your day is just too hectic, make a reading appointment with yourself on your personal time. One professional working parent I coached has made Wednesday night "Reading Night" where she, her husband and their eight-year-old son curl up and read instead of watch television.

When you read, try these tips: separate professional from personal interest reading; make clear decisions whether what you're reading is *worth your time;* read more quickly by reading selectively—check out headlines, subheads, first and last paragraphs; try using a timer or give yourself reading goals, e.g, two journals in twenty minutes; to increase your motivation, tell yourself positive messages about reading, e.g, how reading helps you control your paperwork, saves you time, helps you learn more about your field and makes you feel more professional.

Highlight anything you read that you plan to save so that you won't have to reread the whole thing the next time. I picked up a time-saving highlighting technique from my husband; instead of underlining or highlighting whole sentences horizontally, draw a vertical line (using any writing tool you prefer) alongside a sentence or paragraph. Star any points or paragraphs that are particularly pertinent. You'll be surprised at how fast you can highlight as you read. Also, jot down the name or subject at the top of a paper or article you're saving so that it can be quickly filed or distributed without having to reread it.

FIVE EASY WAYS
TO ORGANIZE YOUR TAX PAPERWORK

Here's a good way to apply the principles, tools and techniques we've discussed thus far, especially if you sweat it out at tax time spending precious weekends trying to catch up on a year's worth of tax-related paperwork and record keeping. Follow these five simple steps:

1. **Create a pleasant, well-equipped work area.** Whether it's a nook, cranny or corner or an office with a door, your work area should be conducive to doing tax paperwork. It should contain all necessary supplies and equipment—such as computer, calculator, pencil, paper and files—within arm's reach. Make sure you have enough work space to spread out your paperwork. (For more on "work space basics," see Chapter 6.)
2. **Set up a simple daily paperwork system to store current bills, checks, receipts and records.** Notice the emphasis on *current*. Generally, you'll want to keep the current year's paperwork

together, especially any tax deductible expense records. File current paperwork so that it's accessible. Select the right filing tools. If you're tight on space or you need portable containers, consider lightweight, plastic file boxes with handles. For faster filing, use different colored folders for different categories. (See also Chapter 7 on filing.)

3. **Separate and store past years' taxes and records.** Most records should be grouped by the tax year and stored separately from current records. Records that you'd refer to by category, such as those for car repair, home improvement and investments, should probably not be filed by the tax year. The main point is keep current records, or those you use most often, most accessible and file inactive information in your filing cabinet or in file storage boxes.

4. **Do record keeping as you go.** Once you've organized your physical records and papers, you're ready for a written record keeping system. Keeping your checkbook register up to date is an important step. But if you have a lot of deductions, you'll want to organize and track this information by category as it occurs. Computer programs and even simple record keeping books can help. If you deduct car or travel expenses, for example, use handy auto expense booklets, which are small enough to fit inside your glove compartment, briefcase or pocket.

5. **To make your system work, be sure to work the system!** Make weekly or monthly appointments with yourself and write them down on your calendar. Create a routine and then reward yourself each time you stick to your routine.

OTHER WAYS TO PUT PAPER IN ITS PLACE!

Are you suffering from a paper mill logjam? If so, you may have a tremendous amount of paperwork to process in your job and/or you probably have some *difficulty making decisions.*

START MAKING DECISIONS

If you're always drowning in paperwork, chances are you tend to avoid decisions. See if one or more of the following seven symptoms apply to you:

1. You're insatiably curious and love to learn new things to the point of distraction.
2. Perfectionism tends to rule in your life.
3. Everything always takes longer than you thought it would.
4. You're creative.
5. You distrust structure and/or authority.
6. You're afraid of making a mistake and taking risks.
7. **You don't have a current, written list of goals that you refer to every day.**

All of these can contribute to decision-making difficulties concerning paper. But remember, number seven is the most important. Making decisions about paper shouldn't be arbitrary. They need to relate specifically to your values and goals in life.

Without goals as a guideline, as a yardstick, it is very difficult to make decisions, including decisions about those papers on your desk.

Difficult decisions about paper often signal ambivalence or conflict about what you want to do now and in the future. "I might need this someday" is such a haunting thought, especially when goals are fuzzy at best. Remind yourself frequently about your goals—every time, in fact, you pick up a paper, a piece of mail, a file folder, whatever. Remind yourself whenever you *put down a paper without making a decision.* And remember, almost always the worst decision you can make is *not* to make a decision because this equation is almost always true: **No Paperwork Decision = Greater Paperwork Buildup.** (See also Chapter 1 on goals and Chapter 5 on collecting.)

PREVENTING AND CONQUERING LONG-TERM PAPER BUILDUP

Certainly, decision making will be a contributing factor to preventing paper buildup.

Controlling your mail will also be a factor. The volume of mail sent by Americans has grown more than 15 percent since 1987.

Americans receive 62 billion pieces of junk mail yearly. Here are some tips to gain more control over your junk mail monster:

- Cut subscriptions to magazines and/or share your subscriptions with others.
- Whenever you order anything over phone, fax or by mail, ask that your name not be sold, rented or traded.
- To remove your name from many national mailing lists write to: Direct Marketing Association Mail Preference Service, Box 9008, Farmingdale, NY 11735.
- Remove your name from company report distribution lists, if you're receiving reports you don't need to see.
- Reduce memberships in associations that no longer meet your needs.
- Contact the Privacy Rights Clearinghouse for its hotline and brochures on reducing junk mail and telemarketing calls and other issues in which technology is affecting privacy: 619/298-3396 or in Calif. only, 800/773-7748. I spoke with this organization, which is very knowledgeable and reliable and is funded by a grant through the California Public Utilities Commission.
- Send $3 for the 16-page booklet "Stop Junk Mail Forever" by writing Good Advice Press, PO Box 78, Elizaville, NY 12523.
- Subscribe to the following service (at $17.50 per household) that will do much of the legwork for you: Stop Junk Mail Assn., 3020 Bridgeway, #150, Sausalito, CA 94965, 800/827-5549.

Some people will go to great lengths to avoid getting mail. I had an interesting encounter with a computer marketing director who had just returned from a trade show to stacks of mail in her office. I called to tell her I would be sending some copy for her approval through the mail. She suggested I fax it or "FedEx" it, anything, as long as it wasn't through the mail. When I explained that it was more convenient for me to mail it, she insisted I address it to someone else in her company (presumably so she wouldn't lose it!).

For existing long-term paper, you have these four options available: 1) trash it, 2) quickly box and store it now and plan to sort it later as a long-term project after reading chapters 5 and 14, 3) read chapters 5 and 14 to do something about it now and 4) create a workable filing system that accommodates resource and reference information you want to keep and go directly to Chapter 7.

Choose an option based on how *important* these papers are to you. **Are they worth your time?**

COMPUTERIZE MORE OF YOUR PAPERWORK

One way to reduce paperwork is use computers more extensively and at the same time, resist the temptation to make all those hard copies. Instead, when the urge to print out hard copy seizes you, back up your work on a computer tape or disk more religiously instead.

A number of years ago I read an article in *PC WORLD* magazine entitled not the paperless office, which may not be realistic, but instead "The Less-Paper Office." The article encouraged readers to embrace computerized work solutions. I have included computerized solutions throughout this book, in virtually every chapter, that can help you reduce or eliminate paper. You can put your calendar on computer (Chapter 2), use scanners as discussed in this chapter along with document management software (Chapter 7), use electronic forms and workflow (Chapters 9 and 11), put your business contacts on a computer database (Chapters 2 and 9), do document sharing and editing in which two or more people work off the same document on computer (Chapter 11), fax directly from your computer to another's computer (Chapter 11) and use e-mail (Chapter 11).

RECYCLING, REDUCING AND REUSING

If after all of the above, you end up with lot of paper that best belongs in the trash can, please reuse or recycle as much of it as you can. And look for ways you can reduce the amount of paper you use.

We accumulate a lot of scratch paper in our office. I always try to reuse paper that has printing on only one side. I use the clean side for taking notes, for printing out drafts and for brainstorming ideas.

Remember to use both sides of a new sheet of paper when xeroxing or printing whenever possible (but always first check with the manufacturer to see whether this could harm your copier or printer). An **auto-duplexing laser printer** makes this kind of printing easier.

Sometimes I get graphically interesting junk mail that I take home for my four-year-old to reuse in an art project.

I reuse mailers, boxes and manilla envelopes and folders. I take large corrugated boxes that I'd be unlikely to reuse to the recycling center. It feels great to make these contributions to our planet!

For other recycling ideas, see the index or chapters 7 and 10.

RESOURCE GUIDE

PAPER MANAGEMENT SUPPLIES AND ACCESSORIES

The selected office products here are handy, dandy items you may wish to add to your work area. Most of these supplies are available in a good office products catalog or store (unless otherwise noted). Good office supply catalogs with hundreds of pages usually have two indexes—one listing manufacturers and the other listing general types of products. I've used the general headings you're most likely to see in these catalogs.

BINDERS AND ACCESSORIES

Besides file folders (which are discussed in detail in Chapter 7), there are many other options to store and organize paperwork.

The **notebook** or **binder** in all its different sizes is still one of the best organizational and storage devices around for paper resources and records *referred to frequently.* Sure, it's easier to throw something in a file, but when you go to find it, the notebook wins hands down.

Use binders to store articles and clippings, updates, product literature, samples, ideas, active client summary sheets, the latest professional or trade information—the list is endless.

As a professional speaker and writer, I keep an **anecdote notebook** with alphabetical tabbed dividers. Under each letter of the alphabet, I have key subject words that begin with that letter. For example, under the letter "I" are the subjects, "Information Management," "Inspiration" and "Insurance." Blank sheets of white paper are labeled with the key words. Short clippings are cut and pasted onto the appropriate page. Longer articles I want to keep are labeled with key words and placed in plastic sheet protectors.

You say you hate hole punching? Then buy the three-hole pre-punched plastic sheet protectors with a margin that allow you to store 8½-by-11-inch papers without additional punching. They're called **top loading sheet protectors**, **page protectors** or **plastic sleeves** and are enclosed on three sides and "load" through the open end on top. See Figure 4-5 for an illustration of 20th Century plastic sleeves.

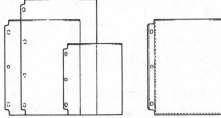

Figure 4-5. Sheet protectors such as these by 20th Century Plastics allow you to store 8½-by-11-inch papers in protective sleeves that are sealed on three sides and large enough so you don't have to hole-punch the papers.

C-LINE makes them in several styles: clear, colored or clear with a colored edge. C-LINE also makes a combination sheet protector with tabs for indexing called "Tabbed Toppers." Or, if you prefer, you can use Avery's Extra Wide Index dividers specially designed for binders containing oversized sheet protectors. The point is if you're using sheet protectors and index divider tabs together, make sure the tabs are not hidden from view.

Pocket dividers are handy for material that is smaller than the standard page size and that you don't want to hole punch.

If you need to organize duplicate sets of binders with tabs but you don't want to bother with typing and inserting labels repeatedly into plastic binder tabs, consider one of the multi-colored index systems on the market that let you simplify the job considerably. The process is simple: you type a master contents page that aligns with the tabs and then you photocopy the page onto blank contents pages. Avery and Wilson Jones make these versatile indexes.

Avery Ready Index is available in either the standard 8½-by-11-inch or 9¼-by-11-inch sizes for binders with oversized items such as sheet protectors. Available in a wide variety of styles, including numerical, monthly and alphabetical, Ready Index works with laser and ink jet printers and copiers. Easy-to-use templates for Ready Index are built into WordPerfect, Microsoft Word and Lotus AmiPro.

Wilson Jones "MultiDex" features a slide out Quick Reference Table of Contents that allows you to see titles without having to flip back to the contents page in the front of the binder. It's available in five different numerical sets—5, 8, 10, 12 and 15 plus 1-31, Jan.-Dec. and A-Z.

If you're tired of three-ring binders that never close properly and can therefore snag important documents, look for binders, such as the Wilson Jones brand with a locking mechanism. You'll find the strongest mechanism in Bindertek's Law Files great two-ring binder that's guaranteed for life and lets you access, insert and remove documents easily. The press-on index tabs can be customized for your business or professional needs. Also available are accessories for filing photos, bulky documents and important originals without hole punching. For more information contact Bindertek (Sausalito, California, 800/456-3453).

For a whole variety of preprinted tabs for nearly every area of law, consider those by Legal Tabs Co. (in Basalt, Colorado, 800/322-3022 or 970/927-3105). The tabs are available on the bottom or on the side, plain or punched (3-hole side or 2-hole top). You can use them in binders or in file folders to organize your legal documents.

To easily make your own custom tabs for notebook dividers, look for Avery's IndexMaker, which comes with tabbed, reinforced dividers and clear labels, ready for laser printing or photocopying. You apply the self-adhesive labels directly onto the divider tabs.

BUSINESS CARD ACCESSORIES

If you attend many meetings and you want a more organized way to keep business cards, start a **business card notebook** with plastic business card sleeves that are tabbed. Label the tabs with either letters of the alphabet or names of organizations and associations. Before you go to a meeting, scan the cards and any notes you made on them.

DO-IT Corporation (South Haven, Michigan, 1/800/426-4822) makes special, self-adhesive strips called "AD-A-TAB card tabs" that you can easily attach to a business card, which will then adapt to your rotary card file. They come in the standard card file size and also the larger 3-by-5-inch size, which is the one I use. See Figure 4-6.

Figure 4-6. An AD-A-TAB card tab is a transparent strip that affixes to business cards to make them fit rotary card files.

For my business cards, I use three approaches: a computer database program, a phone book section in my organizer and a Rolodex card file. I use the 3-by-5-inch size Rolodex covered VIP file (Figure 4-7). The cards are large enough to hold stapled or glued business cards (without having to recopy the information). There's also room for brief notes.

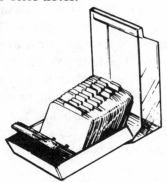

Figure 4-7. The Rolodex covered VIP file is the card file I use.

Rolodex makes a variety of different business card files as well as some useful accessories. To turn your file into more of a resource database, insert special Rolodex plastic divider tabs to divide up your Rolodex into different categories. Use an alphabetical system within those categories, not the entire Rolodex. With several different subject categories, it's often easier to look up listings, rather than trying to remember exact names. You can organize your file with Rolodex colored cards and/or colored plastic card protectors. If your system is used all the time, get the Rolodex plastic sleeve card protectors, which are available in clear as well as colors.

While the most common brand name, Rolodex is not the only brand of card file. There are many brands as well as styles from which to choose. Compare card files available in office supply stores and catalogs.

CLIPS

To temporarily group and secure papers, nothing beats the paper clip. What you may not realize, however, is the variety of clips now available.

See Figure 4-8 for a sampling of multi-purpose clips. Labelon Owl Clips are rectangular clips that hold papers securely and will not catch on other adjacent papers. This type of clip comes in three sizes. Labelon/Noesting Triumph Clamps hold bulky papers securely. **Binder clip** is the generic name for what is probably the most secure, slip-proof clip you can buy. Use binder clips for loose bulky papers that need to be held securely. For a touch of class, use gold binder clips available from Paper Direct catalog (800/A-PAPERS or 201/271-9300). Baumgarten's makes gold binder clips and plastic binder clips, too. **Plastic paper clips,** such as Baumgarten's Arrow and Plastiklips Klips should be used around computers because metal clips can become magnetized and can destroy computer data. They come in a variety of colors and so can be used for color coding different papers. Baumgarten's Plastiklips and Arrow Klips come in a wide variety of colors and sizes. Use Arrow Klips for clipping as well as highlighting and color coding papers.

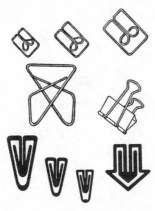

Figure 4-8. Labelon/Noesting's Owl Clips (top) and Triumph Clamp (middle left), a metal binder clip (middle right) and Baumgarten's Plastiklips and Arrow Klip

The **banker's clasp** has a strong grip and is useful for holding bulky papers. The raised short end allows you to easily and quickly slip the clip onto papers. A **magnetic clip** attaches to the sides of metal file cabinets or cabinets and is handy for attaching notes or information. See Figure 4-9.

Figure 4-9. Magnetic clip (left) and banker's clasp

COLOR CODING

For color coding and drawing attention, here are additional products that will help:

Redi-Tags (Figure 4-10) are removable, reusable color-coded tags that have a reusable adhesive on half the tag. They come in 16 different colors, three sizes and many preprinted phrases. Many come in refillable dispensers that can snap together. There is a "general office" series with such tags as "FILE," "FYI," and "RUSH!" There's also a medical series that includes "DIAGNOSIS NEEDED," "SIGN ORDERS" and "COMPLETE HISTORY & PHYSICAL." If your local office supply store or catalog doesn't have this item, call 800/421-7585 or 714/894-4727 for a store location near you.

Figure 4-10. Use Redi-Tags to attract attention. Simply tag where action is needed and remove the tag when the task is finished or the reference is no longer necessary

Post-it Brand Tape Flags by 3M (Figure 4-11) are now available with their own dispensers. Half of the tape flag is colored and may have a pre-printed message such as "Note" or "Sign Here"; the other half is a transparent surface upon which you can write with pencil or pen.

Figure 4-11. Available in 10 colors, easy-to-use Post-it Brand Tape Flags keep your paperwork organized. Use them for quick reference, easy retrieval and handy reminders. They are ideal for color coding, organizing and indexing. On the right are Post-it Pop Up Notes in a new Refillable Dispenser that mounts anywhere and can be removed from the mounting bracket to take it along anywhere. The new Tape Flag Holder (not shown) works the same way.

Signals (see Figure 4-12) are made of plastic or metal and clip securely to record cards, folders or papers to "signal" next action date, type of activity or level of urgency.

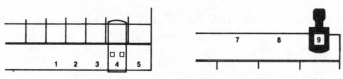

Figure 4-12. Labelon/Noesting's Cellugraf Plastic Signals (left) are transparent (as shown) and are available in 16 colors. Labelon/Noesting's Graffco Nu-Vise Metal Signals stand above a card or folder edge, come in 12 colors and are available in numbered, alphabetical and calendar styles.

Avery's **See-Through Color Dots** are useful for highlighting directly on an item, such as maps, blueprints and graphs, where it's important the information not be obscured. Available in four colors, these ¾-inch dots are removable. One manager uses them on her voice mail log where red dots are for "immediate call backs," blue for "action items" to do now, green for "correspondence" where she needs to send something and yellow indicates "for information only" with no response needed on her part. (If you need more colors and can use permanent, opaque dots, look for Avery color coding labels, which come in 13 colors.)

The CLICK Hi-Liter marker by Avery Dennison is a retractable highlighter that comes in four colors.

To help you keep tabs on your paperwork, try Avery SwifTabs or TABBIES index tabs (Figure 4-13). Both of these products are self-adhesive, durable, plastic tabs that come in a variety of colors and styles. They're also available with preprinted months, numbers or letters. You can write or type on them. Use them on such items as computer printouts, reports or on spiral bound books.

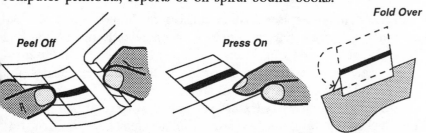

Figure 4-13. TABBIES self-adhesive index tabs (contact Xertrex International, 1530 W. Glenlake Ave., Itasca, IL 60143, 708/773-4160)

And if you're looking for a great selection of paper, envelopes, presentation folders, paper accessory products and even software and hardware solutions, contact PaperDirect for their catalogs: 800/A-PAPERS or 201/271-9300 or write them at 100 Plaza Drive, Secaucus, NJ 07094.

OTHER PAPER ACCESSORIES

Abbot Office Systems carries three versatile paper organizers. **Tarifold Paper Organizers** provide fast, organized access to information that's frequently referred to; they're available in a Deskside Wall Organizer model (shown in Figure 4-14) that displays 20 sheets, Desktop Units (that display 20 to 120 sheets) and Rotary Display Systems (that display either 50 or 100 sheets).

Figure 4-14. Before and after using Tarifold Paper Organizer

The **Multidrawer Box System** consists of durable, stackable file and storage boxes that can be used independently or stacked and locked together and can sit on desktops or cabinets or be used as open shelving. Use this system for forms, literature, magazines and supplies. There are drawer label areas.

Stacking Storage Drawers are versatile drawers that can not only be stacked but also each drawer can accommodate one or two partitions enabling you to section off each drawer into two or three compartments so that you have no wasted dead space. Different style drawers (all with insertable label areas) let you store a variety of materials—literature, forms, binders, supplies, stationery, magazines, reports, disks and multi-media. Quantity discounts are available on these three Abbot products. 800/631-2233 or 201/938-6000. Abbot Office Systems, 5012 Asbury Ave., Farmingdale, NJ 07727

3M Organization Cabinets are new, lightweight, compact cabinets ideal for holding paper, letterhead, transparency films, forms and more. See Figure 4-15.

Figure 4-15. 3M Organization Cabinets come in two styles with labeling windows for item indexing—six-drawer and three drawer. The latter has a removable diskette tray that holds up to 80 3½-inch diskettes.

DESK ACCESSORIES

In the office supply world, the desk accessory category includes everything from basic desk or letter trays to designer desk sets with matching components. As a general guideline, I advise clients to use the *minimal* number of accessories and those with the *smallest* capacity. It's just too easy to start stockpiling stuff.

I also urge clients to lean toward *vertical* rather than *horizontal* containers and whenever possible, to put papers in files rather than piles. Of course, the type of paperwork will often determine which format you should use. A horizontal container often works best for frequently used forms, which often flop over in a vertical container.

But you'll generally want a vertical container for active files (look at the many examples in this section).

Your in-out box or basket system will most likely be horizontal because you're probably processing different sized papers. But remember these tips: keep the depth of containers to a minimum, maintain high access and visibility and *clean out trays regularly.*

Balance good function with good design. Upon getting organized, some clients reward themselves with attractive desk accessories. Check out well-designed products such as those by Rubbermaid in office supply stores and catalogs. Also look at the Hold Everything

stores and catalog (800/421-2264). The Reliable Home Office catalog
is an excellent choice, too, at 800/326-6230.

Desk Files

Take a look at some products to help you set up your daily
paperwork system for your active working files and paperwork.

If your work load fluctuates constantly, you may prefer a modular
system that expands and contracts with your work. The **Rubbermaid
Add-A-File** system has components that snap together (see Figure
4-16).

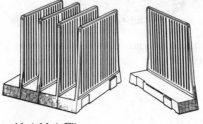

Figure 4-16. Rubbermaid Add-A-File

Step files (Figures 4-17) give great visibility to your working files.
The Rogers Vertical File is a wire step file that comes in chrome or
three Epoxy coated colors. Fellowes Strictly Business Visible Folder
File is a low-cost step file made of corrugated fiberboard with five
tiered compartments that can be used vertically or horizontally.

The Folder and The Holder by Rubbermaid in Figure 4-18 make
maximum use of limited space, accommodate letter or legal size
folders and fold flat when not in use. The Folder holds manila
folders and the Holder handles hanging file folders.

In Figure 4-1 you saw two examples of **desktop file organizers** for
your daily paperwork system. Take a look at a versatile one in
Figure 4-19 that can hold many more hanging files.

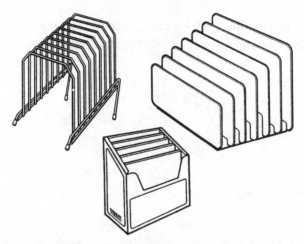

Figure 4-17. A variety of step files: Rogers Wire Vertical Rack, Rubbermaid Maxi Step-Up Step Rack and Fellowes fiberboard Strickly Business Visible Folder File

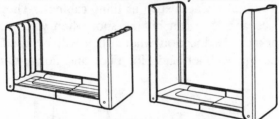

Figure 4-18. The Folder File Holder and The Holder Hanging File Holder by Rubbermaid

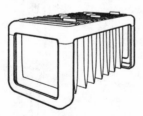

Figure 4-19. Rubbermaid gives you a larger capacity for accessible, hanging folders: the Hot Rack Hanging File Holder, which holds up to 45 hanging letter or legal size folders

OTHER ORGANIZERS

Here are some other items to organize your desk and paperwork, some of which may not be familiar to you.

A **collator** is designed to manually collate documents but I recommend it for large, bulky, *active* client or project files. It's great for CPA or legal files and comes in 12, 18 or 24 expanding sections.

We use it in our office above our printer to store paper, letterhead, folders and mailing envelopes. See example in Figure 4-20.

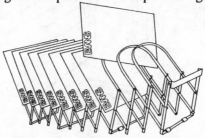

Figure 4-20. Evans recycled aluminum collator

If you're short on work surface, try using **wall mount files**. Sometimes these files are referred to as **pockets** and they can be used on walls as well as on sides of desks. Some come with magnets and attach to metal surfaces such as filing cabinets. They don't take up much space and they can hit the spot when you need a holder for paperwork at the location where they will be used. For some examples, see the Rubbermaid Hot Files and Pockets in Figure 4-21.

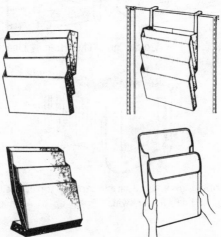

Figure 4-21. Rubbermaid Hot Files and Pockets: Hot File Starter Set and Hot File Hanger Starter Set (top); Hot File Stand and Hot File II Add-On Pocket (bottom)

If you have lots of literature or inserts you're pulling together to put into kits or notebooks, consider **literature organizers and sorters**. Your selection will depend on a number of factors: the number of separate inserts you use, the quantity of each insert you need to have on hand, the space you have available, the frequency of use and your budget. (See Chapter 5 for illustrations of literature organizers and sorters.)

Don't forget your basic **letter trays**, which are useful for in-out boxes or to hold papers to be filed or read. Look for stacking letter trays that leave space between trays and that use supports to connect trays. Some people prefer wire letter trays because you can easily see what's in them; others prefer plastic or wood trays that keep paperwork less visible. If aesthetics are important, select a line that has coordinated desk accessories. Consider getting shallow trays to prevent paper buildup unless you need deep ones for thick folders or reports. See the examples in Figure 4-22.

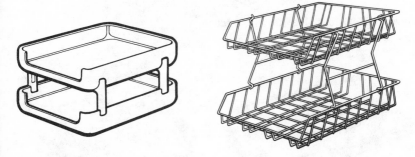

Figure 4-22. Rubbermaid Image 1500 letter trays and Rogers wire desk trays

To keep other materials, manuals and references neatly organized around your computer or desk, consider the Oxford DecoRack in Figure 4-23. To keep your small supplies organized, use a drawer organizer (Figure 4-24). To keep your drawer organizer from sliding around, use 3M brand Mounting Squares or Mounting Tape on the bottom. By the way, 3M also makes an adjustable width drawer organizer (Model C-71) that offers one-hand dispensing of tape and Post-it brand products, as well as spacious compartments for other desk supplies.

Stationery holders are great for letterhead, forms and envelopes and come in many different styles and formats. Some sit out in the open and others, like the Stationery Tray in Figure 4-24, fit inside standard desk drawers.

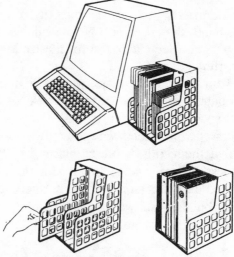

Figure 4-23. Oxford DecoRack by Esselte

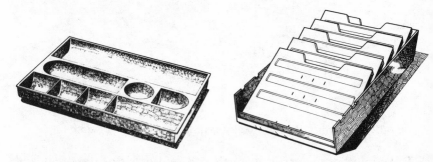

Figure 4-24. Rubbermaid's Catch'all Organizer (left) and Stationery Tray (which can be customized with extra vertical spacers that are included) can fit conveniently in desk drawers.

SCANNERS AND SOFTWARE

There's a great solution to getting those papers off your desk and out of your filing cabinet—scanning paper documents directly into your computer.

The scanner market has really grown and with good reason. The prices have come way down, the quality has gone up and the idea of a paperless office is appealing. Scanners come bundled with OCR (optical character recognition) software but see if you need to upgrade to more sophisticated software (if for example, you'll be canning many documents with graphics.) Without OCR, a scanner would give you an image of the text that you couldn't edit or word process. OCR converts the document from an image into "editable text."

Document management software that helps you with filing and retrieval of the scanned documents on your computer is usually extra (see Chapter 7 for examples).

The scanners I'm including here have all received good reviews. Some of the companies listed make many different models for different budgets. I've focused more on the lower price end. (I have not included business card scanners because as of this writing, they simply aren't up to par; they misread and misspell so many scans that too much retyping time is required.)

Canon IX-3010 is an inexpensive, grayscale flatbed scanner that includes Caere Corporation software that enables the scanner to perform OCR, image editing and photocopying and helps you with document management. **Win and Mac.** $589. **800/848-4123** or 714/438-3000. Canon Computer Systems Inc., 2995 Redhill Ave., Costa Mesa, CA 92626

Envisions 6600S is a color flatbed scanner designed for small, businesses, professional offices, desktop publishers and others who need a versatile flatbed scanner. It scans a page of text or line art at 14 seconds. An optional 50-page automatic document feeder for long documents is available at an additional $449. $529 **800/365-SCAN** or 415/692-9061, Envisions Solutions Technology, Inc., 822 Mahler Road, Burlingame, CA 94010

HP ScanJet 3p is a fast gray-scale flatbed scanner that includes many automatic features. It comes with OCR, image-editing software and can, along with a suitable printer, function as a convenience copier. $399; optional automatic document feeder, $239. **800/SCANJET (800/722-6538)** or 208/396-2551, Hewlett-Packard Co., Direct Marketing Organization, PO Box 58059, MS511L-SJ, Santa Clara, CA 95051-8059

OmniPage Pro is award-winning OCR software that converts printed documents into text in about 50 popular applications and image and file formats. OmniPage Pro trains OCR to recognize difficult-to-read and special characters. A 24-bit color image editor is included so you can edit graphics, too. **Win** and **Mac** versions. $495. **800/535-SCAN** or 408/395-7000, Caere Corporation, 100 Cooper Court, Los Gatos, CA 95030

The **PaperPort** scanner by Visioneer (see Figure 4-25) boasts an award-winning design that accepts almost any size of paper (from business cards to newspapers ranging from two to 30 inches), automatically straightens documents and scans most documents in six seconds or less. Its unique compact design offers a small "footprint" that takes up very little space. It includes OCR software (which can also be used with fax software to help you prepare faxes you send via fax/modem from your personal computer). **Win**, **Mac** and **network.** $399; $49 upgrade to PaperPort for Workgroups. **800/787-7007** or 415/812-6400, Visioneer, Inc., 2860 W. Bayshore Road, Palo Alto, CA 94303

Figure 4-25. The PaperPort Scanner

5

FOR COLLECTORS ONLY: HOW, WHEN AND WHAT TO SAVE

Quick Scan: If you're an inveterate collector or you're in a profession that simply requires you to save many records, documents or resources, this chapter is for you. Here are some guidelines that will help you save only the essentials.

I'm convinced the world is divided into two groups of people–those who save and those who don't. And there has to be a Murphy's Law somewhere that says, "If you're a collector, you're probably living or working with someone who isn't."

I admit it. I'm a collector. Not only do I have many interests and avocations (I suffer from the "Da Vinci Syndrome"), but I have chosen occupations that attract collectors. I have been a school teacher, an editor and a manager. Today I am a professional speaker, writer and consultant and I continue to maintain well-organized resource material.

I am not against collecting. Certain professions demand it. But collecting requires strict guidelines and routines if you ever hope to stay in control.

Consider the degree your collecting habit is taking control over *you*. Recognize that it can be tamed and turned into a constructive resource that will give you a professional edge.

TYPES OF COLLECTORS

Sometimes it's helpful to see the different kinds of collecting traps we fall into. People with a "possession obsession" like to buy new things and add to their growing collection. And once something enters their environment, it remains for the duration.

"Chipmunk collectors" don't go out of their way to purchase new possessions. Instead, they squirrel away everything for the winter—*every* winter. "Waste not, want not" is their motto. Chipmunks were taught to hold onto everything for dear life. Beware of thoughts like these: "I might need this someday" or "Somebody else might need this" or "This could really come in handy."

People who love the printed word are "information junkies." These are people who love to learn, read, write, improve themselves and find out what the experts have to say. And even if you're not an information junkie per se, you still live in an "information age," where there are 1,000 specialized publications every year and 1,000 new book titles each day throughout the world. The sum of printed information is doubling every eight years; it's likely that the millions of computers in the world help contribute to this problem of information overload.

If you can relate to any of these collecting habits (and most of us can), you'll want to keep reading, this chapter anyway. Any of these habits can become nightmares in short order if you don't put a lid on them. The way you do that is by learning to *make decisions* about paper and possessions. But as we discussed in chapters 1 and 2, decisions aren't made in a vacuum.

MAKING DECISIONS ABOUT "COLLECTIBLES"

The secret to making decisions and controlling paper and possessions is simple: know your goals and values. Know what's important to you and what's really worth your time and energy. According to Roy Disney, Walt Disney's brother, "Decisions are easy when values are clear."

Once you're clear about your values and goals, you're ready to establish some stick-to-'em criteria. The problem people have when they're going through papers and possessions is that they aren't using the right criteria. As a result, every item requires a major decision from scratch.

Start by recognizing that there are only three basic decisions you need to make: 1) what to **save**, 2) how to **sort** it and 3) where to **store** it.

TO SAVE OR NOT TO SAVE...
THAT IS THE QUESTION!

If you're suffering from "Discard Dilemmas," the following two general guidelines can help you with troublesome papers:

1. When in doubt, *save* tax, legal or business items.
2. When in doubt, *toss* resource information,
   especially information you seldom, if ever, use.

When you're in a discard mode (or should we say discard *mood*), use these simple guidelines along with the following criteria:

Nine Questions to Toss Out When Deciding What to Save

1. Do you need the item now?
2. Was it used last year? More than once?
3. Will you use it more than once next year? (How likely is it that you will *ever* need it?)
4. Would it be difficult or expensive to replace? Could you get it from someone else?
5. Is it current (and for how long?)
6. Should it be kept for legal or financial reasons?
7. Could someone else use it *now*? (Or could someone else wrestle with this decision instead of you?!)
8. Does it significantly enhance your work or life?
9. Is it worth the time and energy to save?

Go back and star any that you could use. Keep them right in front of you as you make your discard decisions. Add any others that specifically fit your situation.

Or follow the "cardinal office rule" of Richard Riordan, Los Angeles mayor, who advises, "Don't keep it in *your* file if someone else can keep it in *theirs*."

THE SORTING PROCESS

Now that you've established your criteria for saving (or tossing), you're ready to begin the actual process of sorting your collectibles. Your best bet is to make it a game with definite time limits. You can spread out your game over a period of time, doing a little this week and a little next week. Or maybe you prefer to dig right in and work for a few days straight, such as a weekend. Or instead, try this one on for size: pretend you have to move your office in less than 24 hours to a space that is half the size. (Got your adrenalin flowing yet?)

Whichever is your style, choose blocks of time without interruptions, as this is real mental work that requires concentration. Block out at least a few hours. Have on hand the necessary supplies—a trash basket (or barrel), a pencil, a timer, empty cardboard boxes (Fellowes Bankers Boxes or other cardboard file boxes with lids are great) and space to work.

Tackle a small area at a time—one pile on your desk, a file drawer, a section of a file drawer, etc. Begin where the need is greatest. If your file cabinets are packed to the gills, start there. If you haven't seen your desk in years, there's no better place to begin. It's best to choose something small and be able to work through it. Set your timer to establish a reasonable time limit (an hour or less).

Begin by sorting through the designated area, deciding what to save, what to toss and what should be stored elsewhere. As you decide which items to save, sort them in categories based on *types* of items (e.g., books, files, supplies, personal items to take home), as well as *how often* you intend to use them (e.g., daily, several times a week, once a month). **Only things you use or refer to regularly during your working hours should be in your office.**

The process is not simply willpower, of sitting down and forcing yourself to go through your stuff (although a little willpower won't hurt). What you need is a **plan of action**, particularly if you have "long-term buildup." (Chapter 14 will help you design a simple plan of action—you may wish to read that chapter before attempting to tackle long-term buildup.)

Write as you sort. It's helpful to list your criteria and your sorting categories as you do the process. This list, along with a written plan of action, will help you tremendously. Carefully number and label boxes and drawers *as you go*. Keep a written record of any items going into storage.

I use my computer to keep a record of boxes that are stored off site. It's easy to update my word processing document, which is named "Files." I also keep a printout of "Files" in my manual filing system. My boxes are labeled alphabetically (I'll double up on letters should I ever get to "Z," heaven forbid!) I share an off-site storage room with my husband, who uses a numbered box system.

An attorney who is a solo practitioner keeps track of open and closed client files with index card boxes—ones for "Open" files and others for "Closed" files. Each card has the name of a client, the number and location of files for the client and when those files were opened or closed. The cards are filed alphabetically in the appropriate boxes (open or closed).

What if you inherited somebody else's clutter? I received a letter from Sharon Lawrence, a student of mine who ran into this problem several months after taking two of my seminars. She had just accepted a position as a financial management analyst in a California county administrative office. She writes:

> I have a new job and a new challenge to being organized. I left my organized office for a complete disaster area. I couldn't believe my new office; when I walked in, my mouth fell open. There were three inches thick of papers strewn over the entire surface of the desk, a bookcase filled with a year's worth of obsolete computer printouts and two file cabinets filled with five-year-old data, which belonged to other analysts.
>
> I informed my boss that I couldn't function until I had gotten organized. It was hard to know where to begin. By the end of the second day, I had thrown away four trash cans full of obsolete reports and duplicate copies of letters and reports. I had also managed to clear the

> desktop. I was still faced with four piles of paper which had been sorted into broad categories.
>
> Working a little each day for two weeks, I have now managed to organize the piles of information into file folders. I have also given away two file cabinets and distributed their contents to the appropriate analysts.
>
> People now walk by my office and say things like, "Wow, what a difference!" I tell them about your classes and how this is the new me.

This is great, you say, if you know what you're going to need on the new job. But what if the job isn't second nature to you? When Nancy Schlegel became a systems engineer for IBM she waited a year before she tossed out information. "After a year, I knew what I needed and what I didn't and I was in a better position to set up a filing system."

WHERE TO STORE IT

Deciding where to store your records and resources depends on four factors: 1) up-to-date sorting and purging, 2) frequency of use, 3) size, shape and quantity of materials and 4) proximity to related items.

First, have you completed the sorting and purging process *before* you buy that extra filing cabinet or bookcase? Where to house something should only be considered after you decide *if* you should keep it.

Second, the more frequently you use an item, the more accessible it should be. Identify *prime* work areas in your office–those areas that are most accessible. If your desk top and a deskside file drawer are the most accessible areas, do they contain items that you use most often in your office?

Third, the size, shape and quantity of your resources will suggest the types of containers, accessories or pieces of furniture you select to hold those resources. If you have 12 inches of file folders you probably won't be choosing a five-drawer lateral file cabinet. If you're a graphic designer or a printer you may need special cabinets to hold large, oversized art boards.

Fourth, things that go together should generally stay together. Group similar types of books, files and supplies together. Sound like common sense? You'd be amazed to see how many items that are unrelated to each other end up together—sometimes for years.

HOW TO PREVENT LONG-TERM BUILDUP

Having a philosophy about paper helped Kathy Meyer-Poppe when she was Revlon's Corporate Fleet director. Her philosophy was, "File a paper or toss it out—it's either important enough to be filed right then and there or it's not that important. So throw it away."

Bill Butler, president of Butler Consulting Group in Indianapolis, makes it a point to clean one file a day. Butler says, "One file you can manage. As a result, you have fewer files, which means fewer places to lose things."

There are no rules to maintenance. You may like to adopt Butler's "one file a day" or Poppe's "file or toss" routine. On the other hand, once a week or once every six months may work better for you. Or perhaps you want to wait until the need arises—bulging file cabinets or an impending move. Some people tell me the only way they can get organized is by moving—so they actually plan a move every few years!

It can be thrilling to "clear a path" as one client described making headway on her collection. It's also thrilling for me to get letters like the following from Coleen Melton, a California art teacher:

> I'm writing to report to you that my goal is accomplished:
> 20 years of art placed into retrievable order thanks to
> your "Positively Organized!" class and your notes of
> support. I even have my husband wanting to organize his
> filing cabinet, and that is a miracle in itself.

Even lifelong collectors can learn and use the art of organization.

GIVING IT AWAY

Sometimes it's easier to get rid of things if you have someone to whom you can donate items. Often, you can get income tax credits.

For small donations, contact local charitable organizations such as Good Will Industries or the Salvation Army. If you have excess inventory or equipment to donate, contact one of the following organizations: National Association for the Exchange of Industrial Resources, Galesburg, IL, 309/343-0704; Gifts in Kind America,

Alexandria, VA, 703/836-2121; or Educational Assistance, Ltd., Glen Ellyn, IL, 708/690-0010.

RESOURCE GUIDE

(Addresses and phone numbers are included for mail order items and generally *not* for products that are widely available through office supply catalogs and stores.)

ART WORK, BLUEPRINTS
AND PHOTOGRAPHIC MATERIALS

ARTIST AND DOCUMENT STORAGE FILES

Artists portfolios, art folios, art cases, presentation cases are all different names of portable containers for storing, transporting or displaying art work. Check out good office supply or art stores and catalogs.

For storage rather than display, consider the following items available in most office supply catalogs:

For Flat Storage

The Art Rack by Safco (Figure 5-1) is a modular, vertical filing system with eight large compartments. It's 29 by 24 by 36 inches and costs $220. This and other Safco products in this book are available nationwide through office products dealers, industrial supply dealers and art and engineering dealers. For a catalog or more information, contact a local dealer or write Safco Products Company, 9300 West Research Center Road, New Hope, MN 55428.

Safco Portable Art and Drawing Portfolio or **Smead Artist Portfolio** are low-cost, durable files with handles useful for transporting art work, film, drawings and large documents. See Figure 5-2. From $3.85 to $45

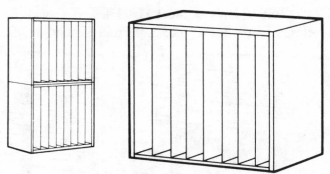

Figure 5-1. The Art Rack by Safco can be stacked vertically, used side-by-side or alone.

Figure 5-2. Safco Portable Art and Drawing Portfolio

Plan Hold is a manufacturer of flat storage equipment that provides many different solutions. Call them for their catalog at 800/854-6868 or in California, 800/432-7486.

Safco 5-Drawer Corrugated Fiberboard Flat Files are economical alternatives to expensive metal files for art boards, blueprints, film, drawings, drafting paper and other oversized documents you want to store flat. See Figure 5-3.

Figure 5-3. Safco 5-Drawer Corrugated Fiberboard Flat Files

Safco 5-, 7-, and 10-Drawer Steel Flat Files come with or without open or closed bases. See Figure 5-4. From $721 to $1,450.

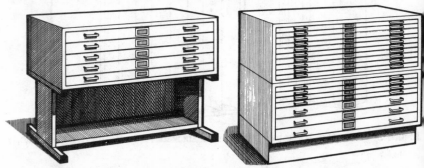

Figure 5-4. Safco 5-, 7-, and 10-Drawer Steel Flat Files

Safco Vertical Filing Systems offer efficient systems for keeping large sheet materials well protected, yet organized and easily accessible. Hanging Clamps form the basic unit and hold up to 100 sheets each. Choose from three systems shown in Figure 5-5: the Drop/Lift Wall Rack, $34; the Pivot Wall Rack, $160; or the Mobile Stand, $360.

For Rolled Storage

Safco Corrugated Fiberboard Roll Files are an economical way to organize and store large materials. The roll file comes in three different tube lengths. **Safco Tube-Stor KD Roll Files** also provide an ideal low-cost system for active or inactive storage. There are two convenient label areas on the inside and the outside to list rolls and locations. Units come with 18 or 32 tube spaces. Built-in tube length adjusters let you customize tube length. $66 to $92. See Figure 5-6.

Fellowes Roll/Stor Stands, Perma Vertical Roll Organizers and **Safco Upright Roll Files** are good choices for deskside filing of rolled documents. They come with four plastic feet to raise the units off the ground. Choose 12 or 20 compartments. From $33 to $37.95. See Figure 5-7.

Plan Hold offers rolled storage solutions. See listing under "For Flat Storage" above.

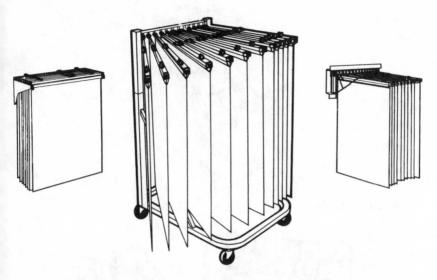

Figure 5-5. Safco Vertical Filing Systems Drop/Lift Wall Rack (left), Mobile Stand and Pivot Wall Rack

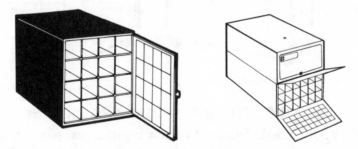

Figure 5-6. Safco Corrugated Fiberboard Roll File and Safeco Tube-Stor KD Roll File

Safco Mobile Roll Files (Figure 5-8) are good for active rolled materials. The units themselves can be "rolled" to areas where they're being used. From 12 to 50 compartments.

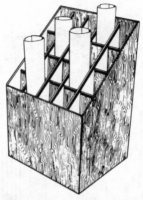

Figure 5-7. Perma Vertical Roll Organizer

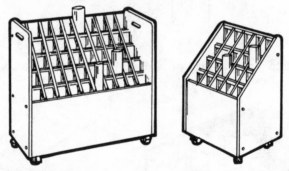

Figure 5-8. Safco Mobile Roll Files

PHOTOGRAPHIC STORAGE–SLIDES AND PRINTS

Abodia Lighted Slide Storage Cabinets organize and store slides for easy access, scanning, editing and assembling, and have a built-in lighted viewing screen. Cabinets hold from 1,000 to 65,000 slides. Call **800/950-7775** for information. Elden Enterprises, PO Box 3201, Charleston, WV 25332

Creative Memories is a great source for photo-safe albums, mounting products and album-making supplies and accessories. The albums have a unique flexible binding that allows addition of many extra pages and provides for stress-free page-turning, keeping pages and photos mounted on them flat at all times. Creative Memories offers a good selection of albums as well as accessories, such as special plastic protectors and the Quartet Ingento Personal Trimmer, a miniature paper cutter that measures five by eight by 1½ inches and includes a two-section storage tray inside for small supplies. Contact Creative Memories at **800/468-9335** or 612/251-3822, 2815 Clearwater Road, St. Cloud, MN 56302-1839.

Light Impressions is a photographic and fine art storage and presentation catalog featuring archival supplies and equipment. A sampling of their products is included in this chapter. To get their catalogs contact them at **800/828-6216** or 716/271-8960, 439 Monroe Avenue, Rochester, NY 14607-3717

The following two Light Impressions items are of special interest to photographers:

Nega*Guard System preserves and indexes hundreds of negatives (see Figure 5-9).

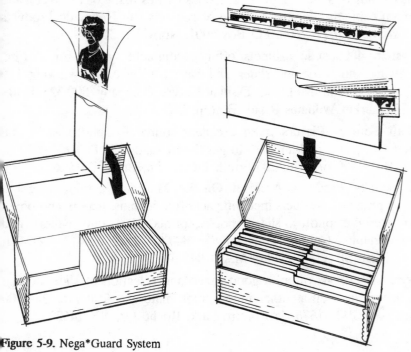

Figure 5-9. Nega*Guard System

PrintFile (Figure 5-10) is a complete negative filing and storage system that provides rapid access to negatives and consists of transparent, polyethylene protectors in a wide range of styles and formats. Many can be filed in binders.

 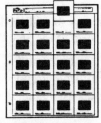 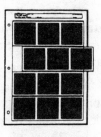

Figure 5-10. PrintFile Archival Preservers come in a wide range of formats for storing negatives and slides. Shown here are sleeves for 35mm negatives, 35mm mounted slides and 120 film negatives.

Simple **slide boxes** to metal **slide cabinets** will hold hundreds or thousands of slides. Light Impressions carries many of the Neumade metal cabinets. For the full line of cabinets call Neumade Products Corp. at 203/866-7600, PO Box 5001, Norwalk, CT 06856.

System 4000 slide cabinets offer a complete system for storing, viewing and retrieving slides and have a viewbox for viewing 120 slides at a time. Multiplex Display Fixture Company, **800/325-3350**, 1555 Larkin Williams Road, Fenton, MO 63026.

20th Century Plastics is an excellent source for photo, slide and negative pages and albums. To get their catalog call **800/767-0777** or 714/441-4500 or write 205 South Puente St., Brea, CA 92621.

University Products Archival Quality Materials catalog offers a wide range of products including acid-free albums, papers and boxes to preserve photos, slides, books, prints, important papers and memorabilia. Contact University at **800/628-1912** or 413/532-9431, 517 Main Street, Holyoke, MA 01041-0101.

Visual Horizons offers a good range and selection of slide storage solutions, as well as other presentation materials. Call 716/424-5300 or fax 716/424-1576, 180 Metro Park, Rochester, NY 14623

FILES AND RECORDS

When you have inactive records, look in your office supply catalog or store under the category "storage files." There you'll find boxes made of corrugated fiberboard that come in a variety of sizes and styles. See Figure 5-11. They usually come with lids. If you'll need access to files, consider getting drawer style storage boxes. Some of these are available with metal reinforcement, which provides greater durability for stacking.

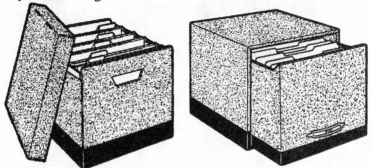

Figure 5-11. Fellowes Portable File and Drawer File

If you have many, many boxes of records you want to store off site, look in the Yellow Pages under headings such as "Business Records Storage" and "Off-site Records Storage." See also Chapter 7 for more information on filing.

If you need permanent storage boxes that are moisture resistent, consider those made by Rubbermaid such as Rubbermaid's File Tote and Trunk Tote File box, which both have see-through tops.

LITERATURE ORGANIZERS

Magazine files or **holders** sit right on a shelf or table and are great for storing magazines, catalogs, manuals or reports. The Oxford DecoFile (See Figure 5-12) is made of high-impact plastic and comes in eight colors (which you could use for color coding different types of literature). Made of corrugated fiberboard, the Fellowes Magazine File costs less but will still do the job. For an easy way to store thin magazines and catalogs in a three-ring binder without punching holes, use the **Magazine/Catalog Organizer** strip shown in Figure 5-13.

Literature sorters and **organizers** come in many different styles and sizes and are great for catalog sheets, brochures and forms that you use frequently or that need to be assembled into kits. See Figure 5-14. See also Chapter 4 for drawer systems by Abbot and 3M.

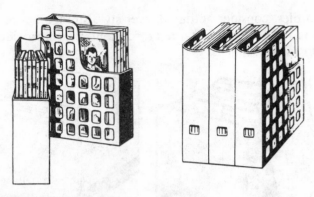

Figure 5-12. The Oxford DecoFile

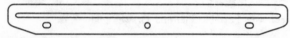

Figure 5-13. The Magazine/Catalog Organizer by Baumgarten's.

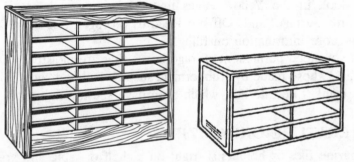

Figure 5-14. Fellowes Literature Sorter (left), Fellowes Strickly Business Mail/Literature Center

DONATIONS OF YOUR OLD COMPUTER EQUIPMENT

As you upgrade your computer equipment you may leave behind some dinosaur machines and software that are taking up precious real estate. The following organizations would probably love to receive your donations: **CompuMentor,** 415/512-7784; **East-West Education Development Foundation,** 617/542-1234; **National Cristina Foundation,** 800/274-7846; and **Non-Profit Computing Inc.,** 212/759-2368.

6

WORK SPACE BASICS: ENHANCING YOUR PHYSICAL WORKING ENVIRONMENT

Quick Scan: Whether you're planning a move or you just have a sneaking suspicion your office design is missing the mark, this chapter will reveal the physical features your office should have to be a more productive, comfortable environment. Many of these features are inexpensive and easy to implement. You'll be amazed to see how the little things can make a big difference in your office, especially if you're one of the 50 million people in the U.S. who now work or will work at home some or all of the time.

Do you feel like everything in your office has been put in place with Krazy Glue?

Once you get used to an office, it usually feels pretty permanent. Everything seems as if it's always been there (and always will be.) But when you become too used to your environment, you don't see the possibilities. Or if you do, you figure you can't do anything about them anyway.

I love the story that stockbroker Alan Harding shared at one of my seminars many years ago. Harding had wanted a window office. As he saw it, though, he didn't need to change offices—he just needed to install a window in a wall that faced the outside. So Harding asked his boss to have a window installed but his boss refused. For most people that would have been the end of it.

Not for Harding. You see, he spent a good part of every day in that enclosed office. He had been with the company awhile and was planning on staying a good while longer. Since he really wanted that window, he decided to spend his *own* money to have one installed—to which his boss agreed.

But that's not the end of the story. After seeing how serious Harding was about the window, his boss then decided to chip in and split the cost. What's more, when Harding came in on a Saturday to physically do the installation, his boss ended up helping. Harding says, "The whole thing wound up as a cooperative effort." It's amazing what can happen when you keep open the "windows of your mind."

There are three types of physical factors related to your office over which you have some control: your physical space, your furnishings and your total environment.

HOW TO ORGANIZE AND MAXIMIZE
YOUR WORK SPACE

Look at where and how your work space is organized. Two space factors come into play: location and layout.

LOCATION, LOCATION, LOCATION

Where is your office located? It sounds like a simple enough question. But you probably could provide many answers.

For example, any of the following could be truthful responses: near the freeway, 40 miles from home, next to the water cooler, on the fifth floor, far away from clients or close to the marketing department.

The last time you probably thought about your location was when you changed jobs or moved to a different office. But so often we just forget about location factors. We may even experience some irritation and not realize that that irritation is directly related to our location.

So just take a moment to think about the location of your work space, to see if there are some aspects that really bother you. Take this little survey. Next to each item, write "O" for Outstanding, "S" for Satisfactory, "N" for Needs Improvement or "NA" for Not Applicable (or not important):

1. Commuting distance
2. Proximity to colleagues
3. Proximity to vendors or suppliers
4. Proximity to your market–clients, customers or patients
5. Traffic flow in or near your office
6. Privacy
7. Noise
8. Lighting
9. Proximity to equipment and supplies
10. Proximity to personal or professional services–e.g., restaurants, shops, attorney, accountant

Take a look at any "Ns" you've marked. Are there any ways you could change or modify undesirable locations? Don't just accept things the way they are, especially if your performance and productivity are really suffering. Be creative–like Alan Harding.

LATITUDE IN YOUR LAYOUT

Now take a look at your **layout**–the location and arrangement of the furniture and equipment within your own office space. There are two essentials of every good office layout: adequate **work space** and **storage space.** Sometimes it's hard to tell, however, if work and storage spaces are adequate, especially if a desktop hasn't been seen in years, filing is less than routine and a move hasn't occurred in more than a decade.

Differentiate between work and storage space. Unfortunately, in far too many offices, the distinction is nonexistent. Work and storage spaces are all lumped (and I do mean lumped) together. You'll be making great headway if you can separate these two basic spaces.

The biggest problem comes when your desktop becomes more a storage space than a work space. Too often the desk becomes a place where things are *waiting to happen*; instead, make it a place for *action*. Think of your desk as an airport runway. If you were a pilot, you wouldn't find spare parts in the middle of the runway. They would be in the hangar. So, remove the obstacles from your work surface and **clear your desk for action!** Get out of the habit of keeping *everything* at your fingertips.

How do you break the keep-the-clutter-close habit? First, **set up appropriate systems for paperwork and projects** (see Chapter 4 on desktop management, Chapter 7 on paper files and Chapter 9 on managing work, projects and information).

Second, **put only those items you *use most frequently***–be they accessories, supplies, furniture or equipment–**closest to you.**

Third, make sure you have enough work space! I generally recommend at least **two surfaces plus adequate, accessible storage space** for most people. The surface right in front of you should be your primary work surface and ideally should contain only things you use every day. This is the area where you are doing your most common work activities. A secondary surface off to the side or behind you could be used as a work area for a particular activity, such as telephoning (unless that's a primary work activity). This secondary area could also provide storage for items you use frequently such as your daily paperwork system, telephone/address directory and stapler.

An **L-shape** layout uses two surfaces–a primary one such as a desk and another one off to the left or right side, which when attached is called a **return.** A return is a small, narrow extension of a desk that is designed to hold a typewriter (or can be adapted to hold a computer terminal). See a desk with a return in Figure 6-1. You can order a desk with either a right or left return.

You can see in Figure 6-2 how to easily create an L-shape layout by putting a table alongside your desk. Or if you don't like using a desk at all, try two tables at right angles.

A **U-shape** layout gives you more work surface and usually more

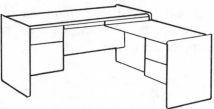

Figure 6-1. Desk with right return

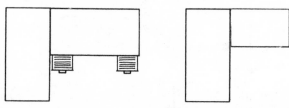

Figure 6-2. L-shape layout with table alongside desk (left) and L-shape layout with two tables at right angles

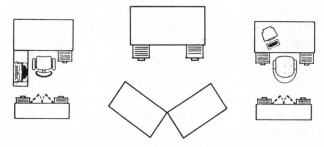

Figure 6-3. U-shape (left), triangular and parallel layouts

accessible storage.

A **triangular** layout takes advantage of a corner, makes good use of angles and plays up the importance of the desk as a focal point. A **parallel** layout places the main work surface, such as a desk, parallel to and in front of a storage unit (a credenza or lateral file cabinet, for example) or another work surface, such as a table. (See Figure 6-3 for these three layouts).

DESIGN YOUR OWN LAYOUT

I use a modified U-shape in my office—I call it a **J-shape.** I have combined modular computer furniture with two work tables and a

printer stand plus two two-drawer filing cabinets and a small
bookcase to provide additional work surfaces and storage space.
Figure 6-4 shows my office layout.

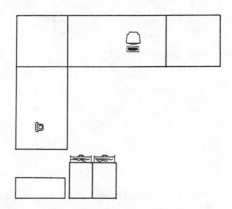

Figure 6-4. My office configuration uses a J-shape layout.

Get objective about an existing or proposed office layout. Make
a quick, little sketch of your layout. Or better yet, particularly if
you're planning a move, buy some graph or engineering paper
(quadrille pads work well), draw an outline of your office to scale
and make paper cutouts of your furniture to scale. Cutouts work
great if you have a small office space and your furniture is going to
be a tight fit. Also, it's a lot easier moving cutouts around on paper
than moving the real things. I've yet to see anyone throw out their
back moving cutouts around.

Another option is to use the award-winning, multipurpose,
business diagramming software program Visio by Visio Corporation,
which has a space planning feature. For more on this program, call
Visio at 800/446-3335 or 206/521-4500.

Even if you're not moving, remember you're allowed to move
things around. I consulted with a public relations executive who had
one of the most beautifully designed and equipped offices I had ever
seen. But she had been designed into a corner.

She had a huge pedestal desk, with a large, cumbersome chair.
Behind her was a custom-built, corner credenza with all kinds of
shelves and drawers, which she never used. Instead the surfaces of
her desk and credenza were piled high with papers.

Why didn't she use the credenza? Simple—she didn't have enough space to easily move the chair and access the credenza. My solution: move the desk farther out from the credenza! Why hadn't she thought of moving the desk? Probably because the designer had indicated where the furniture was to go and there it remained. Also, the desk top was a heavy piece of glass. These factors suggested real *permanence*.

Alexis Kyprianou, a colleague of mine, related how she once had a boss who spent a lot of money on a design that wasn't functional. The boss insisted, "We'll make it work!" What he didn't realize was that it becomes *real* work when the design doesn't work.

Once people are in their offices or have been designed into a corner, the thought of changing a layout simply doesn't occur. Here's a chance to check out your layout. Quickly sketch out the main elements of your office space—furniture, equipment, walls, windows, light sources, plants. Don't worry about scale at this point.

Ask yourself these questions:

- Is your layout convenient?
- Are the things you use most often close at hand?
- Do you have enough storage and work space?
- Do you have enough space for your equipment, especially your computer equipment?
- Do you like the way your office is configured to meet with others—co-workers, clients or customers?
- Does your layout invite irritating distractions? (For example, do you always catch someone's eye as he or she walks by?)
- Do you have different areas in your office for different types of work or activity, e.g., telephoning, computer work, meeting with clients? How and where do you like to do various kinds of work?

All of these factors may enter into the kind of office layout you can live with. Some of these factors are very subtle but their subtlety shouldn't diminish their importance.

PROXEMICS

One subtle factor concerns **proxemics**—the study of spatial configurations and interpersonal relations. Did you know that the seating arrangements in your office influence the relationships you have with your colleagues as well as your clients? Your seating arrangements make subtle statements. If, in the first example in

Figure 6-5, you are "A," sitting behind your desk, and you're meeting with "B," you are in a distinctly authoritarian, powerful position. This configuration may be totally appropriate when meeting with a client but if you're meeting with a colleague, perhaps the side by side configuration in the next example would be more effective.

If you have meetings in your office and you tend to run meetings in which you assert your authority, you would select a rectangular table, as shown in the third example, and sit at the head. If however, you tend to meet informally and you're trying to foster that "good ol' team spirit," select a round table. Of course space considerations as well as purpose will affect your final layout decisions.

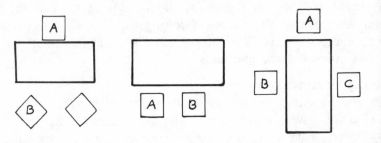

Figure 6-5. These three seating arrangements make three statements.

THE DOORWAY

Decide, too, where to place your desk in relation to the doorway. If you're facing the doorway (or the opening of your cubicle) and you're in a high people traffic zone, you may find interruption is your constant companion. Turning your back to the doorway may appear too severe or even anti-social. You may prefer instead to angle your desk so as not to catch everyone's eye but to remain responsive.

When Kim Villeneuve was a divisional vice president for The Broadway department store in Southern California, she changed her position toward the doorway, depending on the type of work she was doing. Since she needed to remain open to staff most of the day she generally sat facing the door. But when she used the telephone and didn't want interruptions, she would swing her chair around to the credenza behind her. Her telephone sat on the credenza and there she did her phone work without inviting interruption. The credenza became an area designated for important telephone work, without interruptions of people as well as any distracting paperwork on her desk.

YOUR EVOLVING WORK STYLE
Finally, consider how you like to work when you design your layout and remain flexible. As your work style needs change, so should your design.

Dr. David Snyder, a physician in Fresno, California, had a desk in his private office with a credenza behind him. Then he eliminated the credenza. He used his desk to process patient files and other paperwork quickly and efficiently. He said, "I will never have a credenza again—that's where I put stuff I didn't have time to do."

Today he has added a two-drawer lateral filing cabinet behind him. The close proximity of the cabinet gives him access to reference files. He uses the top of the cabinet for his daily paperwork system, which includes a vertical rack that holds active project files.

FURNISHINGS THAT FIT

Walk into your office as if you were walking into it for the first time. Pretend you've just arrived from Mars (some days don't we all feel that way!). Look at your office with fresh eyes and notice all your furnishings—your furniture, equipment, accessories and supplies.

Are they all well-organized, in good repair and well placed? Are they as functional as they should be? Do you have enough storage space?

FURNITURE AND EQUIPMENT
With today's changing technology, workforce and work place location, *flexibility* is a key word to apply to your choice of furniture and equipment. **Modular** furniture (often called "systems furniture") with interchangeable components works great, particularly in today's smaller offices, because it's flexible, can save floor space and yet can increase the amount of work surface.

The flexibility and functionality of modular furniture is particularly important if you'll ever be moving your office. Since buying modular furniture for my office, I have moved twice. Each of my offices required a different configuration. Figure 6-6 shows how I was able to take my original configuration from my old office and simply reverse the components to fit my current office requirements.

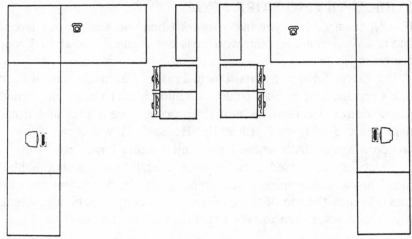

Figure 6-6. I was able to take my old layout (left) and easily reverse it (right) to fit my new office because I have modular furniture.

Figure 6-7 shows you components from The WorkManager System, well-designed modular computer furniture made by Rubbermaid Office Products Inc. Notice that the combination of a single compact pencil drawer and the notched side panels provide completely unobstructed leg-room, making sure you don't wrack up your knees as you swivel to different areas. If you have a mini-tower computer CPU on the floor, place it where it won't obstruct your leg room, such as under a connector, as shown in Figure 6-7. The Work Manager Laser Printer CPU Tower Cart (not shown) is a convenient way to store your CPU tower, laser printer as well as computer manuals and other supplies on three open shelves.

If you need more drawers, consider getting a portable drawer unit or file cabinet on casters. Rubbermaid Office Products Inc. makes a desk height file cabinet with two file drawers and an underdesk file cabinet with a utility drawer and a file drawer. Sometimes such portable units are called **pedestals**. Consider modular work stations, such as the Biotec by Hamilton Sorter. Biotec work tables are available with recessed shelves under each work table for storage

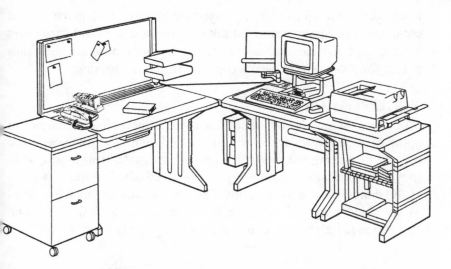

Figure 6-7. The WorkManager System features a variety of modular, computer work station components and accessories, many of which are shown here.

and with convenient half-depth shelves that don't obstruct your movement.

Rubbermaid makes two other modular computer lines, Aspira and SnapEase. The latter assembles very easily (with no tools) and is great for home offices. See Figure 6-8.

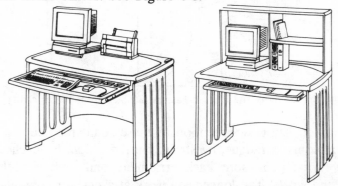

Figure 6-8. The award-winning SnapEase 46" Computer Desk ($229) comes with a full width (46 inches), slide-out keyboard platform that holds keyboard, mouse and pad with compartments for supplies. The optional SnapEase Hutch provides storage for manuals and supplies and is modular so you can configure the shelves and open space differently.

As for equipment, if you're short on space or money and/or you have occasional needs, look at a **hydra**—a multipurpose machine that combines a computer printer, a fax machine, a copier and sometimes a scanner. Separate, standalone pieces of equipment are generally better for moderate or heavy copying, faxing or printing.

ERGONOMICS

Modular systems we've been discussing are a fine example of applying **ergonomics** to office furniture design. Ergonomics is the science of making the work environment compatible with people so they can work more comfortably and productively. Ergonomics looks at the dimensions of work tables, desks and chairs and matches them to the wide range of body sizes and shapes according to certain recommended standards that are illustrated in Figure 6-9.

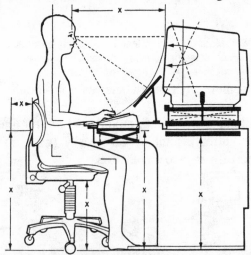

Figure 6-9. Ergonomics—The Human Factors (adapted from Biotec chart)

When you pay close attention to these standards you can avoid such symptoms as fatigue, eyestrain, blurred vision, headaches, stiff muscles, wrist pain, sore back, irritability and loss of feeling in fingers and wrists. The longer you work at a desk or computer, the more you need to consider the importance of correct angles of eyes, arms, hands, legs and feet.

Because you can do almost everything today at the computer, you may find, like many people, you are sitting there for more hours every day than ever before. But this single type of repetitive activity s dangerous physically and mentally. You need to do different things throughout the day. Studies show that repetitive stress injuries (RSI) become more common starting at four or five hours of work in front of a computer every day.

If your work simply demands you spend long hours at a computer, then the suggestions you're about to read are especially critical.

Become a clock watcher and take breaks at least every 30 minutes. Take a "micro break"–which could be a different work activity, a trip to the restroom or some simple stretches or exercises. In fact, there are even computer programs that you can preset that will pop up and remind you to go through a variety of such exercises. One is called "ExerciseBreak" by Hopkins Technology for $29.95 in Windows and DOS formats and $39.95 for the Mac (call 612/931-9376 or write 421 Hazel Lane, Hopkins, MN 55343). Another is called "StrainRELIEF," which includes stretches and eye training exercises, runs on Windows and OS/2 and is available from RAN Enterprises at 800/451-4487 for $69.95. A third is Ergodyne's "Stretch Software," a Windows programs for $45.95, available by calling 800/323-0052 or 612/642-9889.

Use a good **ergonomic chair** whose back and seat are adjustable. A good chair is more than a piece of furniture; it's a necessity for long hours of computer work. A bad one is literally a pain in the back. Adjust the height of your chair so that your thighs are parallel to the floor when your feet are resting flat on the floor. You should have lower back support from the backrest, which should adjust to fit your spine's contours and reach at least the lower part of your shoulder blades so you can relax against it. The seat of the chair should be curved and should have a "waterfall" front or downward-sloping edge. The chair should swivel, have a pneumatically adjustable seat height and back, have arms, have a stable, five-prong base with casters and be upholstered with one to four inches of thickness.

As for brands, *Organized to be the Best!* reader and interior designer Meryl Perloff from San Luis Obispo, Calif., wrote me to suggest some of her reliable sources. She recommends the Steelcase Sensor line for upper end pricing; the Fixtures Furniture Discovery line for medium pricing; and the Hon Company Sensible Seating line for low to medium pricing.

Apply ergonomics from head to toe (see Figure 6-10). Putting an **anti-glare filter** on your computer screen reduces glare, usually ELF/VLF radiation and eyestrain. (VLF stands for Very Low Frequency and ELF for Extremely Low Frequency levels.) A **foot rest** not only supports the feet, but the angle is beneficial for the back and circulation.

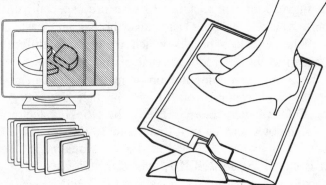

Figure 6-10. From head to toe: Curtis Glass Filter Plus reduces glare 95 percent, absorbs up to 98 percent VLF radiation and comes in seven sizes; FootEase is an adjustable foot rest I use made by Rubbermaid Office Products Inc. that lets you change the angle and height of your feet, thereby benefitting ankles, knees, hips and back.

Don't underestimate the importance of ergonomics in relation to your **computer keyboard.** Do you like the touch and feel of the keys, the sound they make and the design of the keyboard? I like the clickety-clack touch and feel of the keys on my Dell keyboard (which is manufactured by Alps) as well as the raised dots on the "F" and "J" keys, which keep my fingers in correct alignment. But I'd prefer that the function keys were on the left as on my previous IBM keyboard. While life's a tradeoff, you can easily buy a replacement keyboard for your computer if you're not happy with the standard issue.

In fact, your keyboard is one of the most important factors that determines just how happy you are with your computer as a whole. It's not expensive to replace your keyboard—it will cost you anywhere from $60 to $150.

Remember, too, that good ergonomic *work habits* will make a big difference in addition to selecting the right furniture and equipment. Be sure to stay at least 28 inches (about an arm's length) from your computer monitor, especially if it's a color monitor. (Electromagnetic fields are considerably weaker at that distance.) You should also maintain a distance of 4 feet from the sides or back of any other monitor in your workplace, even if a wall separates you from the other monitor, because electromagnetic fields are strongest there. (Keep laser printers and copiers also about four to five feet away from your body.) Some studies show that electromagnetic fields emitted from monitors (and other equipment) at unsafe distances may be linked to health problems.

Check to see if your monitor gives off too much static (which typically is not a problem with newer, low-radiation monitors). There are two telltale signs. First, there may be an accumulation of dirt on the plastic in and around a monitor that's very difficult to clean. Second, if after your monitor has been on for a few hours you turn it off and run the back of your hand over the screen, you should not hear popping, crackling sounds; if you do, then your monitor is giving off too much static. When there's too much static, an invisible cloud of microscopic particles floats in front of the screen and can cause eye irritation. According to computer expert John Dvorak, you should consider buying a new monitor if yours is giving off too much static.

It's also a good idea to pause every 20 minutes or so to look away from the screen and to change your close-up focus by looking at distant objects in order to prevent eyestrain.

How you use your keyboard, especially if you use it many hours every day, can have an adverse physiological effect on your hands. There are several ergonomic measures you can take to prevent hand disorders such as tenosynovitis and carpal tunnel syndrome. Take a five-minute break every hour to relax your hands. Wrists should be straight while typing and at the same height as your elbows. As you're typing, you may want to rest your wrists on a **wrist rest**, which either is built into your keyboard or you may need to use an additional wrist rest accessory. I'm using a comfortable, padded wrist rest attached to a platform called the Daisy Wrist Rest from the Daisy Wheel Ribbon Company (800/266-5585 or 714/989-5585.) I find it's very comfortable using my keyboard on this wrist rest/platform, which I place on my lap, with my feet supported on a foot rest. This also positions me more than 28 inches from the screen. (See also Computer Accessories for more on wrist rests.) For wrist rests and other products discover your own **comfort level.**

Positioning and **placement** of equipment is an ergonomic factor that also relates to left- or right-handedness. At my Positively Organized! seminars I'll often ask participants whether their telephone should go on the right or left side of the desk if they are right-handed. Answers are usually evenly divided between "left" and "right." The correct answer is "left." If you're right-handed you'll be writing with your right hand. So place the phone on the left so that the phone doesn't get in the way. You'll want to hold the phone with your left hand to your left ear, leaving your right hand free to write.

Consider, too, how you like to turn your body in relation to equipment. Do you prefer a computer or typewriter on a left or right hand return? Where do you want to place the copy stand and materials—on the left or right side of your computer or typewriter? (I have my copy stand on the left, which seems ergonomically to make sense since I read from left to right). Most people just don't stop and think about the things that they use every day.

Check to see that your work surfaces are the right height from the floor. Your keyboard should sit on a surface that's generally 26 inches from the floor but your writing work surface should be 29 inches high.

The **accessibility principle** should influence your decisions about equipment placement, too. Even a work surface has areas that are more convenient than others. Angle your computer, for example, off to the side for occasional use; place it right in front of you for frequent or constant use.

Trying it on for size is an important principle when shopping for workspace equipment as well as for clothes. Never buy a chair from a catalog; you should "test sit" any chair you buy. When it comes to keyboards, mice and trackballs, you should play with them first or if a mouse or keyboard is standard issue with your computer and you're less than pleased, then go out and test drive some others and don't be afraid to switch.

I personally think that posture and positioning are critical factors in preventing RSI, carpal tunnel syndrome, tendinitis and "mouse shoulder." The latter often results from reaching for a mouse and using it too much. But good design of keyboards, mice and trackballs may be just as important and may also build in some positioning features. Look for shapes and configurations that fit the size of your hands and fingers and for any features that reduce the amount of work your fingers, hands and arms need to do, e.g., some mice and trackballs are eliminating double clicking. As one article pointed out, no matter how ergonomically designed a product is, final selection boils down to personal preference because one size or style does not fit all.

Here are some brand name models that have received noteworthy attention: Lexmark Select-Ease keyboard; Maltron Ergonomic keyboard from Applied Learning Corp.; the FlexPro, also known as the ergoLogic keyboard; Ergonomixx MyKey keyboard; Health Care Comfort Keyboard System; Kinesis Ergonomic Keyboard; Kensington Expert Mouse trackball; Logitech MouseMan Cordless and TrackMan Voyager; the TrackPoint II device built into IBM's notebook computers; CH Products Trackball Pro; MicroSpeed WinTRAC trackball; Appoint's Gulliver mouse (for use with a desktop and a laptop); and Logitech's Kidz Mouse (which fits children's small hands).

CREATING AN ERGONOMIC PHONE AREA

Set up a separate, clear phone area where you can handle calls without the distraction of other work. When you don't have to shuffle through other tasks and projects, you can really focus on each call. Your area should have enough writing surface and be close to files and other telephone information you may need. Telephone equipment should ideally include: a clock (or if necessary, several clocks for different time zones); a timer (if you have trouble keeping track of time and length of calls); a voice mail system or a telephone answering machine; a speaker phone with on-hook dialing, automatic on-hook re-dialing and automatic memory dialing; and a **telephone headset** if you're on the phone at least two hours every day and/or you need your hands free for writing or typing while on the phone.

I've used a headset for years. Figure 6-11 shows a typical headset configuration. The small price tag for a headset is certainly well worth it for convenience as well as for your health, too. A telephone headset can help prevent neck and back aches and trips to the chiropractor. For more information, see the "Telephone Accessories

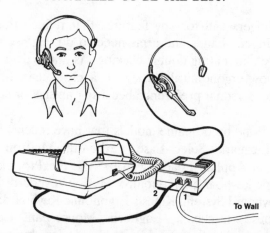

Figure 6-11. The Plantronics SP telephone headset by Plantronics (California), which makes a complete line of quality headsets and can be reached at 800/544-4660 or 408/426-5858.

and Features" section later in the chapter, as well as "Accessories and Supplies" in the Resource Guide.

Use the speaker phone when you're on hold so you can do other work while waiting. You can also use it for a conference call in your office, provided that confidentiality isn't a problem and the speaker phone echo doesn't bother the person(s) on the other end.

ACCESSORIES AND SUPPLIES

In my consulting work I notice that clients either have too few or too many accessories for their paperwork, telephone and computer. Those who have too few generally lump their work all together on the desk, on tables, on shelves, in drawers and on the floor. Those with too many (if one pencil holder is good, six are better) collect accessories along with good intentions. They buy a new accessory every time they're inspired to "get organized." Soon the accessory becomes just another catchall rather than a clearly defined tool. The original purpose is too soon forgotten.

Remember, to keep it simple; sometimes the simplest, least expensive accessories can save you a lot of money. You might even avoid the "$12,000 paper clip." It's the little things that count as one man found out after losing two $12,000 copiers because of paper clips that somehow became lodged inside. This man now uses a $3 magnet attached to a piece of Velcro tape on his copier to hold paper clips. (By the way, we use Velcro tape to attach a writing instrument to each of our office phones or any place where a pen or pencil has a way of just walking off by itself.)

Any time you add a new accessory to your environment, define its purpose and *get in the habit of using it*. And from time to time, check to see if it's doing its job. If it has outlived its usefulness, *get rid of it!*

Let's look at some of the most useful work space accessories (see also chapters 4, 5 and 7).

PAPERWORK ACCESSORIES

One of the most versatile paperwork accessories is the **expanding collator**. It comes in plastic or aluminum with 12, 18 or 24 slots. If you're a CPA or an attorney, use it for large, bulky active client files that you're referring to daily or several times a week. (While it's always safer to put client files away each night in filing cabinets, using the collator is a good intermediate step for anyone who is still piling files on couches and floors.)

Use the collator near your copier or computer printer to store large quantities (up to 500 sheets) of different types of paper.

You can always use the collator for its original purpose, too—collating! It's great for assembling or sorting literature and handouts. (See Chapter 4 for an illustration of a collator.)

The **stationery holder** is a wonderful accessory to hold letterhead, envelopes, forms and note paper. Some stationery holders are designed to fit inside a desk drawer; others sit on top of furniture or on a shelf. Place a stationery holder where you'll be using it.

Magazine files or **holders** are indispensable boxes for storing catalogs and directories as well as magazines. They're usually made out of plastic, acrylic or corrugated fiberboard. (See Chapter 5 for some illustrated examples.)

If you use a typewriter or computer, use a **copyholder**. See Figure 6-12. There are many different types but the main idea is to get one that can be placed at the same focal distance as the screen. It's hard on the eyes to keep refocusing to accommodate different focal lengths. The Curtis Clip attaches to the monitor and swings out of the way when not in use. It may not be feasible to use such a clip all the time; you'll probably want to have at least one other standard

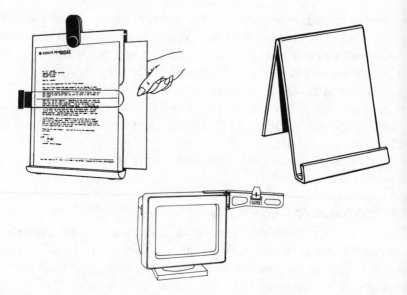

Figure 6-12. Oxford CopyKeeper (includes a sliding guide and side storage compartment for "to-be-typed" materials); Oxford CopyCaddy holds thicker material; Curtis Clip can attach to either side of your computer and gives you good ergonomic positioning.

copyholder (see Figure 6-12 for two examples).

If you have wall partitions, consider installing a **wall unit paper management system.** As office space decreases into more flexible, partitioned "cubicles," using vertical wall space for accessories makes sense. Wall systems help you get paper off your desk and yet make it accessible and organized.

If you do a lot of hole punching, stapling, folding or trimming, consider getting accessories to help you automate these processes. **Electric hole punches** and **staplers** can save you a lot of time. (Panasonic and Acco Swingline have several good models; Swingline even has a 5,000-staple cartridge that's easy to load and eliminates frequent refilling.) **Letter folding machines** are available from Legal Tabs Co. in Colorado, 800/322-3022 or Premier in Indiana, 219/563-0641.

Don't forget about color coding. Small colored adhesive dots on locks and keys will help save you time.

TELEPHONE ACCESSORIES AND FEATURES

Selecting a basic telephone today has become a major decision given all the different features and accessories that are available. Look for these features:

- speaker phone with on-hook dialing
- automatic on-hook re-dialing
- automatic memory dial
- compatibility with your headset, telephone answering machine or other telecommunications equipment.

If you're on the phone a lot (at least one to two hours a day) or you have any neck, shoulder or back trouble (or want to prevent such trouble!), a telephone headset is the answer. Besides being more comfortable, a headset frees up your hands to take notes, handle paperwork or operate a keyboard. I always use a headset whenever I do interviews for articles or seminars or when I know I'll need to write or use a keyboard during the call. If you don't like the look or feel of a headset, at the very least use a **shoulder rest**, a device that attaches to your telephone handset and allows you hands-free movement. (One neurologist believes that cradling the phone for just three or four minutes while taking notes is enough to stress the neck and cause muscle spasms.)

Make sure your headset is compatible with your phone equipment. Some headsets will not work with all *electronic* phones. (If your phone has any of the typical bells and whistles—redial, speaker phone, memory dial—it's electronic.)

Where do you buy a headset? Radio Shack has headsets, as do many stores that sell telephones and other electronic equipment. Look for headsets in mail order catalogs, too, such as The Sharper Image from San Francisco. Office machine dealers may have them, also. Again, I can't emphasize enough the importance of compatibility. Very often sales people will not be aware of compatibility problems, so either bring your phone to the store to check it out or if you order a headset, make sure it is completely refundable.

My favorite source for telephone equipment and accessories is the HelloDirect mail order catalog. Their service and support is excellent. I used them for my current telephone headset, the HelloSet Pro (my Dual Pro model is $189) and the handy Touch-

N-Talk handset on-off hook device ($9.95 when ordered with any HelloSet headset). This quality business headset comes with a lifetime warranty. The amplifier is guaranteed to work with any phone (it's been field tested on more than 400 different phone terminals) and it has a handy mute button (great for private side conversations or when a sudden cough comes on). Contact Hello Direct at 800/444-3556 or 408/972-1990, 5884 Eden Park Place, San Jose, CA 95138-1859. See Figure 6-17 on page 147.

A **telephone answering machine** is a must for most homes and small offices. There are many on the market today with a variety of features from which to choose. Here are some features that are nice to have:

- ability to pick up messages off site by dialing a code
- ability to change outgoing messages off site
- if you have two phone lines, a two-line answering machine that can answer either line
- a machine with a computer chip instead of a tape

A computer chip provides better sound quality and lets you play back, repeat or skip messages instantly without having to wait for the tape to forward or rewind. I use AT&T's Digital Answering System 1545, which is loaded with features that are perfect for a small office. Voices and messages are "digitized" on a microchip. There are four voice mailboxes you can use along with your own multiple outgoing messages. (As in a voice mail system, each mailbox can be used for different announcements or for leaving messages for different individuals or departments.) This machine was a recent "Hot Pick for the Home Office" in *PC WORLD* magazine and is available through Hello Direct.

And to maximize your telephone time, use a **clock** placed strategically in front of you. And if you frequently place calls to another time zone, use a second clock specifically for that time zone. A **countdown timer** (available at an electronics store or use a simple cooking timer) will help you consciously choose how much time you want to spend on each call.

COMPUTER ACCESSORIES

Protect your eyes. Make sure your screen has an **anti-glare filter** (as mentioned earlier). Purchase an anti-glare filter at your local computer store or through one of the catalogs listed at the end of the chapter.

I'm using a 3M Anti-glare/Radiation Filter that blocks 99.9 percent of ELF/VLF E-field radiation, stops static charge and dust buildup and has a unique universal mounting system.

Polaroid makes an excellent glass circular polarizer filter with anti-reflective coating. (For names of dealers call 800/225-2770 or in Europe, 31-053-821911.)

Set your monitor on a **tilt stand** if you need to adjust the proper angle of the screen to your eyes.

Avoid eyestrain by using at least a 17-inch monitor, which offers high resolution and lets you work more comfortably with more windows on your screen. Ideally, you should try out a monitor before you buy; computer expert Lawrence Magid suggests viewing small black type against a white background to judge overall resolution and quality.

Protect your ears. Enclose a noisy letter quality or dot matrix printer in a **sound cover** if the sound from your printer is disturbing to you or co-workers or can be heard during telephone calls. Check that your sound cover and stand have slots in the right places for feeding paper to and from your printer. Your sound cover should also come equipped with an automatic cooling fan and have a conveniently located switch.

Protect your floppy diskettes. Buy **plastic diskette boxes** with divider tabs to store programs, files and backups on disks.

To guard against the possibility of electrical power disturbances wiping out data, use a **surge protector**, also called a **surge suppressor**. Typically, you use a surge protector for computers and printers but it's also useful for copy machines, faxes and other equipment. Service calls fell by 51 percent at Arizona State University after surge protectors were installed on copy machines.

Adapt a desk return that's too shallow with a **keyboard extender** or a **keyboard drawer** as shown in Figure 6-13 that mounts under the desktop and conveniently pulls out. Another type of keyboard drawer is a stand usually made out of steel upon which you place your cpu (central processing unit) and monitor and there's a space underneath to store a keyboard drawer, which pulls out when in use. A keyboard drawer is a space saver and depending on the type, can be a good accessory to lower a keyboard that's too high for comfort-

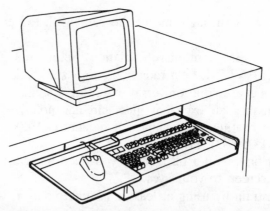

Figure 6-13. Rubbermaid Office Products Inc. makes a keyboard extender called the Underdesk Keyboard Drawer, which is shown here with their MouseDeck—this is a comfortable, efficient way to use and store a keyboard and mouse together. The MouseDeck slides on tracks to accommodate left- and right-handed users.

able typing.

Articulating keyboard arms are similar to underdesk keyboard drawers but they usually have different adjustable positions.

Look for a keyboard drawer or arm that either has a wrist rest built in or can accommodate one. Look, too, for accessories that will position your mouse as close to the keyboard as possible so that if you're using a keyboard drawer or arm, you're not reaching for your mouse on the desktop. Rubbermaid Office Products makes several such products: the Mouse Tray that attaches to the side of their Underdesk Keyboard Drawer, the MouseDeck (as shown) and the Underdesk Mouse Tray. Look, too, for a mouse pad that has a built-in wrist rest. PC Compatibles makes such a pad and calls it a Mouse Push ($15.95, 800/487-0781, fax 203/384-1932, in Connecticut).

If, like me, you work with the keyboard on your lap, consider the Mouse Arm by Ring King Visibles (Figure 6-14). This ingenious mouse pad ($42.95) attaches easily to almost any armrest and lets you move the mouse more with your forearm, not your wrist, thereby reducing neck, shoulder, arm and wrist strain. I've evaluated this product firsthand and it definitely gets the Susan Silver Seal of Approval! (Reach Ring King Visibles at 800/272-2366 or 319/263-8144).

For lap users who prefer the keyboard and mouse all on the same

Figure 6-14. The Mouse Arm by Ring King Visibles.

plane, Fox Bay CarpalRest Wrist Support with Mouse Area combines a comfortable, padded fabric wrist rest with a platform to support your keyboard and mouse. (It's available through Daisy Wheel Ribbon Co., 800/266-5585, which is where I saw it.)

Speaking of the keyboard, if yours is located in a dusty or dirty area, protect it with a "keyskin," a special, thin, molded, plastic membrane that allows keys to be clearly visible, protected and usable. Also, be sure to cover your computer when it's not in use.

Straighten up your computer cables and wires—for aesthetics as well as safety—with cable management accessories. Velcro USA Inc. makes a "Wire Management" line of clips, ties and covers that will keep cables in their place.

APC's PowerManager ($135) gives you power control, cord management and guaranteed surge protection for life. Lift the lid and you can neatly wrap the cords inside the unit (as shown in Figure 6-15). You can control up to five peripherals (six outlets total) directly from your desktop. Surge protection helps prevent hardware damage and data loss. The Pow6T model adds telephone protection that prevents spikes and surges from reaching your modem, fax, answering machine and telex equipment via phone lines.

KEEPING SUPPLIES IN ORDER

Deciding what supplies to buy isn't as much a challenge as keeping your supplies organized and stocked. The following will help:

- Organize your supplies for easy access, keeping the most frequently used most accessible.
- Group supplies by type as well as by frequency of use.
- Label supply shelves, drawers or cabinets and/or use color coding.

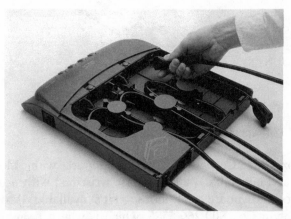

Figure 6-15. APC PowerManager lets you remove the cover and neatly wrap cord inside.

- Replenish supplies regularly and systematically and have one person in charge of the ordering process. Develop a form like the one in Figure 6-16 to simplify the process.
- Place a re-order chart near supplies for people to indicate whenever a supply is getting low or for special requests.
- Place re-order slips strategically close to the bottom of supply boxes: whoever gets a slip turns it in to the person who orders supplies.
- Prepare a "frequently ordered items" form for each vendor you use, listing items and stock or catalog numbers; refer to these forms to speed up the ordering process.
- If you use forms in your office, consider putting the master on an overhead transparency sheet and placing it on the bottom, that way no one will use the last form and the master is always within easy reach to make more copies

With regard to printer paper and toner cartridge supplies, I'd like to recommend that you use recycled products but you should probably check with your printer manufacturer, especially if you're under warranty. Your printer warranty may not cover damage from a remanufactured cartridge or from using recycled paper. Two major printer manufacturers, however, currently have instituted model recycling programs for laser printer cartridges: Hewlett-Packard (800/527-3753) and Canon (800/962-2708).

```
                    OFFICE SUPPLY REQUEST FORM
_____
_____

                                        Date:  _____

Requested by:  _____   Due by:  _____

Department:  _____   Estimated Cost:  _____

*Department Manager's Approval:  _____
(When cost estimated exceeds $25)

Description of Goods:  _____

_____

_____


Note:  Office supplies are ordered twice a week - Tuesday and
       Thursday only.  Visits to Price Club are limited to once
       every two weeks, please keep this in mind when ordering
       supplies.  Your lack of forethought does not constitute
       an emergency on our part.
```

Figure 6-16. This office supply form was developed by clients after participating in one of my office training programs.

As for paper, there is a definite move to switch to recycled paper. The entire California court system for one has mandated "the use of recycled paper for all original documents filed with California courts." Knowing that 50 percent recycled paper is less likely to jam than 100 percent may help but you should still ask your manufacturer(s) what is best for your printer as well as your copier.

YOUR TOTAL ENVIRONMENT

How do you feel about your office space? Do you feel comfortable there? Is it *you*? Is there something about it that rubs you the wrong way (or the right way)?

There are five important environmental factors that affect how you feel about your office space: aesthetics, air, comfort and safety, lighting and privacy. See to what degree any of these environmental factors influence your feelings.

AESTHETICS

If you spend at least one third of every week day in your

office—that's at least eight hours a day—you deserve to have a working environment that's aesthetically pleasing.

COLOR

Many studies have revealed the "psychology of color," showing the effect of color on our emotions and state of mind. They have found for example, that red excites us; in fact, when red is used in restaurants it is supposed to make us salivate! But used in moderation, red can be a great accent color, particularly for a sales or marketing office where you want an upbeat atmosphere.

Blue is perhaps the most universally pleasing color and is generally a calm color, depending on the shade, of course. Grays browns and other neutrals are even more subdued. All three can work well in professional offices.

Burgundy and deep forest green are rich colors that can work well together or separately in professional offices, too. They can be used as main or accent colors.

Use of "trendy colors" can give a more contemporary feeling which may be important for your type of office. You do run the risk, however, of having those colors go out of style more quickly Use of more traditional colors and color schemes avoids this problem and may convey a more permanent, solid business environment. Base color decisions on the nature of your business, who comes into your office and your own particular preferences.

Choose light and dark colors to enhance your space. Lighter colors tend to open up space and work well in smaller offices. Darker colors make rooms feel smaller, cozier and more intimate. They work well in large office spaces that could otherwise appear too intimidating or sterile.

Don't ignore the impact of color. The question to ask is, What are the right colors for you?

PERSONALIZATION

Color alone is not enough. Your office is not just a place to work. It should be a reflection of you. It needs to be personalized with objects you love.

In fact, why not have objects you love around you, such as art photos or plants? Just remember, they should complement not clutter your work space.

If you've become bored with your office, consider moving personalized objects to different places. We all need variety; just moving things around or changing objects from time to time can make a big difference.

AIR

What can you do about the air you breathe? First of all, be aware of it. Second, see if you can change any unpleasant atmospheric conditions or adapt to them.

AIRBORNE TOXINS

The most obvious toxin in the air is cigarette smoke. Some studies have shown that cigarette smoke is more harmful to someone nearby inhaling "secondary" smoke than the smoke inhaled by the actual smoker. If smoke is a problem for you, stay away from it!

Many cities and companies now specify that smokers go outside or to other specially designated areas to smoke. If your city or company doesn't have such requirements, consider working toward establishing them. Sure it'll take some of your precious time, but isn't your health precious enough? At the very least, make sure that office workers who smoke have an air cleaner or purifier unit on their desk to remove at least some of the smoke.

As far as other toxic substances, such as asbestos, read your newspaper to stay current on new discoveries and legislation. Notice, too, whether you experience certain symptoms such as nausea and dizziness only in your office environment. Invisible toxic substances pose a real problem in detection and in identification but we're bound to see more research on this in the future.

Consider putting in some plants. A study by NASA found that plants can remove up to 87 percent of toxic indoor air within 24 hours. One estimate puts nearly a third of all new office buildings at risk of indoor air quality problems.

Plants can absorb common office pollutants that include: formaldehyde (from particle board, wall paneling, plywood, furniture and carpeting); trichloroethylene (from some inks, paints and varnishes) and benzene (from tobacco smoke and some plastics, inks and oils). According to the book *50 Simple Things Your Business Can*

Do to Save the Earth, use at least one four-to-five-foot plant per 100 square feet. Good plants to use with fluorescent lighting include: philodendrons, golden pothos, English Ivy, peace lily and mother-in-law's tongue. Spider plants and flowering plants such as azaleas and chrysanthemums work well with more light.

TEMPERATURE

Here's one of those factors that is far easier to adapt to than to change. I can't tell you how often I have complained to facilities managers about the temperature, which for me is almost always too cold in modern buildings, where you are at the mercy of a thermostat that either isn't working or is adjusted to somebody else's body!

I used to work for an aerospace company. Our department was on the same thermostat as the computer room. It was always "freeeezing" in the office. I kept a little portable heater on under my desk. (Fire regulations where you work may prohibit this solution.)

My office today doesn't usually get cold enough for a heater, but I keep an extra sweater in the office at all times, particularly during the summer when the air conditioning tends toward the cool side. I also close off most of the vents in my office in the summertime when the air conditioning is running fast and furiously. If your office is too hot, your only option may be to keep complaining or work at home if possible. But recognize that temperature is a factor in your productivity and your attitude toward your workplace.

COMFORT AND SAFETY

Fifty percent of disabling office accidents are the result of slips or falls–most of which could have been prevented.

Keep floors clear of cords, cables and other objects. Even a rubber band on the floor can be a hazard. One office worker slipped on a rubber band, breaking his arm in two places and crushing his elbow. He lost six weeks of work.

Our discussion of ergonomics in this chapter certainly relates to comfort and safety. Check out your chair and your equipment according to the ergonomics chart and criteria discussed earlier.

I recommend that whether you work for yourself or someone

else you should become more responsible for your own safety. As of this writing, ergonomic regulations and programs are coming under less scrutiny by the government. Learn what you can to protect yourself and if an employer doesn't provide what you need, you may wish to provide it for yourself or look for another more ergonomic workplace.

LIGHTING

Lighting is related to comfort and safety, as well as aesthetics. Select the right **amount**, the right **kinds** and the right **direction** to make lighting work best for you.

Make sure you have enough light. Some offices are too dark and depressing. Interior offices usually need additional lighting. That one panel in the ceiling just won't do it.

Make sure you don't have too much of the wrong kind of lighting in the wrong places. If you're using a computer terminal, all those overhead fluorescent lights could be causing irritating glare. Better to use a lower level of overhead lighting combined with **task lighting**, localized sources of lighting for specific tasks or areas. An example of task lighting is a desk lamp that sheds light on desktop paperwork only and stays off the computer screen.

Balance fluorescent lighting with either a natural light source (a window) or incandescent lighting. Fluorescent lighting by itself is very hard on the eyes.

In addition, some research studies indicate fluorescent lighting may be emitting harmful ultraviolet rays that cause such symptoms as fatigue and dizziness. Some retail stores are putting **ultraviolet shields** on their fluorescent lights. You may also consider replacing your fluorescent lighting with **full spectrum lights**, also called **health lights** or **Durolights**.

PRIVACY

The last environmental factor concerns the need for privacy in your office. Privacy usually comes from some sense of *enclosure*, which can include visual as well as sound barriers. Having some barriers, be they walls, movable panels, plants, bookcases or file cabinets, is important for most people.

For one thing, effective communication needs privacy. Studies have shown that employees who sit in an open, "bull pen" environment tend to communicate less freely. On the other hand, employees who have some measure of enclosure and privacy tend to communicate more freely and openly.

Privacy also can improve productivity. Most people need to have their own space to focus, concentrate and shut out some of the distractions. A smaller, more controlled environment is also less stressful for most people.

RESOURCE GUIDE

FURNITURE AND EQUIPMENT

Whenever possible, see furniture and equipment "in person." At the very least, get color chips of finish or fabric or actual samples. *Never* buy a chair without sitting in it first. Suppliers are listed from different parts of the country; you can often save significantly on shipping when you order in a geographical area that's nearby.

BIOTEC SYSTEMS is the line of modular, computer furniture that I have in my office. To get the name of your local representative or to receive a free copy of the BIOTEC Design Guide call 800/543-1605 or 513/870-4400 or write Hamilton Sorter Co., Inc., 3158 Production Dr., Fairfield, OH 45014

Business & Institutional Furniture Co., Inc. mail order catalog includes the lowest prices on furniture (they'll meet or beat any price) and guarantees all products for 15 years. 800/558-8662. 611 N. Broadway, Milwaukee, WI 53202-0902

Environmental Protection Agency (EPA) Energy Star Program provides you a list of computers and peripherals that are energy-efficient. Call 202/233-9114 if you want a copy mailed to you or an abbreviated list by type and manufacturer is available via fax.

National Business Furniture is a mail order catalog that offers a substantial selection of furniture at discount prices with a guarantee for 15 years (except for normal upholstery wear). They offer 10,000 different products. **800/558-1010**, 222 E. Michigan St., Milwaukee, WI 53202-9956

Rubbermaid Office Products Inc. offers dozens of microcomputer work station components and accessories that are as attractive as ney are functional. **800/827-5055**, 1427 William Blount Drive, Maryville, TN 37801-8249

ACCESSORIES AND SUPPLIES

Allsop Inc. manufactures a line of computer and office equipment accessories and supplies that include diskette cases and computer cleaning kits. **206/734-9090**.

Curtis Manufacturing Company, Inc. (Rolodex) manufactures more than 100 computer and electronic accessory products, which are available through dealers. **800/955-5544** (New Jersey)

Daisy Wheel Ribbon Co. is an excellent direct mail source for computer supplies and accessories with great customer service. **800/266-5585** or 909/989-5585 (California)

Hello Direct is an excellent catalog of telephone productivity tools that I have used and recommended. See Figure 6-17. **800/444-3556** or 408/972-1990 (California).

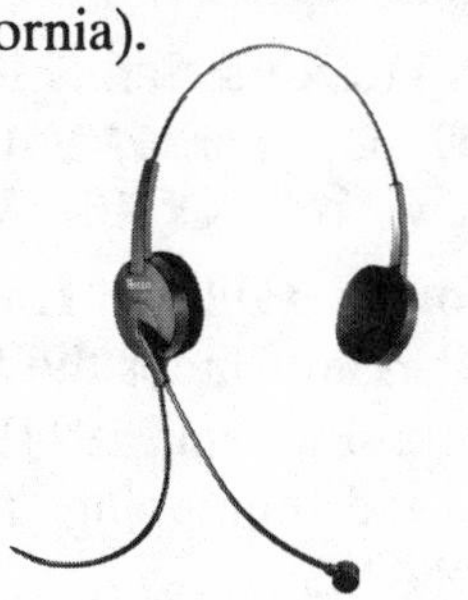

Figure 6-17. I use Hello Direct's Hello-Set Dual model headset (shown here) with the Pro Amplifier and Touch-N-Talk device (not shown)

Inmac's award-winning mail order catalog offers one of the best selections of quality computers, supplies, accessories, furniture and data communications products at great prices. **800/547-5444** (California)

Reliable Home Office is a beautiful catalog that features many attractive desk and office accessories for your office at home as well as at work. **800/621-4344** (Illinois).

Secure-It, Inc. makes Kablit locks and cables to help you prevent theft of valuable computers and peripherals. **800/451-7592**

BOOKS AND OTHER READING

Cumulative Trauma Disorders: A Manual for Musculoskelet
Diseases of the Upper Limbs (Bristol, PA: Taylor & Francis, 198?
was edited by Vern Putz-Anderson of the National Institute fc
Occupational Safety and Health and is considered to be one of th
best books on RSI (Repetitive Stress Injuries).

How to Survive Your Computer Work Station (Kerrville, Texa
CRT Services, Inc., 1990) by Julia Lacey shows specifically how t
prevent and eliminate physical, vision and stress problems related t
computer use. $14.95 plus $2 shipping by check only. **800/256-437?**
PO Box 1525, Kerrville, TX 78029-1525

9 to 5 Fact Sheets contain valuable information about good offic
design, particularly for computer workers. To get the fact sheets an
a complete listing of other work-related books and reports ca
216/566-9308. 9 to 5 National Association of Working Women, 61
Superior Ave. NW, Cleveland, OH 44113

VDT News, The Computer Health & Safety Report is an outstandin
bimonthly newsletter. $147 per year. **212/517-2802.** PO Box 179?
Grand Central Station, New York NY 10163.

Working From Home, Fourth Edition: Everything You Need t
Know About Living and Working Under the Same Roof by Paul an
Sarah Edwards (New York: Putnam, 1994) has several exceller
chapters on setting up and equipping a home office spac¢
Paperback, $15.95. **800/788-6262**

Working Until It Hurts is an excellent video on RSI. Subtitled "Ho\
Computer Technology is Disabling America's Workers," this video
available for $89 plus $3 shipping (and tax in California) fro
California Working Group, PO Box 10326, Oakland CA 9461(
510/547-8484

7

UP-TO-DATE
PAPER FILES
AND BEYOND

Quick Scan: They're out of sight, out of mind. Or so you'd like to think until one fateful day when you can't find that all important document. Or until your files are so full that it's physically dangerous to pry open files to slip in just one more paper. Find out how to organize your files so that they become an ally, not an enemy. Discover which filing supplies can make a world of difference. While the main emphasis is on your own personal filing system, this chapter also includes information useful for larger or special office filing systems.

For most people, paper files are like skeletons in the closet—bad secrets that no one likes to talk about. Who wants to admit that files are bulging with out-of-date papers, that they are difficult to handle and retrieve and that very often files are misplaced or even lost?

Then there are the *piles*—the papers that never make it into the files. They sit on desktops, in bookcases, on tables, on file cabinets, and yes, even on the floor. Let's see how your files stack up.

HOW DO YOUR FILES STACK UP?

Here's a quick quiz to rate the state of your filing system. Check "yes" or "no" after each question.

	YES	NO
1. Is filing a real chore?		
2. Would it take a long while to catch up on your filing?		
3. Do you often have trouble finding and retrieving papers —often enough to cause irritation?		
4. Do you keep many papers and/or publications "just in case" someday you may need them?		
5. Is your filing system characterized more by randomness than careful planning?		
6. Are your files inconveniently located?		
7. Do you frequently have trouble deciding what to name files or where to file papers?		
8. Is it difficult to tell what's in each file drawer without opening it up?		
9. Are you afraid to attempt retrieving a document from your files (or piles) while someone is waiting in your office or you're on the phone? (Would you prefer to look without the time pressure of "beat the clock"?)		
10. Are you copy machine happy—do you make unnecessary duplicates of papers?		
11. Are all your filing cabinets/drawers stuffed to the gills?		

If you have at least three "yes" responses, keep reading!

Below are some typical excuses I hear from people who explain why their files are usually not as functional as they should be. See if you relate to any of the following:

- I don't have a secretary.
- I don't have time/I'm too busy putting out fires.
- Setting up a system is menial, clerical work.
- It's not my job.
- I don't know what to call things.
- I'm creative and my work style is "organized chaos."

THE THREE FILING PHOBIAS

Besides these excuses, there are three fears people have when it comes to files and piles. I call these fears the "3-Ds" because they each start with the letter "D."

First, people are afraid of Decisions. If you don't know what to call papers, you'll end up calling them nothing. Papers then collect in unnamed stacks and piles, as well as in drawers and in-boxes.

Second, people are afraid of Discards. Heaven forbid you should throw anything out—you might need it someday.

Third, the fear of Disappearance haunts many. "Filing a paper in my system is like filing it in a black hole—never to be seen or heard from again," one new client told me.

Now that we've psychoanalyzed some filing phobias, here are some valid reasons for *making the time* to set up or revamp your deskside files. Check any that apply to you:

- You look and act more professional and competent when your information is organized.
- Organized information helps you plan your activities.
- It's easier to get work done.
- You feel better when you know where everything is. You have more control over your work.
- You save time looking for things.
- Accessible, fingertip information is a key resource for your productivity, professional image and peace of mind.
- Add some reasons of your own, making them relate specifically to your goals. What will a good filing system help you achieve or accomplish?

FIVE EASY STEPS
TO AN ORGANIZED FILING SYSTEM

Most people in the workplace are foggy when it comes to filing systems. They haven't been "office trained." They don't realize that the clerical work of filing is only a part of an organized filing system. The *mental*, conceptual work is the most important aspect of a good system.

Most people also don't know where to start. What follows is a blueprint to guide you in designing or revamping your system. Here are the five main steps I use with clients:

1. Categorize any existing files as "active" or "inactive" and pull inactive files from your existing filing system.
2. Write out your filing system categories and subcategories on *paper*. Get input from any others who'll be using the system.
3. Physically set up the system. Have all supplies on hand as you prepare file labels and purge, consolidate and arrange file folders.
4. Put the finishing touches on your system. Label drawers and prepare a file index or chart for yourself and any others who have access to the system. If others are involved, introduce the system at a special training meeting.
5. Maintain your system by sticking to a routine.

We'll go into more detail about these five steps after becoming more familiar with the thought process behind every good filing system.

A CLOSER LOOK AT THE FIVE-STEP PROCESS

There are three essential questions to answer about each paper or file:

1. **When** is it used? How many times a day, a week, a month, a year do you handle it?
2. **What** is it? Under what category(ies) does it belong?
3. **Where** should it go? Near your desk? In storage? In a filing cabinet? Which drawer? A notebook? The trash?

Steps One through Three will deal with these questions.

STEP ONE: ACTIVE AND INACTIVE

Files should be categorized on the basis of *frequency*, that is *when* or how often they are used. There are two basic types: **active** and **inactive**, sometimes also called **open** and **closed**.

Active (or open files) belong in your office because you will refer to each of them at least several times a year. You will either add to these files or retrieve something from them. Examples include your financial records for this year and active client or customer files.

Working files are active files that are used most often—daily or several times a week. They should be the most accessible to you at your desk or work station. They can go on a credenza, a side table next to your desk or inside the most accessible file drawer. The most active working files can be part of your daily paperwork system, described in Chapter 4.

Inactive, closed or storage files are used infrequently, if at all, and should usually be kept out of your office. If you opt to keep these files in your office, put them in the least accessible locations—in the rear of a file drawer, on a top shelf or in an area separate from your main work area. Whenever possible, remove files to someone else's office or to a designated storage area on or off site.

As you begin to sort through any existing files, be thinking of these two basic categories: active and inactive. Go through your existing files and weed out all the inactive ones and either discard or store them. By the way, this file sorting process should be done quickly by looking at file names only. *Do not sort through papers in files at this time.*

Now that you've sorted through your files, you're ready to tackle any piles of paper you may have accumulated. Go through these piles *quickly*, pulling active and/or important papers. Don't spend hours and hours going through piles, however, or you'll never create your filing system. These five steps will help you streamline the process:

1. Get yourself a countdown timer. (An egg timer is fine or you may prefer an LCD countdown timer available at an electronics store such as Radio Shack.)

2. Quickly sort through piles using the timer. This is not the time for a thorough analysis of each and every paper. As my friend and colleague Maxine Ordesky says, "Separate the treasures from the trash." For our purposes here, "treasures" are any papers that will go into active files or any important documents that you *must* save and file. Set aside for now "semi-precious" papers that may go into storage. As far as what "trash" to toss at this time, apply my two **Discard Dilemmas** rules: a) when in doubt, *save* legal, tax information and b) when in doubt, *toss* resource information. (For more information on purging, see Chapter 5.)

3. Clear the decks. Put your "semi-precious" papers temporarily in records storage boxes with lids (such as Fellowes Bankers Boxes). Label the outside of the box "Inactive Papers" and add any specific description of the contents, unless they're just miscellaneous. Try to keep the filing area as clear as possible—that way you'll be able to think and work more clearly.

4. For your "treasured" papers, think about category and file names and jot a name on each paper in pencil. If any of these papers could go in existing file folders, file them now. If they need folders of their own, quickly put these papers in folders and jot a name on the file folder tab in pencil. Or use removable Post-it brand File Folder Labels for temporary labels. If you have no extra file folders on hand or there are too few papers for their own folder, then paper clip related papers together and jot a future file name down on the top paper or on a Post-it label in each grouping.

5. In summary: spend most of your time on *important* papers.

STEP TWO: THE NAME GAME

Once you have the two most basic groupings of active and inactive you are well on your way.

Now you're ready to identify *what* are the major areas or divisions of your work and/or your work-related information. Start thinking in terms of the largest, *broadest* categories for your active files.

Naming categories and then files is the most critical element to setting up an organized system because it will aid in *retrieval* of information. Human beings are much better at storing information rather than retrieving it—whether it goes into our brains or our file cabinets. Just as our memory works best by connecting to related information, so, too, will a file naming system work when we make those connections.

One estate planning attorney who is a sole practitioner with a personal computer has designated four main areas of information: Clients, Business Operation, Estate Planning Information and Personal Computer Resources/References. A management consultant has these three categories: Business Administration (which includes client files), Resource Information (for seminars and articles) and

Marketing/Business Development. A computer systems engineer has files for Communications, Software Applications and Hardware.

Here is a listing of general categories. Check any that might apply to your work. Add your own at the end. Remember to select the *broadest subject areas* (not necessarily specific file names) that apply to you.

Accounts, Customers, Clients or Patients
Background/History
Business Administration
Communications (in company or organization)
Contacts
Legislation
Management
Marketing
Products
Projects
Reference
Research
Resources
Samples
Staff
Support
Volunteers

To start breaking down these broad categories into subcategories and specific file names and to help you visualize their relationship to one another, you may want to try two exercises.

First, it may be helpful to make a picture or chart of your major category and subcategory names. You can draw an **organization chart**, also known as a "tree directory" in computer circles. Suppose you have three major categories called People, Products, Promotion. Your chart might look like the one in Figure 7-1.

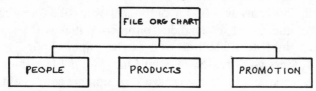

Figure 7-1. File Organization Chart

Writing in pencil, you would then draw lines and fill in the boxes with the next largest, broadest category names. Figure 7-2 shows how it might look now.

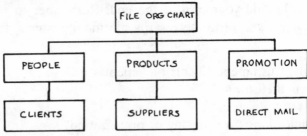

Figure 7-2. Expanded Organization Chart

A second exercise may be helpful if you're just setting up your system for the first time (or it feels like the first time). Use **colored index cards** with one color for each of your major file categories. Put each file name on the appropriately colored card and put it with the other cards. Spread out the cards and arrange them alphabetically or by subject. You can use the cards later to make up your filing system labels and also right now as you design your system on paper.

DESIGNING A SYSTEM ON PAPER

A filing system on paper serves as a blueprint that charts out all category, subcategory and file names and shows how they all fit together.

If you have a computer, a word processing program will be helpful at this step. Besides being able to easily move words around, many word processing programs such as WordPerfect let you sort (arrange) words alphabetically.

Start with one of your major category areas. Use the File Chart shown in Figure 7-3, which is a form to help you easily list your file categories and names and show how they are related. When completed, the chart will be an outline of your filing system.

Use the File Chart as a guide (photocopy it if you wish). Look at your existing file folders as well as the paper-clipped groupings and new folders you created in Step One. See if file names suggest themselves to you. Look for patterns, groupings, combinations that

Figure 7-3. FILE CHART

MAJOR CATEGORY (OR DRAWER NAME):

HEADING	SUBHEAD	SUBHEAD

go together. Be creative but don't create file names that you won't remember later. Don't try to think of *every* file name right now; this is not your final system—it's only the beginning.

Using a pencil (or your computer), write down a major work category from your filing system. Now complete what you think will be the main headings. Leave plenty of space between headings as shown in the Figure 7-4 example. Select names for headings that make sense to *you* (and anyone else using the system). Stick with unadorned nouns for headings, if possible.

Look at Figure 7-5 to see two levels of subheads that have been added.

As you chart out headings and subheads you'll start to see which names belong together and which ones need additional subheads. You're creating your own file design. Don't get too carried away with elaborate headings and subheads. Often one heading and one level of subheads are plenty. Keep your design simple!

Now complete the file chart for one *major category only.* Then, when you're ready, do a chart for each of your other major

Figure 7-4. MAIN HEADINGS

MAJOR CATEGORY (OR DRAWER NAME): Resource Info.

HEADING	SUBHEAD	SUBHEAD
Contacts		
Manuals		
Products		

categories in your filing system. Remember, nothing is etched in stone; your file chart is only a guide. If your file charts are on computer, you may now wish to alphabetize any headings or subheads that are actual names of clients, companies, vendors, etc., or you can wait to do it in Step Three.

Figure 7-5. ADDED SUBHEADS

MAJOR CATEGORY (OR DRAWER NAME): Resource Info.

HEADING	SUBHEAD	SUBHEAD
Contacts	Stores Consultants Service	Answers on Computers
Manuals		
Products	Hardware Software	

STEP THREE: PUTTING IT ALL TOGETHER

Where files will go in your system is a combination of *what* types of files they are, *who* uses them, *when* they are used and *how much room* you have. You should now know approximately how much room you have after having completed Steps One and Two because you've determined how often files will be used, purged your system of unnecessary inactive files and identified all your active file names.

One of the most important aspects of your filing system is location. Here are some guidelines to consider when deciding upon where to put your files:

- The more files are used, the closer they should be to your desk or main work area.
- Keep like files together. Group files by subject, type or frequency of use.
- Choose appropriate media to store your information—perhaps you want to use notebooks or boxes rather than file folders. Maybe you have large, bulky or odd-sized items that require special filing solutions.
- Security may be a factor; take any necessary precautions to secure confidential information.
- Select the appropriate cabinets or equipment.

With regard to cabinets, I suggest you start with what you have on hand. If you're starting from scratch, estimate the number of filing inches you have now and project, if you can, over the next several years. Look at your available floor space and your current or projected office layout to determine what will physically fit in your space (allowing space also for drawers to be pulled out).

Vertical cabinets will generally give you a few more filing inches per floor space than **lateral cabinets** but you need space into which you can extend the vertical cabinet drawers. Some people prefer the look of lateral cabinets along with being able to use the drawers either side-by-side or front-to-back. Whether you choose vertical or lateral, look for cabinets with high quality rolling or gliding mechanisms, built-in glides to accommodate hanging files and tilt-proof or non-tip safety features.

You can almost triple the number of files in the same floor space if you choose **open shelf file cabinets**. Besides holding a large number of files, these cabinets give you easy access to files. I would recommend you get flip-front doors so that you can close and lock cabinets. (Bindertek's Law Files described in Chapter 4, work great in an open shelf filing system.)

Now you're ready to physically set up your system—a time-consuming task that's nice to share with someone else, if you have such luxury.

Decide if you want to use **color coding** in your system. A simple color-coding scheme by drawer or by major category can be helpful, especially when you go to refile a folder. We use blue hanging folder tabs and file folder labels for our business and administrative files, for example, and yellow ones for our resource information files. You're less likely to misfile a folder in the wrong drawer with color coding. You can also see at a glance the type(s) of folders in a particular drawer. (For more elaborate color coding, see "Special Office Filing and Information Management Systems" near the end of the chapter Resource Guide.)

Make sure you have the right supplies on hand (see also the chapter Resource Guide). Here's a typical "shopping list" I suggest to clients, followed by comments describing why these items are important:

- One box of hanging file folders (generally 25 to a box); they come with or without tabs; get them without tabs if you're going to use color coding
- Hanging "box bottom" file folders, one-inch capacity, one box of 25, no tabs included
- Hanging box bottom file folders, two-inch capacity, one box of 25, no tabs
- Plastic tabs for any hanging folders that don't come with tabs; tabs come in two-inch or 3½-inch lengths—I prefer the 3½-inch size; if you're going to color code your files, get colored plastic tabs or buy colored plastic windows (to use with any clear plastic tabs you may already have on hand)
- Third-cut *interior* folders, (100 per box); interior folders are cut lower than ordinary manilla folders so that the folders sit inside the hanging folders without sticking up; they come in a variety of colors; third-cut folders work with the standard file folder labels you'll be getting; for more about "third-cut" and "fifth-cut" see page 178.
- Self-adhesive file folder labels; if you're color coding your files, buy the colored labels

To make full use of your headings and subheads, use **hanging file folders**, especially the one- and two-inch **box bottom folders**, which work great as your major headings. Inside each box bottom folder, place several **interior folders**, specially cut manila folders that can serve as subheads. If possible, avoid using only one interior folder per hanging folder; too many hanging folders will take up too much space and you also won't take advantage of the heading/subhead classification system, which adds to greater retrievability. (Check the Resource Guide for descriptions and pictures of these different folders.)

Pull out your File Chart (or your index cards, if you used them). Go through each heading and subhead and indicate which of the headings and subheads will take regular, one-inch or two-inch hanging folders. Put a "1" by any that you think will be up to one-inch thick and a "2" by any that will be up to two inches thick. Those with 1s will take one-inch box bottoms and those with 2s, two-inch box bottoms. Write "H" for any of the remaining headings or subheads that would take regular hanging folders; otherwise they would automatically get interior folders. (Most of your subheads will probably take interior folders.)

With your File Chart or index cards as a guide, type or print your hanging folder labels using all capital letters. (For more ideas about labeling, see Figure 7-6 as well as the Resource Guide section on "Labeling Systems.")

Insert the labels into the hanging folder plastic tabs (or if you're using Avery hanging file folder labels, attach them directly to the outside of the tab). Put in order the hanging folders you had marked on your File Chart. Insert the plastic tab on the inside front cover at the far left for headings. For hanging folders with subheads, you may wish to place the plastic tab a little over toward the right, as shown in Figure 7-7. Also note that you should stagger any tabs that would block other tabs. If your box bottom folders require that you insert cardboard reinforcement strips on the bottom, add them now. Set up your new hanging folders in a file drawer. Place existing file folders inside the new hanging folders.

Now type labels for new interior folders. Before you affix them on the interior folders, place the three types of folders in front of

Figure 7-6. CREATIVE LABELS FOR HANGING FOLDERS

Colleague Beverly Clower of Office Overhaul uses a Kroy **lettering machine** to create large, legible labels. She uses 18- and 24-point size wheels in the Helvetica bold, all caps, font style. The 24-point size is for headings and the 18-point size is for major subheads. Kroy produces black lettering on clear (or white, if you prefer), self-adhesive strips cut to size. Each strip is then affixed to the white label insert.

If you have access to a **personal computer** with some desktop publishing capabilities, you could prepare your label names with the font and style of your choice. Print them directly on an 8½-by-11-inch sheet of "crack 'n peel" (self-adhesive paper used for labels). Avery's Labelpro software program is helpful if you have a laser printer.

Or if your printer won't accommodate crack 'n peel, print onto your normal paper, which will become the master. Then use the master to photocopy onto the crack 'n peel (make sure your copier will accept crack 'n peel—most high speed copiers should).

You might also try photocopying onto "65 lb. card stock," a heavier grade of paper that you could use instead of the furnished white label inserts. (Check compatibility of card stock with your copier.)

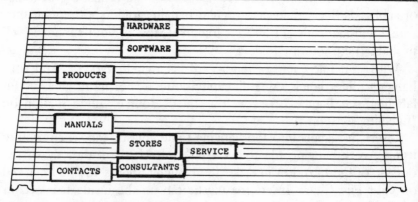

Figure 7-7. Position hanging folder tab headings on the left and subheads to the right. Notice that the tab subheads, "Consultants," "Service" and "Stores" are staggered for greater visibility.

you: left-cut, center-cut and then right-cut (assuming you are using third-cut folders). Pull folders in order of left-cut, center-cut, and right-cut. Don't always start at the left every time you come to a new hanging folder; keep going where you left off. That way you won't end up with a lot of extra right- or center-cut folders when you're done. In addition, you will maintain good visibility in your system by staggering folders in this way. Now affix the labels.

For even greater visibility and versatility, consider MAGNIFILES, which are V-bottom or box-bottom hanging files that come with special 11-inch long transparent (colored or clear), durable, magnified plastic indexes that run the full length of the file. Besides greater file name visibility, these file indexes give you plenty of room for file titles–five times the space of conventional tabs. Index strips come in white, full color or color tip styles. MAGNIFILES are available from Abbot Office Systems, 800/631-2233 or 201/938-6000, 5012 Asbury Ave., Farmingdale, NJ 07727. See Figure 7-8.

Figure 7-8. MAGNIFILES (right) from Abbot Office Systems provide greater file name visibility.

For interior folders that will be handled frequently and will risk dog-earing, cover the label area with either self-adhesive plastic that you'll have to cut to size or, better yet, use pre-cut label protectors listed in the Resource Guide and as shown in Figure 7-9.

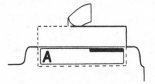

Figure 7-9. Smead Seal & View transparent label protector

ARRANGING FOLDERS

You can arrange your file folders in a number of ways: alphabetically, numerically or by frequency of use. You might even arrange your folders in a combination of ways. For example, you might use a basically alphabetical setup but group frequently used folders in a special, accessible location, for example, in the front of your file drawer.

Certain kinds of information work better alphabetically. For example, client or customer name files work best in an alphabetical system.

On the other hand, subject files do not always have to be in strict alphabetical order. It may be more convenient to place files you use more often in a more accessible location, irrespective of alphabetical sequence. Frequently used subhead files, too, may be placed out of alphabetical order within their hanging folders.

Numerical filing is a better method if you need to arrange files by date (e.g, purchase orders) or by number (legislative bills). Numerical filing is also useful when you want to keep files more confidential (it's more difficult to tell what's in a numerical file). A file index may be needed, however, in order to readily locate material. The index should be kept in a different location apart from the files to ensure their security.

Whichever method(s) you select, place all your interior folders into their respective hanging folders. Put any remaining, unfiled papers left over from Step One into appropriate folders.

FINE TUNING

You may have noticed that your existing files haven't yet undergone a complete and thorough purge. There's a good reason for this. It's better to set up a *functional* system first and fine tune later. Do your fine tuning now.

Go carefully through each of your existing, *active* folders in your system. Do you really need this information? How accessible does it have to be? Could a folder be consolidated with another folder? Use a timer and allot a specified period of time, from 15 minutes to an hour and a half on a given day. Or try giving yourself a goal, say, five folders in fifteen minutes.

You may find you need to add new labels (or delete others). Add them to your File Chart in a different color. Don't take time out to type or print the labels right now. Jot down subheads in pencil on new folders.

When you have completed the purge for one complete subject area, type or print any remaining labels and attach them to the new folders.

STEP FOUR: FINISHING TOUCHES

Now that you've physically set up your system, make sure you can tell the types of files you have in each drawer without having to open each one. You need a summary of your file drawer contents. Such a summary could be as simple as labeling each drawer with main headings.

Beverly Clower makes a "key to the files," which is a map or diagram of file cabinets and drawers. See Figure 7-10.

KEY TO THE FILES

Cabinet 1:   Cabinet 2:
Next to Shirley's Desk   Next to Ann's Desk

OFFICE ADMINISTRATION GENERAL INFO/SOURCES	BOARD OF TRUSTEES MINUTE BOOKS COMMITTEES
INSURANCE PERSONNEL	CONTRIBUTIONS FINAN. ASSISTANCE
AGREEMENTS/CONTRACTS	ESTATE FILES
REPORTS/STUDIES	BUILDING PROJECTS

Figure 7-10. A "key to the files," such as the one above, is distributed to everyone in an office using or accessing an office filing system.

A simple listing on paper, such as your File Chart or a "file index," could suffice. Better yet, keep a listing on your computer that can be easily updated. Be sure to print out at least one "hard copy" on paper. It's important to have computer listings for both active as well as inactive files in storage boxes. I call my inactive file computer listing "storage," which I have broken down by Box A, Box B, etc.

Train anyone who will be using your filing system. Have a special meeting or training session to introduce the system. Distribute a file index, file chart, key to the files or other listing. If appropriate, show how to borrow files by leaving an **out guide** in the place of the missing file. See Figure 7-11.

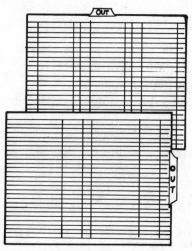

Figure 7-11. Two different styles of out guides, which function as library cards for your filing system

STEP FIVE: MAINTENANCE

The trick to a productive filing system is a regular maintenance program by you or someone you designate. Your program should be fairly routine and involve only a minimal amount of time—famous last words! But let's see how it can be done.

Start by making some decisions in advance about your file maintenance program. Answer the following questions:

1. Who's going to do your filing?
2. Will you file some or all papers "as you go"? Which ones?
3. If you plan to file papers in batches, how often and when specifically will filing occur?
4. How many times a year will you purge files and transfer formerly active files into storage? During which months or quarters?

Too many professionals and offices have *no* filing maintenance guidelines. Don't wait until an emergency, crammed file cabinets or a move forces you to take stock. It may be too late or you may be in the middle of a top priority project that prevents you from devoting what will now require a large chunk of time.

Set up your own maintenance system. Decide how many minutes a day or a week you (or someone you designate) will spend on it. Which day(s) will you choose and which time(s)? Be specific. Until your system becomes routine, write down your maintenance tasks on your daily to-do list or in your planner. Take a look at the Quick Chart (Figure 7-12) for other ideas.

Figure 7-12. QUICK CHART: FILE MAINTENANCE TIPS

Here are some tips to make filing easier:
- Immediately after you read a paper or an article you want to save and file, jot down the subject or file name in the top right corner. This will save you time, especially if the paper is not filed right away so that you or an assistant don't have to re-read the paper before it's filed.
- If the information in the article will probably be obsolete after a period of time, indicate a discard date in the top left corner. This will help you easily toss old papers without having to reread them.
- As an experiment, keep track of papers or files that you actually go back and refer to. Jot down an "R date"—the date you referred back to a paper or file for information. At the top of the paper or file write "R" followed by the date. If you start to see several R dates, maybe you need to move this information so that it's more accessible. On the other hand, seeing no R dates, you may decide to discard more papers and files. If nothing else, R dates may show you how often or little you actually refer to files.

The longer you wait to either set up or implement your maintenance system the easier it is for paper to accumulate once again. Get tough on paper!

The hardest part of maintaining your filing system is maintaining enough incentive. You have to believe this is a top priority or you'll keep putting it off. Filing systems often get put on the proverbial back burner until you've run out of filing space or a crisis occurs. Don't let that happen to you.

THREE FILING TIPS FOR EVERY MANAGER

If you're a manager or you work for one, you need to help implement three key ideas related to your co-workers and your office filing system.

First, **take your office filing system seriously.** Filing is not just clerical busy work. It's a vital database without which your office or department could not function.

Evaluate your current systems, including the central filing system as well as individual filing systems. Begin by using the five steps we've just discussed. See if there's any duplication of effort, e.g., is everyone keeping a copy of internal memos that could be filed in one central location?

When she was a manager, CEO Kathryn Johnson created the "vanguard system" in which each of her staff became a specialist in a particular subject area and maintained files in that subject. Because each staff member was "in the vanguard," filing became easier, reading loads were lighter and department morale was boosted. Johnson still uses the system today with her current staff.

Second, **reduce paper to be filed and stored through systematic records management/purging, paper reduction and recycling.**

One company has records management guidelines with retention schedules that culminate in an annual event called "Pack Rat Day." This event encourages all departments to review their records for storage or disposal according to the company guidelines. Each department tracks all "pack rat material" on a log sheet, which, along with records for storage or shredding, are turned in to the Records Systems department, the sponsor of the event. There is a Pack Rat Day celebration with refreshments, live music and departmental "Reformed Pack Rat Awards."

One aerospace company has had "Operation Roundfile" every year in which employees clean out their files and offices, tossing as much paper as possible. The company also has paper reduction programs throughout its divisions. One division came up with a motto, "Paper doesn't grow on trees—it *is* trees." This division set a goal of reducing photocopies by 20 percent, lines of computer print by 50 percent and mailing lists by 25 percent.

Smart managers are recognizing that it's more productive and profitable for their organizations as well as for the environment to cut down on paperwork and paper-generated communications in the first place. Look for ways to communicate using less paper, e.g., through electronic mail, voice mail or routing one memo (instead of making copies of the memo).

Set up a policy to reduce paper in your office or organization. Adopt a **purge prevention policy** such as the one developed by Derrick Crandall, president of the American Recreation Coalition in Washington, D.C. Crandall implemented what he calls an "ongoing, self-policing, purge prevention policy" to limit office file cabinets to two lateral five-drawer units. He explains, "It's so easy to become a walking encyclopedia of nonessential stuff. It's more time effective to go elsewhere for information, even if it takes 24 hours to get it than having to purge files in two to three years. It's a terrible waste of time to prune that stuff—better to deal with it the first time around."

Many organizations have instituted major recycling programs, not only to recycle paper that would ordinarily be thrown away, but also to buy paper products, such as file folders, made from recycled fibers. Esselte Pendaflex Corporation makes EarthWise, a complete line of filing supplies made from 100 percent recycled fiber, which should be available through your office supply dealer (or call Esselte at 516/741-3200). The Quill Corporation direct mail catalog now features recycled products, including file folders (800/789-1331 or 708/634-4800).

To get a better idea of just how important recycling is with regard to conserving our natural resources and saving energy, money and landfill space, see Figure 7-13.

Figure 7-13. DO YOU KNOW THESE PAPER FACTS?

- Each American uses about 580 pounds of paper a year, the highest per capita consumption in the world.
- To produce one ton of virgin paper, it takes 3,699 pounds of wood, 216 pounds of lime, 360 pounds of salt cake, 76 pounds of soda ash, 24,000 gallons of water and 28 million BTUs of energy. This process also produces 84 pounds of air pollutants, 36 pounds of water pollutants and 176 pounds of solid waste.
- Each ton of paper made from recycled fibers saves approximately 17 trees, 4,100 kilowatts of energy, 7,000 gallons of water, 60 pounds of air pollutants and three cubic yards of landfill space.

Reprinted courtesy of Esselte Pendaflex.

The third filing tip is **value the importance of training.** Smooth functioning office filing systems don't happen by accident. They take careful planning and training.

Whenever more than one person is using an office filing system, you need to set up at least one training session and preferably two. The first session introduces the logistics of the system—how files are named and arranged and how and when they are filed and by whom. This is a good time to introduce the out guide and distribute a file index.

If you are at all concerned that there will be some resistance to the system, suggest that everyone "try it out" for the next couple of weeks and then meet again at a second meeting to discuss and evaluate the system. The more people are a part of any system, the more likely they are to accept it. You must, however, be open to their ideas.

If more managers would follow these simple tips, more offices would have better organized filing systems.

RESOURCE GUIDE

BOOKS AND BOOKLETS

Alphabetic Filing Rules published by the Association of Records Managers and Administrators (ARMA), 4200 Somerset Dr., Ste. 215, Prairie Village, KS 66208. This booklet provides guidelines for establishing a consistent, documented filing system, whether or not you have a manual or automated system. 800/422-2762 or 913/341-3808. $12 for members; $17 for non-members.

Guide to Record Retention Requirements published by Commerce Clearing House, Inc., PO Box 4766, 4025 W. Peterson Ave., Chicago, IL 60646. This 448-page guide tells businesses and individuals that do business with government agencies exactly which records must be kept, by whom and how long. It contains the National Archives and Records Administration's Office of Federal Registers's digest of federal regulations covering recordkeeping by the public. 800/248-3248. $17.50.

How to File Guide published by Esselte Pendaflex Corp., Clinton Rd., Garden City, NY 11530. A great little full-color booklet with lots of photos, examples and information about filing tips, supplies and systems. 516/741-3200. Paper. Free.

The Organized Executive: by Stephanie Winston (New York: Little Brown, 1994). The chapter on filing is an excellent resource. Paperback $11.99.

Records Management Handbook with Retention Schedules. Fellowes Manufacturing Co., 1789 Norwood Ave., Itasca, IL 60143, 708/893-1600. While geared for large office filing systems, this booklet provides useful records retention/purging information applicable to smaller systems. Free.

Taming the Paper Tiger by Barbara Hemphill (Kiplinger Books). You'll find some excellent paper management tips here, especially for your personal paperwork. Paper. $11.95. **800/727-7015**

Technical Publications Catalog lists the 93 publications available from the Association of Records Managers and Administrators (ARMA), 4200 Somerset Dr., Ste. 215, Prairie Village, KS 66208, 800/422-2762 or 913/341-3808.

FILING SUPPLIES

FOLDERS

Hanging folders are the mainstay of frequently used filing systems. They provide easy access to paperwork, good visibility and an organized way to group files.

They are typically made of durable, two-tone green paper stock but many hanging folders also come in other colors and are made of other materials such as plastic or the more environmentally sound recycled fibers used in Esselte Pendaflex EarthWise folders, which contain the highest percentage of post-consumer content available today.

Special scoring in the middle of the flaps and on the bottom makes these folders more useful (see Figure 7-14). Scoring in the middle allows you to bend back the flaps so that the folder can be propped open in the file drawer until contents are reinserted. Scoring and folding at the bottom let you square off the v-shape bottom to increase the folder's storage capacity.

To really increase the capacity so that you can more easily use the hanging folder as a container for several file folders (or for catalogs), use a **box bottom folder**, which, depending on the manufacturer, comes in one- to four-inch capacity, letter or legal

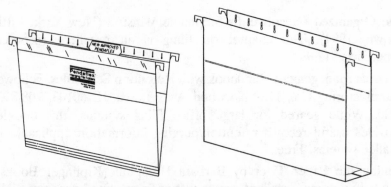

Figure 7-14. The classic Pendaflex hanging file folder (left) now is reinforced along the top and bottom with a durable poly-laminate and Smead Flex-I-Vision box bottom folder with reinforcement strip at bottom.

size, and two-inch for computer printout size. Pendaflex box bottoms come in the standard green or in other colors. Special cardboard strips reinforce the "bottom" edge of box bottoms. On the Smead box bottom the strip is pre-installed. See Figure 7-14.

The Pendaflex Hanging Box File is a blue box bottom with sides that prevent papers and other materials from slipping out.

The Pendaflex Hanging File Jacket lets you file small items with standard-size papers so that they won't slip out. Notice the easy-access, cut-away front. See Figure 7-15.

Pendaflex hanging folders also come in a variety of different sizes to handle a variety of items, such as invoices, x-rays, computer printouts.

Interior folders are special file folders cut shorter to fit inside hanging folders without obscuring hanging folder tabs. Esselte Pendaflex Corp. makes them in two lines: the Pendaflex line, available in manila and ten two-tone colors to match Pendaflex hanging folders, and the EarthWise line, in five earth-tone colors.

For manila folders that are handled frequently and are used more outside the filing cabinet than inside, consider getting those with **reinforced** tabs such as the one shown in Figure 7-16. Better yet, consider getting **plastic file folders** that are made in different colors

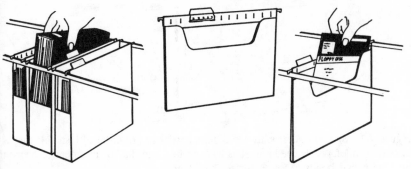

Figure 7-15. Pendaflex Hanging Box File and Pendaflex Hanging File Jacket

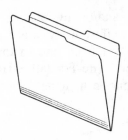

Figure 7-16. This Smead manila folder with the reinforced "two-ply" tab has extra durability. Notice the scoring along the bottom which permits 3/4-inch expansion.

and styles by JEFFCO, Inc. 800/248-3453 or 520/722-0800, 1671 S. Research Loop, Tucson, AZ 85710-6708

If you want papers you file to be more secure, less likely to fall out and easier to locate, consider two-hole punching papers in **fastener folders**. They're essential for important papers that have legal or tax implications where you just can't take a chance on losing any paper. Generally, you'll put papers in reverse chronological order–i.e., the most recent papers are on top. Hole-punched papers take up less space, which is particularly important in businesses where bulky files are the order of the day. See Figure 7-17 for examples of fastener folders. (You can buy folders with the fasteners already attached or buy the folders and fasteners separately, which is more economical.)

Wherever you'd use several fastener folders for one client or project, the **partition folder** is great. The partition folder, also called a **classification folder**, is made of heavy duty pressboard, and lets you group related papers together in different sections of the folder by either attaching two-hole-punched papers to fasteners on either

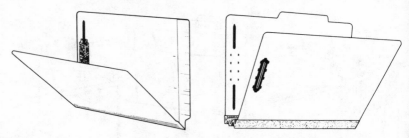

Figure 7-17. Smead folders with two different styles of pre-installed fastener: the "K" fastener (on left) is clinched into slots by eight tabs and the "B" fastener has a strong fiber base that bonds to inside surface of folder

side of each partition and/or by placing unpunched papers in between the partitions. Different styles are available from different manufacturers. You can get from one to three partitions, some of which are pocket dividers. The Pendaflex Hanging Partition Folder is really two folders in one—a hanging folder and a partition folder. (See Figure 7-18).

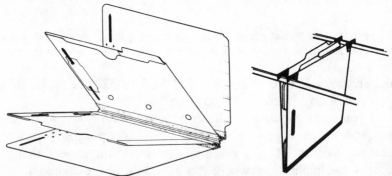

Figure 7-18. This Smead Classification Folder (left) comes with pocket style dividers and is also available in four bright colors; on the right is the Pendaflex Hanging Partition Folder.

If you frequently pull files out of the filing cabinet and take them to different locations, you may want to use folders that have sides to protect the contents. The **file jacket** comes in two styles—flat or expansion (see Figure 7-19). File jackets can be used within your filing system or as part of the daily paperwork system discussed in Chapter 4. Oxford file jackets come in manila and in ten colors.

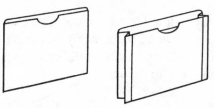

Figure 7-19. Oxford Manila File Jacket (left) and Expandable Manila File Jacket

Much sturdier than the file jacket, the **file pocket** in Figure 7-20 has accordion style sides called "gussets" that allow for more expansion and use. The file pocket can fit inside a file cabinet, on a shelf or in a metal collator (see Chapter 4). The file pocket will hold several related file folders together or other bulky materials, including catalogs and books.

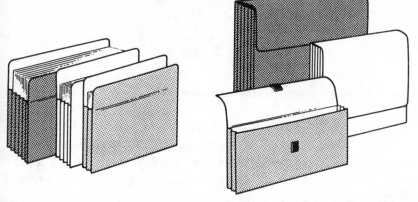

Figure 7-20. Wilson Jones ColorLife File Pockets (left) come in five bright colors. Wilson Jones ColorLife Expanding Wallets with single pocket and multiple pocket styles include easy-to-use "Gripper" Velcro closures.

The **expanding wallet** is similar to the file pocket except it usually has a flap with a clasp, tie or an elastic cord. It is useful for carrying, transporting or storing records. Wallets come with or without internal dividers or "pockets." I use wallets with pockets to store my annual tax and business records. See Figure 7-20.

The **expanding file** or **accordion file** is similar to the wallet in terms of construction, except it's larger and you can get it without a flap. The expanding file is a box-like, multi-pocket file with preprinted headings such as A-Z, 1-31 and Jan.-Dec. Figure 7-21 shows an example. If you're looking for an extremely durable material for an expanding file, check out CaseGuard in the All-state catalog (800/222-0510 or 201/272-0800). Speaking of materials, take a look at Figure 7-22 to see the different types and grades of materials available for file folders.

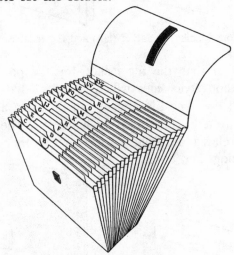

Figure 7-21. Wilson Jones ColorLife Expanding File

Check out the new Oxford Plus line of reinforced expanding products. These file pockets, expanding wallets and expanding files feature unique rip-proof gussets that are four times stronger plus special reinforcements at other critical wear points to prevent tearing, fraying and bursting.

LABELING SYSTEMS
Labeling systems are useful for file folders as well as a variety of other office applications.

Kroy's labeling and lettering systems range from portable models to more sophisticated keyboarded desktop systems (see Figure 7-23). You can make colored labels for not only filing systems but also for such items as maps, overhead transparencies and video disks. In business for 20 years, Kroy pioneered labeling systems.

If you're going to be doing many file folder labels, look into either Avery LabelPro Software for Windows or DOS if you own a PC and a laser, ink jet or dot matrix printer and MacLabelPro

Figure 7-22. FILE FOLDER MATERIALS (Reprinted with permission of Esselte Pendaflex Corp.)

---

3 COMMON TYPES OF PAPER FOR FOLDERS:
Manila is semi-bleached stock that resists tearing, folding and bursting. It's available in 9½- and 11-point thicknesses (more about point sizes momentarily).
Kraft is durable, smooth, unbleached stock that offers greater strength and rigidity. The tan color resists soiling. It comes in 11 and 17 points.
Pressboard is hard, dense, long-lasting stock that offers superior strength and comes in 25 points.

MORE ABOUT POINTS AND FOLDER PAPER STOCK
Bearing in mind that a point represents a thickness of .001 inch....
9½ points   Medium weight.
11 points   Heavy weight. Available in manila and kraft.
17 points   Extra heavy weight. Available in kraft.
25 points   Superior weight and thickness. Available in pressboard.

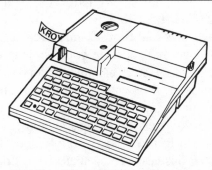

Figure 7-23. The Kroy DuraType 240 is about the size of a desktop calculator, has a typewriter-style keyboard and provides high-quality print on adhesive, laminated tape in 10 colors and a range of type styles and sizes. The retail price is $169. Contact Kroy at PO Box C-12279, Scottsdale, AZ 85267-2279 or call 800/733-5769 or 602/948-2222.

if you own a Macintosh. The software has 150 pre-set layouts for Avery products including index dividers, card products and file folder labels. One layout, for example, lets you print file folder labels that are 30-up on an 8½-by-11 sheet.

Sample labels for file folders as well as for a variety of other uses (such as disks and mailing addresses) are included with the software and the manual. LabelPro is a real time-saver and very reasonable at $99.95–assuming you don't have to go out and buy the computer and printer! For more information contact Avery at 20955 Pathfinder Road, Diamond Bar, CA 91765, 800/252-8379. There's also a technical support help line should you need it.

And here are two simple tips to prevent label sheets from curling in your laser printer, which can cause faded and broken type on labels. Before printing, first pull each sheet firmly over the edge of a table, label side up, to create a curl in the opposite direction. Second, use the printer's manual feed to print one sheet at a time.

OTHER SUPPLIES

You'll need **hanging file frames** to support your hanging folders unless your filing equipment already has them or glide rails built in. Traditionally such file frames come notched at half-inch intervals that you can break off to fit your drawer; but since most never break off easily, I recommend having your supplier cut them to size for you. Better yet, get the Pendaflex SpeedFrame that requires no tools, snaps together, easily adjusts to letter or legal size and fits all standard 24-to-27-inch file cabinets.

The Pendaflex Links and Stop Clamps are useful accessories that will help you manage and separate your hanging file folders. Made of stainless steel, links fasten hanging folders together to prevent between-folder misfiles. Stop clamps fasten to frame rails to separate groups of folders or to keep folders from sliding along the frame.

Smead makes **self-adhesive vinyl pockets** in seven different sizes which you can attach to the inside of file folders. These pockets can hold such items as business cards, microfiche, floppy disks, photos, diskettes or any loose item that needs to be kept with the file.

Hanging folder **tabs** generally come "fifth-cut" or "third-cut." The "cut" refers to the width of the tab in relation to the folder. A third-cut tab, for example, is cut one-third the width of the folder, allowing the tabs of three folders filed back to back to be seen at one time. Since the tab is used for labeling, select the size that will best do the job. Use third-cut if you need a larger label surface. Pendaflex Tabs come in clear (white) and seven colors. Or if you prefer, get the clear Pendaflex Snap-On Tabs. They're easier to attach but if you're using color coding, you'll need to also buy and insert Pendaflex Colored Plastic Windows. Use these windows, too, in any existing clear tabs that you'd like to color code. Pendaflex Printed Label Inserts let you save labeling time. Inserts are printed A-Z for name, subject and alphanumeric filing; states for geographic files; and months (Jan.-Dec.) and daily (numbered 1-31) for follow-up, sequential or chronological filing.

If you're looking for a quicker way to produce hanging file folder tab titles, Avery offers two different options. Avery Hanging File Folder Tabs allow you to write or type on the tab. You then simply peel the reinforced tab from the backing sheet, fold it in half and insert it into any fifth-cut hanging file folder.

You can also make the tab titles using your laser or ink jet printer or typewriter with Avery WorkSaver Inserts for Hanging File Folders. Just key or type your titles, print, separate and insert them into the plastic tabs. A unique side-by-side folding format lets you print or type both sides at the same time.

Label protectors will help you keep file folder labels and tabs clean and resistent to wear and tear. Smead Seal & View Label Protectors, available in three sizes, are made of a transparent laminate and should be available in your office supply catalog. (See Figure 7-9.)

You can also get label protectors by mail order from the Finance Business Forms catalog (800/621-2184) and the SYCOM catalog (800/356-8141 or in Wisconsin, 800/356-9152). If you only need a few and don't mind cutting them yourself, look under "Protectors" in an office supply catalog and then look for clear, self-adhesive, plastic sheets that you can cut to size.

SPECIAL OFFICE FILING
AND INFORMATION MANAGEMENT SYSTEMS

If you're planning to design a filing system for a large office or an office with special information management needs, the products in this section could be helpful. Other places to look for local assistance with your filing or information needs is in the yellow pages under "Filing Equipment, Systems and Supplies," "Microfilming Service, Equipment and Supplies," "Optical Scanning Equipment," "Bar Code Scanning Equipment" and "Data Processing Equipment."

MORE ON COLOR CODING

If your office is a medical office, for example, and has many, many files you'll probably select a more elaborate color-coded system that uses different combinations of colored, self-adhesive letters or numbers to quickly identify folders and prevent misfiles.

If you file patient files by their last name, for example, you woul probably take the *first two letters* of their last name and pu corresponding self-adhesive colored letters on the folders. Each lette of the alphabet in such a system has a color. For example all th "Ss" are orange, the "Is" green and the "Ms" purple. Take my las name, "Silver." My folder would have an "SI" on it where the "S" i orange and the "I" is green. When you file or retrieve the "Silver folder, it's much faster to go directly to "SI" than to check throug all the last names that begin with "S." If the next folder is "Smith you'd see an orange "S" and a purple "M." Color coding file folder lets you find and file them more quickly.

There are other codes you can attach as well to folders, such a yearly codes or colors that signify a type of patient.

The following companies make a whole line of special color coded tabs: ANCOM Business Systems (Ohio, 800/847-9010); Jete Systems (Ohio, 800/321-8261); Smead (Minnesota, 612/437-4111 TAB Products Co. (800/672-3109 ext. 3304 or in California, 800/742 0099 ext. 3304); and Wright Line (Massachusetts, 800/225-7348 Ask if there are local representatives to help you design your system

SPECIAL FILING EQUIPMENT

High-density mobile filing systems equipment, consisting of heav lateral filing units that usually run on mechanical floor tracks an all but eliminate wasted aisle space, are useful for large, centralize filing systems. Four manufacturers of these systems are: Karde Systems, Inc. (800/848-9761 or 614/374-9300 in Ohio); Lundia (i Illinois, 217/243-8585); The Spacesaver Group (800/492-3434 o 414/563-5546, Wisconsin); and White Office Systems (201/272-8888 New Jersey). Jeter, TAB and Wright Line also offer special filin equipment that can handle both small and large systems.

Wright Line is best known for its computer media filin accessories and equipment that store and organize items such a printouts, computer tape reels and diskettes.

AUTOMATED FILING SOLUTIONS

Because information continues to proliferate both in paper form, a this chapter has discussed, and in computerized files (as you'll see i upcoming chapters), your office may need a **document management system** that may include software and hardware components.

The term "document management" can refer to different types of systems and software, all of which involve use of a scanner. One type is focused more on scanning and storing *images* of documents, which you then index with keywords of your choice. With a stored image of a document you do not have editable text that you can word process.

Another type of system goes a few steps further. It takes the image and runs it through an optical character recognition (OCR) program that turns the image into a text file (that you can edit) and also indexes every word in the file. Such a system has search capabilities that let you search for any such file based on any words or phrases they contain (not just a few keywords). If desired, you can also turn the electronic file back into the original image and print it out on paper. In this way you don't have to store the original paper because it's stored in the computer either as a graphic image or as text (which may contain graphics).

For these types of systems you'll want to look for **document management software**, sometimes also called **document image management software**. Some of these programs also have workflow capabilities, such as document image routing, tracking all file creation and editing and document sharing. (See also groupware in Chapter 11.) The following software products have received good recent reviews: File Magic Plus for Workgroups by Westbrook Technologies (Connecticut), 800/949-3453 or 203/399-7111; MarcoPolo by Mainstay (805/484-9400); PaperMaster by DocuMagix Inc. (California), 800/362-8624 or 408/434-1138; PageKeeper by Caere Corp. (California), 800/535-7226; ImageFast by ImageFast Software Systems (Virginia), 800/899-6665 or 703/893-1934; PC DOCS by PC DOCS, Inc. (Florida), 800/933-3627 or 904/942-3627; Saros Document Manager (Washington), 206/646-1066; and SoftSolutions by Novell (Utah), 801/226-6000.

When document management is more involved with keeping track of records and the use of bar coding, it moves into the area of **tracking software** or **records management software**. One major HMO uses customized records management software called Image-Trax from Document Control Systems, Inc. to track x-rays as they move from department to department and from desk to desk. We're talking about x-rays at more than ten medical centers and 50 medical offices with a patient base of several million. (Call 800/428-DOCS or 714/961-0193 to contact Document Control Systems in California.)

If you're serious about document management, you're going to need more than one of the low-priced, slow scanners discussed in Chapter 4. They're fine for occasional use or for desktop publishing needs but they aren't designed for heavy duty document management needs. Another caveat is make sure you have enough disk storage space for document management. Here's a tip: you can save space by deleting images after they've gone through OCR, provided you only need the text and not the image. Select a system that will grow with you because you won't want to change systems and waste time converting your system's files to another system.

Find out just how much time is involved with the various steps in the document management process—initial scanning, running an image through OCR, searches and printing. Determine whether the investment in time and money warrants your use of document management, to what degree and by whom. Do your homework—selecting a document management system takes some research and planning. And ask about references, current reviews or awards.

For a more sophisticated document/file database, use a **CAR** or **Computer Assisted Retrieval** system that lets you locate documents through the use of computer-stored indexes. A CAR can be particularly helpful if you're using microfilmed documents in your office—such as microfilm or microfiche. The Canon CAR System, for example, lets you index your documents as you transfer them to microfilm for quick retrieval.

Micrographics offers options to copy paper documents onto more compact media where the information takes up less physical space and also is easily retrievable. A 4-by-6-inch piece of microfiche holds several hundred documents and a roll of microfilm holds 4,000 to 5,000 documents. **Optical disk technology** can store 50,000 pages on one side of a disk.

The Canofile 510 made by Canon is a desktop electronic filing system that is comprised of a main unit with a mass storage built-in magneto optical disk drive, a large, LCD display keyboard and optional laser beam printer. A solution to large-volume filing, the system scans, stores, retrieves and prints out image information that would otherwise be stored in a filing cabinet.

8

POWERFUL
COMPUTING:
ORGANIZING YOUR
PERSONAL
COMPUTER FILES

Quick Scan: Gain full value from your PC or Mac by discovering different ways computer files can be organized to help you work more easily and find files and information more quickly. Read this chapter, too, to learn how and when to back up your files. And if you want to protect yourself against computer disaster, because yes, it can happen to you, you'll learn important computer housekeeping, file maintenance and recovery strategies. You'll learn different tips as well as which computer products can help. This chapter is for anyone who is using or plans to use any of the following personal computer operating systems or environments: DOS, Windows, Windows 95, Macintosh or OS/2.

One day, when the glow of using a computer wears off, you may discover you're having trouble getting around your computer hard drive. Files are hard to find. Naming and organizing your files is confusing. Somehow you thought the computer would make everything easier, certainly easier than dealing with all the paperwork on your desk and in your cabinets.

The bad news is that just like paper files, computer files need to be accessible, up-to-date, properly categorized and regularly maintained. You and your computer can slow down dramatically whenever computer file organization and maintenance is poor (or nonexistent).

But the good news is both you and your computer will function better when your personal computer files are in good working order. And it's not hard to learn how to organize your files.

BASIC COMPUTER FILE ORGANIZATION STRATEGIES

No matter what operating system or environment you're using, there are several basic strategies to keep in mind.

HAIL THE HIERARCHY

The most important one is to use a **hierarchy** when you organize your files. A hierarchy lets you create categories and subcategories into which you can put your application (program) files you buy and data (document) files you create. Using a hierarchical filing system helps you better manage the large numbers of files and folders that come with the increased hard disk storage that's now available.

Such a system lets you group files logically by categories called **directories** in DOS and **folders** in the Windows, Mac and OS/2 systems. You can also create subcategories called respectively **subdirectories** or **folders "nested" inside folders.**

Said another way, a personal computer hierarchical system gives you a way to graphically (visually) organize and see different levels and sublevels of the work you do. The big danger is not to get carried away and create too many levels, subdirectories or folders nested in folders. **Limit your number of levels, subdirectories or nested folders.** Beware of creating too complex a system that takes too much time to use. In general, you don't want to go more than three levels deep.

You also want to make sure you don't accumulate too many documents or applications in any one folder or directory. When that happens, files can become difficult to find. That's when you may need to subdivide large folders or directories into smaller ones. But if you have too many small ones, your system can become too complex. It's all a matter of balance and good design.

To keep your system as simple and as accessible as possible, follow two guidelines. First, limit the number of documents or applications you keep in each folder or directory, especially a folder or directory that you use frequently. One rule of thumb is to create a new folder or directory every time you accumulate more than 20 files.

The fewer files you have in a folder or directory, the faster it is to find files—especially the files you use most often. And that's the secret: **keep files you use most often, most accessible.** It slows you down if a folder is crowded with files you rarely use. Yes, you can use the search utilities but that's just adding another step. Also get in the habit of moving old or rarely used files to archival or storage folders and disks.

SEPARATING PROGRAM AND DATA FILES

Keep programs and data separate. Think of applications as tools and your data or documents as the products you create with the tools. It's far easier and faster for your backup routine to back up only data files that change, not applications that don't. There are a number of ways to separate and organize program and data files.

You could put each program file in its own separate folder or subdirectory (e.g., one for your word processing program and another for your spreadsheet program). You may also want to group these program subdirectories on their own "logical" drive as well because it simplifies backup routines. A logical drive is an area of your hard disk that you've "partitioned off" or defined as "C," "E" or any other letter of the alphabet (except usually "A" or "B," which are generally reserved for your floppy drives, and "D," which is used by CD-ROMs). A "physical" drive means you actually have a separate physical drive. A floppy drive is a physical drive and two hard disks are two physical drives. But C and D drives that are both located on one physical hard disk are logical drives.

Group your data files in other separate folders or subdirectories (e.g., one for each client or for the type of work) on another logical drive. If you are a professional writer, for example, keep your word processing program in its own folder or subdirectory on one logical drive and keep your articles in at least one other subdirectory on another drive. As a professional writer as well as a consultant and speaker, I have subdirectories called "BOOK," "WRITE," "CONSULT" and "SPEAK," all under my WordPerfect data subdirectory called "WP." See Figure 8-1.

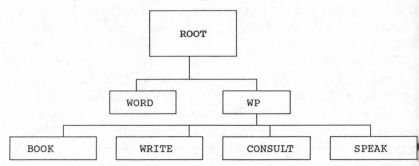

Figure 8-1. On my computer I keep my WordPerfect program in its own separate subdirectory, "WORD." I keep data files in their own subdirectory called "WP," which then in turn has grouped data files into their own task specific subdirectories. WORD and WP are on the same level; the four subdirectories shown here are also all on the same level, but one level down.

If you have too many folders or subdirectories, however, you may want to put data and program files in nested folders or on the same subdirectory "branch" as shown in Figure 8-2.

If you share your computer with other people who are using the same programs, it also makes sense to arrange programs followed by data. For an example of what your organization might look like, see Figure 8-3.

IT'S ALL IN A NAME

Consistency and brevity are more important than creativity when it comes to personal computer file, folder or subdirectory names.

As an organizer, I have liked the original DOS eight-character (plus three-character extension) limit on file names because it has forced people to come up with a file naming system. A good system uses consistent codes or abbreviations. I have used initials followed

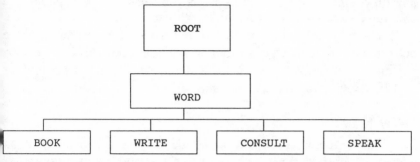

Figure 8-2. In this arrangement, the application program resides in the subdirectory, "WORD." The data file subdirectories are under the WORD subdirectory.

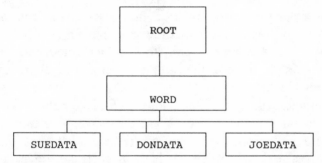

Figure 8-3. Subdirectory organization with shared computer word processing program

by a dash and an abbreviation for many of my file names. For example, I use the "C-" prefix before correspondence and the "H-" prefix before seminar handout materials. For example, the file C-ARCO contains all correspondence to ARCO and the file H-ARCO contains a seminar handout custom developed for ARCO.

Even if you're able to use long file names, I recommend that you begin each file name with a short, codified, abbreviated version that's followed by a clear descriptive phrase. It will save you time in the long run to use this kind of naming system.

You may also want to use a naming system that's parallel to your paper filing system. Mine are loosely parallel to one another. I prefer more subject-oriented naming schemes; I have a speaking subdirectory, for example, as well as a file drawer devoted to that subject. Some people I know have alphabetical client files on paper and on computer. See if there's a way you can make your paper and computer systems more consistent with each other.

It may be helpful, too, to put the file name of a document at the bottom in very fine type so that it will print out on a hard copy version. Later on, you'll know immediately where on your computer that document was created and stored.

PATH NAMES

Just like a person, each individual file has both a name and an address. A **path name** is both the name and address of a computer file.

A name alone is not enough. Both a person and a file need more than a name to make them truly accessible. An *address* is necessary to locate a person as well as distinguish one person from another. John Jones on Maple Street isn't the same person as John Jones on Elm Street. An address is a *path* to someone's door, starting with the state, going to the city, then to the street and number and finally to the individual.

A computer file needs an "address," too. A **path name** is the address for a computer file. Your computer locates a file by following a path from the "drive" you're in (usually "A" or "B" for floppy drives and "C" or "D" for hard disk drives), on next to the first level and through any sublevels (subdirectories or folders) and finally to the actual file name. You can click your way through the path with a mouse or just type it, if you prefer.

Just as the U.S. Postal Service likes to use certain abbreviations, so does your computer. When typing out a path name, start with the letter name of the drive you're in followed by a colon. Use a backslash symbol \ every time you want to indicate the different parts of your path name. The first backslash indicates the first level or **root directory**. Each additional backslash tells the computer to go down to a new subdirectory level. The last name is the file name itself.

Here's an example. Go back to the chart in Figure 8-1. C:\WP\BOOK\CHAPT1 is the full path name for my Chapter 1 file. C is the drive name for my hard disk, the first \ stands for the root directory, **WP** is the first-level subdirectory, **BOOK** is the second level subdirectory and **CHAPT1** is the actual file name.

And just as there can be a John Jones who lives on Maple as well as one who lives on Elm, so, too, you can have the same file name (or the same file) in two different subdirectories. If I wanted, I could have a copy of CHAPT1 in my WRITE subdirectory, too. The path name lets you locate the correct file. Your computer will not, however, let you create the same file name if it already exists in the same subdirectory you're in.

You also can't have two first-level subdirectories with the same name, for example, C:\BOOK and C:\BOOK. But with two different first level subdirectories, you could have two second level subdirectories, as well as files, with the same names. For example, the following would be acceptable:

C:\BOOK\LETTERS\MAY96 and C:\WRITE\LETTERS\MAY96

To keep your path names simple, however, keep down the number of subdirectory levels. Depending on your operating system or environment, you may need or prefer to type out the complete path name to "call up" (retrieve) a file, you'll want to do as little typing as possible. You'll also want to keep your mouse clicking down to a minimum.

Build some consistency, rather than creativity, into your subdirectory and file names. Try to make directories or folders parallel by using the same names and sequence of names. For example, if you have consulting clients, each client might get their own subdirectory or folder with the following names: PROPOSAL (for proposals), CORR (for correspondence) and REPORTS. Use consistency in naming files, too. Use the same abbreviations, such as adding the ".ltr" extension to all files that are letters.

DOS IS NOT DEAD YET

I believe DOS will be with us in one form or another. Many closet DOS users will continue to operate their DOS programs on older machines or on newer machines under Windows, Windows 95 and OS/2.

If nothing else, some important DOS terminology related to organizing computer files will continue to be used. The "path names" concept is from the DOS world.

The "directory tree" is another. It's called a directory tree because such a diagram resembles a tree—an upside-down tree to be exact.

The illustrations in this chapter start with the "root directory," which is indeed upside down. This is the first and main directory; all other directories "branch off" from the root.

Technically, there is only one directory, the root directory. All the other directories are really **subdirectories.** All of your subdirectories grow and expand as you add files to them.

A directory or subdirectory (the terms are often used interchangeably) or a folder is a specific area on your disk that stores files, usually related files. Compare it to a drawer or a section of a drawer in your filing cabinet that holds a particular grouping of files. All subdirectories are related to one another, too, because in the tree-structured directory system, they all descend ultimately from the root directory. Some subdirectories are on the same level, some have their own subdirectories and those subdirectories can have their own subdirectories, ad infinitum.

If the terms "root directory" and "subdirectory" are still confusing, compare them to their counterparts in a paper filing system. Think of the root directory as your entire filing cabinet with no dividers for major sections or categories. All contents will be thrown together unless you include groupings such as dividers or drawers called subdirectories in the computer world.

The directory tree system is similar to the one you set up for your paper files in Chapter 7. In a well-organized paper filing system you group related files together under headings and subheads. You do much the same thing with your computer files, whether they're on floppies or your hard disk, when you group them in subdirectories.

You can draw a picture of your tree directories, just as you drew a chart for your paper files in Chapter 7. Think of this drawing as a "family tree" for your computer that shows how everything is related. The Directory Tree Chart in Figure 8-4, adapted from my computer's tree-structured directories, will help you see the relationships between five of my major subdirectories.

The graphic directory tree representation in most operating systems and programs typically shows a tree with the root directory (and folder icon) of the drive at the top and different level folders (subdirectories) branching out as you travel down the tree. You may

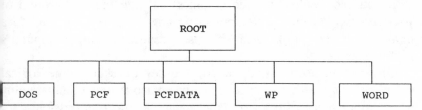

Figure 8-4. Directory Tree Chart adapted from my computer

also see the term "hierarchical folders" replacing the term "directory tree."

THE GRAPHIC ADVANTAGE

While there will always be DOS diehards among us and while this operating system, first created in the early 80s, has done much to bring us all into the era of personal computing, it's time to move on to newer **graphic user interface** (GUI) ways of working. The idea is to make computing more "intuitive," easier to work directly on a program and system that's graphic, friendly and understandable without having to first pour through technical manuals.

Let's give credit here to Xerox who invented many of the graphic elements in today's GUIs, including **icons**, the little pictures that represent programs and files. And of course, Apple has been the real GUI pioneer with its Macintosh.

But before we get caught up in the graphic euphoria, it may be well to see if we're using icons and graphics to their best graphic advantage.

ORGANIZING YOUR DESKTOP

Unfortunately, clutter isn't limited to your desk; it can also accumulate on your computer **desktop**, the main staging area on your computer screen where you lay out your computer work using windows and icons. I'd like to share some thoughts on how to better arrange it so it's more functional for you.

First, check out the overall appearance. Is it too cluttered or busy for your taste? Is it interesting enough? Do you have too many icons? Are they grouped logically together?

If you use "wallpaper," the graphics that line the background of your screen, you may prefer not using any because it can add to a more cluttered look and it also reduces your computer's performance.

Group your icons in alphabetical order or using some logical grouping. Play with the spacing between icons and eliminate any unnecessary space. Keep icon label names as short as possible.

Group everyday programs and/or files together or use special features that bring them up automatically. For Windows, the way applications are placed in the StartUp program group will determine the order in which they load. *PC WORLD* editor Karl Koessel described how he would arrange for his calendar Schedule+ to load last so that his calendar would be on screen when Windows was done loading; cc:mail loaded next-to-last, so that once he checked his appointments and closed his calendar, he could then see his e-mail in-box. For Windows 95, put Shortcut icons on the desktop for programs or files you use constantly. Macintosh System 7 lets you drag a file icon "alias" onto the desktop, which can take you directly to the file.

See the Resource Guide for utility programs that can help you further organize and customize your desktop and file management.

BACK IT UP!

You can't talk about computer organization without talking about backups. For our discussion here, a backup is a duplicate copy of computer data (programs and files) that is stored on another medium besides the primary one you're using. There are two parts to making backups: establishing a **backup routine** and selecting a **backup device**. The backup device or medium you select isn't half as important as whether you actually use it.

WHY BOTHER?

Why do you have to bother backing up your work when you have a hard disk—isn't it solid as a rock? Computer expert Paul Somerson responds by saying, "Hard disks used to be expensive and unreliable. That's all changed. Today they're inexpensive and unreliable."

You never backed up your filing cabinet; why should you back up your computer files? First, the chances of wiping out your computer data are much greater than losing your hard data. Second, it's so easy today to back up. (And why tempt fate anyway?)

Backups are *insurance* for valuable, current data that would either require more than an hour to re-enter or would be next to impossible to re-create exactly as inputted the first time. Whenever I'm producing original, creative material, I not only save it on my hard disk, I save it on a special backup floppy as well. That floppy goes home with me each night.

By the way, since I'm saving this material frequently and using two different media to do so—a procedure that requires many steps—I use a **macro** to automate the process. A macro is a quick, shorthand method of doing many computer steps with just a few keystrokes. With WordPerfect, my word processing program, I'm able to create a "save" macro that lets me press just two keys (the Alt key and the letter "S") to quickly perform an operation that would normally require pressing at least 35 different keys!

Besides making additional copies of important information, backups can serve as **archival storage** for less important information that is not being used and is taking up too much space on your hard disk. Once you've backed up this archival information, then you can delete it from your hard disk or a working floppy. Make two archival backup copies if the information is very important and keep the copies in separate locations—for example, at home and at the office.

Good backups will let you conduct business as usual even if your hard disk crashes or your entire computer is in for repair. Don't wait until a crash to get serious about backing up. As writer Wes Nihei observed in *PC World*, "Backing up files is a lot like dental hygiene: by the time you get serious about flossing and brushing, it's usually too late."

HOW OFTEN, HOW MUCH?

Your backup routine depends on how often files change, the number of files you modify a day, the kind of information or applications you use and how easy your backup device is to use. It may also depend upon whether you keep any hard copy that would enable you to re-create computer files. Based on these criteria, check any of the following that you think would apply to your situation:

- Each day back up any data, subdirectories, folders or applications you have modified that day.
- Have two rotating sets of complete backups where the most current set is off site (at home, for example, if your office is not in your home). As soon as you make your most up-to-date backup, take it off site and bring back the older backup set.
- Do a full backup every day.
- Do a full backup every week.
- Do a full backup every month.
- Do a full backup every four to six months.
- Have three complete sets of programs and data: one you're working with on your primary computer and two current backups—one on site and an additional backup kept off site.
- Assuming your active program files are on one "logical drive" of your hard disk (as discussed earlier in this chapter), do a full backup at least once a year and store it off site. It's faster to back up program files that are in one location and you're also backing up all that time-consuming customization you've done for each program.
- Check for reliability *before* you need it by trying to restore backups periodically.
- If you're a corporate user and you're on a network, ask your network manager if personal data will be backed up or if you'll need to do your own private backup; also find out if there are any corporate policies regarding transporting any backup data to and from home.

Data processing departments generally keep daily files Monday through Thursday, make a weekly backup on Friday and do a monthly backup every fourth week. Copies of weekly and monthly backups are kept off site as well as on site. My recommendation is **always have at least one complete, current backup off site.**

TYPES OF BACKUP
Your backup routine should include **selective** as well as **complete** or **full** backups. Complete or "full" backups are used to copy the

entire contents of your hard disk and would be useful if you had a system failure and you had to restore the data on your hard disk.

Backup devices do complete backups in one of two ways: **image** or **file-by-file**. Image backups make a mirror-image copy of your hard disk, are very fast and can back up copy-protected programs. The disadvantage is that you might not be able to restore an image backup to a different hard disk other than the original. (If, for example, your hard disk crashes and can't be repaired, you may possibly be unable to transfer your image backup to a new hard disk.)

File-by-file backups, while slower, don't have that problem. Not only are they more reliable, they also make it easier to find backed-up files. You can also restore individual files without having to restore the entire hard disk. New technology is aiming for faster, file-by-file backups. File-by-file backups can be used for selective as well as complete backups.

Selective or partial backups are used to copy individual files, programs or data. An **incremental** backup is a type of selective backup that copies only files that have changed since your last backup. If your backup device can do incremental backups, you will save time–keep this feature in mind when you select a backup device. A **differential** backup is like an incremental backup except it will overwrite a previous version on your backup medium.

You would make incremental backups if you needed to save each version of a file because you might need to refer to one of these versions or you need an audit trail. If you don't need to see old versions, but only the current, most up-to-date version, use differential backups. I use differential backups because I generally work with the same files over and over and only need to see the latest versions. Differential backups save me time and space.

ADDITIONAL TIPS FOR A BETTER BACKUP ROUTINE

Following these simple backup tips can save you many headaches down the long haul. Check off all the ones you already do; circle those you will incorporate into your routine after reading this section:

• Always back up new software.

- Always back up newly *installed* software, particularly if you made any special installation procedures. (Also keep a hard copy record of the answers you gave to installation questions in case you need to reinstall the program.)
- Make sure you have a backup of your backup software so that you would be able to restore files after a crash.
- Make an emergency floppy to get you up and running again on another computer (Norton Utilities has a Rescue Disk feature that would help you create such an emergency floppy).
- Make two backups of files that change every day. Make the backups as you go, saving each file twice, once on your hard disk and once again on a floppy. Or make your backups at the end of the day from a daily, written list of modified files.
- Carefully date and label all backup media; use color coding if necessary. If you make daily backups on floppies, use a different color label or diskette for each day of the week, for example, red for Monday's disk, orange for Tuesday's, etc.
- When you install a backup device, test it out with some junk files before betting your life on it.
- Use dated hard copy as important backup.
- Have at least two current sets of all important work—one should be off site.
- Try to select a backup program that can also be run from a floppy, such as Fastback Plus, and keep it with one set of backup disks. That way you won't have to reinstall the program before restoring files.
- Whenever possible, exclude unnecessary files such as README, BAK or TMP files and do not back up system files.

BACKUP AND STORAGE DEVICES

All backup devices are one of two types—**disk** or **tape**. Disk devices are generally faster in terms of backup speed than tape devices. It's also easier and faster to locate backed-up data on a disk. But disks usually cost more and sometimes hold less data than tapes. Tape backup devices use a magnetic tape similar to the kind used in audio recording. Most backup tapes are housed in cartridges.

SELECTION CRITERIA

Before you select a backup device, consider the following criteria:

- ease of use (if it's not easy to learn and use, you won't bother with it)
- speed (how much of your time will it take; how fast is it in different modes of operation—with or without compression, with or without verification?)
- capacity (be sure to match the capacity of your hard disk with the size of your backup tape or other device; how much do you need now and in the foreseeable future?)
- portability (are you going to be removing and transporting the device frequently and if so, how far?)
- operator monitored (or does it "run in the background" by itself?)
- compatibility (with other office computers and/or your network)
- security
- performance
- reliability/verification (what kind of "error checking" does it have?)
- additional hardware required (the cost factor aside, what kind of space do you have for more hardware?)
- file-by-file or image (you may need both, but at the very least have file-by-file)
- cost (what are your budget restrictions?)

Go back and check off all the criteria you *must* have and compare them to your budget and your information needs to determine the price you're willing to pay. Also see if you like the software that comes "bundled" with your backup or storage hardware; if not, there are several excellent software packages. Some of the best are PC Tools for Windows, Fastback and Norton Backup (all by Symantec—800/441-7234 or 503/334-6054), Dantz's Retrospect (800/225-4880 or 510/253-3000) and for network backup, Palindrome's Backup Director (708/505-3300) and Cheyenne Software's ARCserve for NetWare (800/243-9462 or 516/484-5110).

Be aware that even as you read this page, new and updated backup and storage technologies are emerging. But don't forget your trusty box of diskettes, which may be all you need if you have small scale data file backup.

THE REWARDS OF
COMPUTER HOUSEKEEPING

Regular computer housekeeping, especially computer file maintenance, is essential to the health and performance of your computer. Not only will it be easier to find files, but you can improve the productivity and speed of your computer–particularly your hard disk.

What's more, if you never do maintenance and your hard disk fills up with files, you're just asking for a computer crash.

BIGGER IS BETTER, RIGHT?

If you've ever been tempted to substitute a bigger hard disk for computer housekeeping chores, think again. You may have also been tempted at one time or another to buy another file cabinet for all your papers and files. Or perhaps you've bought a bigger house to accommodate all the "stuff" you've accumulated (you may remember the famous George Carlin routine).

If you're behind in your housekeeping, a bigger hard disk is just going to make matters worse. Just as with file cabinets, you can only tell how much space you need *after* you have purged your files. Once you've cleaned out your hard disk, see if you have 75 percent or more filled with current programs and files. If so, a larger or additional hard disk may be very appropriate.

By the way, when was the last time you cleaned out your hard disk? Have you *ever* cleaned it out? Since for most of us, out of sight means out of mind, it's particularly easy for computer files to accumulate. With the availability of larger and larger hard disks, this will continue to be a problem.

There are three reasons to take the time and trouble to clean out your hard disk:

1. to speed up your computer
2. to speed *you* up (locating files becomes difficult when your directories or folders are full of files that you aren't using)
3. to make more room on your hard disk.

A SQUEAKY CLEAN HARD DISK

The best computer file maintenance is done as you go—deleting duplicates and out-of-date files, storing inactive files on backup media and having a backup routine that you use regularly. But if you're like most people, you'll probably need to sit down once every six months to a year and do a thorough spring cleaning. Where do you begin and how do you proceed? Here are some useful steps:

- Before you do any "house cleaning," print a hard copy of your root directory so you can see at a glance all the names of your subdirectories or your first level folders.
- Go through each main subdirectory or folder and see if you recognize any files you can delete. (Now's the time to remove those extra backups that your word processor may automatically make.)
- Look more closely. Are there any files you're no longer using but you'd like to keep in archival storage? If so, back these up on floppies, tape or whatever backup medium you're using. Or perhaps you have a backup device or program that can "tag" these specific files and back them up collectively. For files that are very important, make *two* archival copies that are kept in different locations.
- Consolidate any files you can—i.e., group separate, related files together in one new file or a folder. For example, instead of having every letter in a separate file, group all 1996 letters together or all letters to a client together. In the DOS and Windows environment, a file could take up more bytes of memory even though it looks in your directory listing as if the file only has X number of bytes. (Each file under DOS, Windows, OS/2 or Macintosh is allocated a certain minimum number of bytes, whether or not those bytes are actually used.)
- Examine your largest files and decide how often you use them. Perhaps they can be stored elsewhere.
- Look for any subdirectories or folders that only contain a few files. See if you can move these files elsewhere and delete these subdirectories or folders, which even by themselves take up space.
- Print a hard copy of your latest **catalog** (a listing of all your directory or folder files) and keep them near your labeled

backup media. If you back up your hard disk with a program that contains a catalog feature, print out the catalog when you complete your backup (I always do this after each full backup).

Just as with manual systems, try to keep most accessible only the files you're regularly using. Only these files should be kept in your current subdirectories or your folders. It's so easy to start stockpiling files that you never use. When you do, you'll soon discover you have trouble finding files that are needed.

After eliminating, transferring and consolidating files, your computer may *appear* neat and tidy, but chances are that many files are probably **fragmented**, which means that the information in each file is scattered in different places over your disk. The more you use your hard disk, the slower it becomes. The reason for this is that every time you want to save information, your computer stores the information wherever it will fit. (Windows, in particular, produces many fragmented files.)

Your computer stores pieces of information in **clusters,** wherever it can find room on your hard disk. The information in a file may start out as one cluster but through use, the file becomes many clusters that are scattered all over the hard disk. This results in slower access time, which you'll notice especially when you call up a file.

The more fragmented your files are, the more clusters you'll have on your hard disk, the more your computer slows down and the more you need to **optimize** your hard disk using a software program such as DiskExpress II, a highly rated program for the Mac by Alsoft, Inc. (713/353-4090) or The Norton Utilities (800/441-7234 or 503/334-6054). Optimizing restores your hard disk's original speed by consolidating file clusters.

An optimizing program or a program with an optimizing or de-fragmenting feature can reorganize the clusters on your hard disk, grouping them all together. Some experts suggest optimizing at least once a week. Optimizing not only keeps your access time from slowing down, but it also saves wear and tear on your computer. If your disk is optimized, your computer doesn't have to scramble around looking for all the clusters of a file and therefore, your computer doesn't have to work as hard.

With regard to using **compression**, which removes any extra spaces much like concentrated orange juice removes most of the water, I generally recommend against using it to compress data files on your hard disk. It's fine, I think, for backup programs or for compressing applications on your hard disk. It is problematic at best for data files on your hard disk. Large hard disks (at least a gigabyte) have also come way down in price, as have other media storage devices, making compression a much less needed option. You can partition a large hard disk into smaller logical drives (discussed earlier) to avoid wasting space on the hard disk (i.e., smaller logical drives use smaller clusters—clusters may take up the same amount of space whether there is 1 word or 1,000 words in a file). So, smaller clusters can avoid leaving unused and unavailable space on your hard disk.

If you're after a clean hard disk, you may want to remove unnecessary files that any Windows program you install has a habit of leaving around in your directories. You could use the popular uninstall program called logically enough, UnInstaller by MicroHelp (800/777-3322 or 404/516-0899) but use it with care and, as computer expert Richard O'Reilly advises, *read the manual first*. Consider also the highly-rated Uninstall-it! by Landmark Research International Corp. (800/683-6696 or 813/443-1331). Clean Sweep by Quarterdeck Office Systems (310/392-9851) may be the safest uninstall program with its built-in safety features (Quarterdeck is also known for great technical support).

With the widespread emergence of **viruses**, nasty computer programs that are inserted secretly and designed by "hackers" to cause great damage to data and/or computers, you need a good anti-virus or virus detection program to protect yourself. Viruses are spreading because of the proliferation of computer networks and increased information sharing and on-line services. You might have a virus right now and not even know it because it can lurk for years until an event or date triggers its devastating consequences. You take a chance any time you insert a new floppy disk into your computer or download program files from bulletin boards. Unfortunately, new crops of viruses continue to appear.

So what can you do? Get at least one good anti-virus program (two would be better) and scan your hard disk initially and whenever you use any new files, programs or disks. For Windows, DOS, OS/2 and networks check out the award-winning Integrity Master by Stiller

Research (800/788-0787 or 314/256-3130), VirusScan by McAfee Associates (408/988-3832) and Norton Anti-Virus by Symantec (800/441-7234 or 503/334-6054). If you use a Mac, consider the award-winning Virex by Datawatch Corporation (508/988-9700).

To protect your files from unauthorized use (just as you wouldn't give a house key to just anyone), you might want to limit access to your computer files. In an office situation, you could set up password protection through different programs. One award-winning program for the Macintosh, called FileGuard by ASD Software (909/624-2594), is a full-featured security product that offers access privileges for multiple users. There is a version for Macintosh PowerBook users called PB Guard. If you have a computer in your home office and you want to limit access to your kids, Edmark's KidDesk (800/426-0856 or 206/556-8400) may be just the answer.

To protect yourself from theft, or rather to help you recover your computer after it has been stolen, you can alter one of your key files—your AUTOEXEC.BAT, which is a batch file that has all the commands you want carried out every time you "boot up" (start) your computer. Mike Hogan wrote in a *PC WORLD* article to add the following five lines to your AUTOEXEC.BAT:

```
Cls
Echo THIS PC IS STOLEN
Echo CALL YOUR NAME
Echo YOUR PHONE NUMBER
Pause
```

Alternately, he suggests, you could create an OWNER file that includes your name and phone number; he says to hide this file, if possible. You should have an OWNER file (or maybe one called LOST & FOUND) for your notebook computer as well; perhaps you should add the offer of a reward if your computer is "found."

Check the chapter Resource Guide under "Hard Disk and Data Maintenance and Recovery" if you're serious about keeping your hard disk humming. Consider regularly using full-featured hard disk maintenance utilities such as The Norton Utilities by Symantec (800/441-7234 or 503/334-6054) or Gibson Research's SpinRite (714/362-8800), which can test and repair a host of maladies.

FLOPPY ORGANIZATION

Most of our discussion about computer file organization has focused on your hard disk. But chances are good you'll still be using floppy diskettes (also called floppies, diskettes or simply disks) from time to time because the floppy is not dead yet. In fact, it's a very handy backup device especially for current files you're working on. It's also a very stable storage medium; unlike a backup tape, whose data can decay in two to ten years (check with the manufacturer), a floppy's data could be good indefinitely—which is true for both the 5¼- and 3½-inch disk. (But the latter is more durable with its hard plastic casing.) Here are some tips to prevent you from floundering in floppies, as well as tips to save you time and aggravation.

As a general rule, separate program files from your data files. This can save you time during backup by letting you easily exclude program files (which don't usually change once you've installed them). Group data files together by subject, task or client or by a common subdirectory or folder name.

Keep floppies in plastic storage cases specially designed for floppy disks. Get the kind with plastic dividers and stick-on labels to group different types of files. For extra security, buy cases with locks and keys (see Figure 8-5).

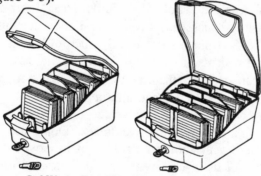

Figure 8-5. Fellowes SoftWorks Disk Files, 50- and 100-capacity with locks

Keep a set of up-to-date, printed **directories** for all your floppies. As used here, a directory is a table of contents for your floppy. It's a good idea to keep a set of printed directories in a nearby notebook or folder. Hard-copy directories can save you the time of inserting floppies and scanning the contents when you want to see what's on them.

If you have hundreds of files, you may want to consider color coding. You can use colored diskette labels or buy diskettes that come in colors. Sentinel and Verbatim make diskettes in different colors.

For temporary labeling or color coding, use removable labels or dots or a strip of removable tape over a permanent label. Whenever you label a diskette, always date it. In fact, anytime you work on a disk, write the date of that work session on the label. Use a thin, permanent felt-tip marker, such as a Sharpie pen, that works well.

Keep your floppies away from heat and magnetic fields. Avoid leaving floppy disks in your car or on top of your TV, monitor, modem or windowsill. Keep them away from telephones, stereos, headphones, magnetic paper clip holders, magnetic copy holders, metal paper clips, electric pencil sharpeners, electric cables and cords and all other devices that could have magnetic fields.

Worried about x-ray machines at airports? You don't have to be but avoid the walk-through security devices, which have damaging magnetic fields. Whatever you do, be careful about handing disks to a security guard, who may be standing at the back of the metal detector, where there are magnetic fields that could cause damage to data.

Be careful how you handle 5¼-inch floppies. Never bend or paper clip a disk jacket, which can prevent the disk from spinning freely in the drive. The best place to hold a 5¼-inch disk is at its corners. If you touch the disk itself, you may leave an oily residue from your fingers that can damage this disk as well as leave a residue on the drive's heads that could damage another disk.

If you use floppies often, consider using a floppy disk drive cleaning kit that cleans the drive heads. Don't use it too often, however; twice a year should be sufficient in most cases.

Remember, *all* disks can wear out from normal use. Never rely on only one disk to hold important information indefinitely—always have another copy.

And finally, when you buy diskettes, buy the best. You don't have to buy the most expensive, but whatever you do, avoid generic, dirt-cheap disks, that carry no manufacturer's name. These disks are said to have high failure rates—as high as 20 percent. High quality disks have no more than a one percent failure rate. Also, if you want to save some time, buy pre-formatted disks.

CD-ROM ORGANIZATION

Chances are your CD-ROMs are proliferating with all the information available on CD-ROM disks and the use of CD-ROMs by software publishers. And you may also be using **CD-Rs**, recordable CD-ROMs that are useful for special purpose backups (such as distributing databases throughout a company or keeping several different versions of a lengthy document all together but off of your hard disk).

CD-CABIN is a valuable software program that automatically logs and indexes all of your CD-ROMs. This CD-ROM manager manages your whole CD-ROM library, giving you virtually instant access and letting you search easily across CDs by group, title, file category and annotations. It's available from The Aldridge Company (800/548-5019 or 713/953-1940).

To increase the number of CD-ROM disks that are physically available on your computer, you'll want to get a **CD-ROM changer** or **juke box**. Pioneer New Media Technologies (800/444-6784 or 310/952-2111) is the "pioneer" in this product line. They make two six-disk CD-ROM changers and two 18-disk juke boxes. The disk changer and juke box use a plastic **magazine**, a caddy with swing-out trays (six for the changer and 18 of them for the juke box). And here's a way to store and organize your CD-ROMs: you can get several magazines and use a different one for each category or subject matter of disks, for example, one for business data and another for entertainment.

Besides organizing your CD-ROM disks, such magazines also reduce handling. A simple fingerprint, not to mention a scratch, on the data side of a CD can mar the data and make it operate poorly. The data is on the shiny side, not the label side. If you ever have to put a CD down on a table, put it label-side down. Always hold a CD by its edges. Never stack unprotected CDs.

Always store a CD in something—be it the plastic jewel case or cardboard sleeve it comes in, a special CD-ROM storage wallet (available through computer outlets and music stores) or even extra Tyvek disk sleeves or vinyl holders from old 5¼-inch disks (you can also buy these inexpensive sleeves separately). You should label sleeves with a felt-tip pen if you can't see what's printed on the CD;

if the CD isn't preprinted, label it, too, with a permanent felt pen Don't put a label on the CD.

If you do need to clean a CD, only use soft, lint-free material or cleaning pads, which you can buy at music and stereo stores (cleaning materials for audio CDs will work for data CDs).

To prevent loss of conventional memory or upper memory blocks when running CD-ROMs, consider using Multimedia Cloaking by Helix Software ($39.95), 718/392-3100. It was recommended close to press time by *PC Magazine*, if you have a PC without Windows NT or OS/2.

DISASTER PREVENTION

Good organization, computer housekeeping and backup can help prevent some disasters. Here are a couple of other tips that can help.

When you upgrade your system, avoid, if possible, adding more than one thing at a time. Most importantly, wait until whatever you add, be it a new software program or some new hardware, works well for you. Adding anything new can create problems and it becomes difficult trying to unscramble problems and affix any responsibility to a particular product (or a company).

RESOURCE GUIDE

Note: Always check with vendors for the latest version of software products and the compatibility with your existing hardware and software. "Suggested retail prices" are used; for most products look for lower "street" and special marketing prices. The following abbreviations are used and are in boldface for easy reference: **Win**=Windows; **Mac**=Macintosh; **Net**=network; **DOS**=MS-DOS or PC-DOS; and **OS/2**=OS/2 Warp. Many of the software products are widely available through computer dealers and software stores or can be ordered directly by calling the listed number. See this chapter and the index for other products.

FILE MANAGEMENT, INTERFACE ENHANCEMENT AND SHELL UTILITY PROGRAMS

The following utilities will help you better manage your personal computer files and enhance functions and features in your operating system or environment. They have excellent recent reviews in major publications. As of this writing many of these are for Windows; check whether Windows 95 versions are available.

CursorPower lets you redesign and resize your cursor. **Win** and **OS/2.** $49.95. **702/831-1108.** North Shore Systems Inc., Nevada

Dashboard is an award-winning shell with a simple push-button control panel, taskbar, shortcut menus, "fly-over help," Quick Launch buttons and Resource Gauge that make Windows more intuitive. **Win** and **Win 95.** $49.95 **800/370-8963** or 408/439-0942. Starfish Software, 1700 Green Hills Road, Scotts Valley, CA 95066

DESQview: The Multiwindow Software Integrator offers a mouse-and-Windows environment that lets you operate up to nine programs simultaneously and switch quickly between programs. DESQview comes with **QEMM-386,** a memory manager, and **Manifest,** a system analyzer. **DOS.** $129.95. **310/392-9851.** Quarterdeck Office Systems Inc., 150 Pico Blvd., Santa Monica, CA 90405

DiskTop is a highly-rated, Mac file management utility in a desk accessory. It allows you to find, list, delete, rename, copy, move, size, launch, shut down, restart and set the attributes of files on any disk without leaving the current application. It's quicker than returning to the Finder. **Mac.** $99.95. **800/346-5392** or 515/225-3720. Prairie Group, 1650 Fuller Rd., West Des Moines, IA 50265

Drag and File is an easy-to-use File Manager replacement and viewer with some additional utilities. **Win** and **Win 95.** $69.95. **800/280-3691.** Canyon Software, 1537 4th St., #131, San Rafael, CA 94901. Shareware version available on BBS & CompuServe

HiJaak Graphics Suite lets you browse, search, find, view, create, draw, edit, capture, scan and print powerful graphics; it has file format conversion, image management and file management features. **Win.** $99. **800/374-6738** or 203/740-2400. Inset Systems Inc., 71 Commerce Dr., Brookfield, CT 06804

Jasc Media Center allows you to organize your multimedia files by creating albums. Files within each album may be arranged in a variety of ways. Albums can even be merged together. This program also lets you catalog your multimedia files using keywords and comments. The program keeps track of file locations on removable disks such as floppies and CD-ROMs. **Win.** $39. **800/622-2793** or 612/930-9171. JASC, Inc., 10901 Red Circle Dr., Ste. 340, Minnetonka, MN 55343

MasterJuggler is a highly rated program that lets you easily open over 300 font suitcases, view their contents by name, face and size, and compress fonts to save valuable disk space. **Mac.** $69.95. **713/353-4090**, Alsoft, Inc., PO Box 927, Spring, TX 77383-0927

Norton Desktop has an excellent set of file management tools plus a collection of other useful utilities. **Win** and **DOS.** $179. **800/441-7234** or 503/334-6054. Symantec Corp., 10201 Torre Ave., Cupertino, CA 95014

Now Utilities is a highly-rated Macintosh set that enhances the Macintosh operating system, improving efficiency and making Mac features easier and faster to use. *MACWORLD* magazine called three modules—Now FolderMenus, Now Menus and Now SuperBoomerang—"almost indispensable." **Mac.** $89.95. **800/237-2078** or 503/274-2800. Now Software, Inc., 921 S.W. Washington St., Ste. 500, Portland, OR 97205-2823

OnFile (see Figure 8-6) offers users an easy way to organize and quickly find their files. Based on a fun and easy-to-use book metaphor, OnFile lets you organize files by topic, project, application type or any way you prefer. OnFile gives you more information about your files; for example, you could choose up to 100 characters for a file name, enter summary descriptions and view fields without opening the associated application. **Win.** $49.95 **800/234-2500** or 408/986-8000 Software Publishing Corp., PO Box 54983, 3165 Kifer Rd., Santa Clara, CA 95056-0983

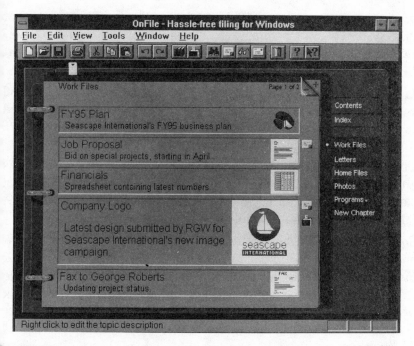

Figure 8-6. OnFile gives you an easy way to organize and quickly locate files.

Outside In/for Windows is an award-winning file viewer utility and file manager that integrates well with standard e-mail systems. The Windows 95 version offers hundreds·of additional file viewers and lets you print a document from a view. (Systems Compatibility Corp., the software manufacturer, supplies the basic viewers that come with Windows 95.) **Win** ($89) and **Win 95** (under $50). **800/333-1395** or 312/329-0700. 401 N. Wabash St., Ste. 600, Chicago, IL 60611

PC Tools is a multi-award-winning utility program that is jam packed with features including powerful file and desktop management and one of the best programs for disk backup and data recovery. It has received nearly every editorial award possible in its class. **Win** and **DOS**. $179. **800/964-6896** or 503/690-8088. Symantec Central Point Software, 15220 Greenbrier Pkwy, Ste. 150, Beaverton, OR 97006

PowerMerge is a powerful, highly-rated Mac file management and file synchronization tool that helps you keep files, folders and disks organized and up to date. Designed with PowerBook, multiple Mac, and multiple disk users in mind, PowerMerge automatically synchronizes and updates files between any Macintosh computers or disks via network or removable media. **Mac.** $129. **714/757-1787** Leader Technologies, 4590 MacArthur Blvd., Ste. 550, Newport Beach, CA 92660

Praxim is an award-winning program that offers a powerful command line interface to Windows for those who prefer the speed of the command line. **Win** $39.95 **800/634-9808** or 512/328-0100. Wesson International Inc., Austin, TX

SpinWizard is a well-designed substitute for Program Manager. As an organizer, I really like its unique, compact, eight-sided cylindrical carousel that holds up to 96 programs, files and macros. **Win.** $79. **800/460-7746.** Tanisys Technology Inc, Austin, TX

Square One is a highly-rated Mac program that puts the programs and files you use every day on one handy, icon-palette. Move your mouse to a corner or hit a hot key, and your palette jumps to the front. You can launch, switch, hide or quit any program with a click or a keystroke. **Mac.** $74. **800/824-6279** or 310/449-1481. Binary Software, 2118 Wilshire Blvd., Ste. 900, Santa Monica, CA 90403

TabWorks is built around the familiar and intuitive notebook metaphor that lets you organize your files and your work in any way that makes sense to you—for example, by project, function or client. Documents and applications are easily and quickly accessible on your personalized, tabbed notebook and TabWorks can launch them automatically. Fast and easy text search and password protection are two new features. (Xerox pioneered the tabbed notebook concept.) **Win** and **Win 95.** $49. **800/909-4446** or 510/412-1426. XSoft Division of Xerox, 3400 Hillview Avenue, Palo Alto, CA 94303

Tree86 is sophisticated, network-compatible file management tool that sorts files in 10 different ways and has pull-down menus, instant access to single or multiple drives, text search and can copy, move and find duplicates. $94.95. **Win** and **DOS.** $94.95. **800/548-5019** or 713/953-1940. The Aldridge Co., Inc., 2500 CityWest Blvd., Suite 575, Houston, TX 77042

VirtualDisk is highly-rated disk-cataloging software that automatically builds a complete catalog of all your disks and files as they're encountered by your Mac. It tracks removable disks, including floppies, cartridges and opticals. It also offers efficient label printing ising several standard Avery label formats. **Mac.** $69. **503/848-7112.** Continuum Software, Inc. 1075 NW Murray Rd., Ste. 307, Portland, OR 97229-5501

XTree Gold is the award-winning file manager I use (I have used XTree programs for more than 10 years). Considered to be the granddaddy of file managers, its tree directory representation can't be beat. XTree Gold continually adds many new features since the original XTree was released in 1985. **Win and DOS.** $99.95. **800/964-896** or 503/690-8088. Symantec Central Point Software, 15220 Greenbrier Pkwy, Ste. 150, Beaverton, OR 97006

HARD DISK AND DATA MAINTENANCE AND RECOVERY

A number of specialized programs and services will help you keep your hard disk clean and correct specific file and data problems you may encounter on your computer. See this chapter itself for other products.

Disk Historian is an award-winning program that cleans up your hard disk and speeds up your PC. It keeps track of every file on your computer, telling you how many times and when each file was last used, if at all. It then previews the content of any file and compresses, off-loads or deletes the unused files to increase space. **Win.** $59. **800/388-2761** or 805/967-9853. Solid Oak Software Inc., PO Box 6826, Santa Barbara, CA 93160

Ontrack Data Recovery Inc. charges $200 for an initial diagnosis and between $200 to $600 for data recovery. It takes three to five days. **800/752-1333** or 612/937-5161 in Eden Prairie, Minnesota

QEMM is a highly rated memory manager that has novice and experienced levels. **DOS and Win.** $99.95. **310/392-9851.** Quarterdeck Office Systems Inc., 150 Pico Blvd., Santa Monica, CA 90405

Solutronics is a computer repair service specializing in components for IBM, Compaq and Apple machines. **800/875-2580** or 612/943-306. 7255 Flying Cloud Dr., Eden Prairie, MN 55344

WINProbe is the award-winning Do-It-Yourself Troubleshooter toolbox for Windows. It will help you optimize memory and suggest

the best Windows setup for your system. It now includes CD Certif
and NetCruiser. **Win.** $99. **800/683-6696** or 813/443-1331. Landmar
Research International Corp., 703 Grand Central St., Clearwater, Fl
34616

READING, REFERENCE & RESOURCE INFO

The following directories, tools and magazines are excellent source:
of computer information, providing news and views on the lates
programs, features, updates and versions.

Claris Solutions Alliance Guide is a complete, well-organized guid
to Claris products, services and partners. **408/727-8227.** $14.95. 62:
pages.

Computer Select on CD-ROM is published monthly and contain:
computer related articles (abstracts or full text and spreadshee
tables) from over 140 publications as well as product announcements
product specifications and vendor contact information. There ar
more than 70,000 hardware, software and data communicatior
products and more than 12,000 manufacturers' profiles. **212/503
4400.** Computer Library, One Park Avenue, New York NY 10016

Datapro Software Finder is an updated-quarterly CD-ROM tha
profiles 30,000 business, professional and technical software package:
for micro, midrange and mainframe systems. With nine differen
search criteria, including key words, you can quickly identify product
that meet very specific requirements. Profiles give you all the basi
facts at the touch of a key: price, systems compatibility, memor
requirements, network support, vendor contact information and a
detailed description. It's ideal if you make software buying decisions
It's also available in hard copy editions. I used the three-volume
loose-leaf **Datapro Directory of Microcomputer Software,** a
comprehensive and easy to use resource with more than 18,00(
software packages, to update software products for this book
800/328-2776 or 609/764-0100, Datapro, a unit of McGraw-Hil
Information Services Co., 600 Delran Parkway, Delran, NJ 08075

Macworld Magazine is a user-friendly Macintosh magazine that's fu
to read. I really like their "Buyers' Tools" feature, which is a
cumulative listing of Editors' Choice winners and all hardware and

software that has been rated by their star system. **800/288-6848** or 303/604/1465. PO Box 54529 Boulder, CO 80322-4529

MICROREF Shortcuts! and Keyboard Templates will help you find and learn commands for popular software programs. The handy quick reference booklets and templates are available at computer, software and book stores or can be ordered directly from the publisher. $2.50 for Shortcuts booklets; $10.95 for templates. **800/553-2212** or 708/498-3780. Educational Systems, Inc., 706 Landwehr Rd., Northbrook, IL 60062

Microsoft Business Source has a toll-free phone line with free answers to software and hardware questions. **800/60-SOURCE**

PC Magazine, The Independent Guide to Personal Computing, comes out every two weeks and features in-depth product reviews and industry trends. The "Editor's Choice" designation helps you quickly spot winning products and programs. A one-year subscription (22 issues) costs $49.97. **800/289-0429** or 303/604-7445. PC Magazine, PO Box 54093, Boulder, CO 80322

PC WORLD is a user-friendly monthly publication that features more practical (rather than technical) PC product reviews and articles. $29.90 for one year. **800/234-3498** or 303/447-9330, PC WORLD, 501 Second St., San Francisco, CA 94107

The Software Encyclopedia provides the street map you need to navigate through the maze of software that makes up the information superhighway. This two-volume set lists more than 18,000 software programs in every format from disk to CD-ROM and is updated annually. I used it to update this book and found it to be a very helpful, reliable resource. Paperback, $234.95. **800/521-8110** or 212/337-6934. R.R. Bowker, A Reed Reference Publishing Co., 121 Chanlon Rd., New Providence, NJ 07974

Software Support Inc. provides third party software support 24 hours a day, 365 days a year on over 150 leading software applications for Windows, DOS, Macintosh and OS/2 platforms, as well as operating systems support and advanced technical support for selected products, such as Lotus Notes. Call for pricing. **800/756-4463** or 407/333-4433. 300 International Parkway, 3rd Floor, Heathrow, FL 32746

9

MORE WAYS
TO MANAGE YOUR
WORK, PROJECTS
AND INFORMATION

Quick Scan: Discover specific tools and systems to keep track of the detailed information related to work, projects, people, resources and records. If just too many of your office details are slipping through the proverbial cracks, you could profit from a simple system or two. Here are some ideas that can help.

Let's face it. Life keeps getting more and more complicated each day. So many details to take care of and so much information to manage. How *do* you stay on top of it all?

Some people are lucky. They can delegate the details to someone else. But whether you can delegate or not, you still need sound organizational tools and systems to manage your high-demand work load.

Why? If you're like most people, you probably do or supervise plenty of paperwork, record keeping and follow-up activities in your work, all of which generate many layers of information. When you can manage information effectively, you'll make a professional, last ing impression on people. It says you care about **quality** and **service**. It says you *care enough to follow up and follow through*—which is quite a feat in the midst of an ongoing information explosion that we all face each day.

Effective follow-up and follow-through require *systems* to organize details and see the big picture, too. Systems can be manual or computerized. Generally, it's best to start out using manual systems first (even if you have a computer). While complexity may necessitate a computerized system later on, start first with a manual one. The trick is to keep systems *simple*—as simple as possible.

Remember, too, a computer will not get you organized. Start planning logically and systematically on paper and then if necessary (and only if necessary) find a computer solution that conforms to you, not the other way around.

And should you happen to be fortunate enough to have an assistant, remember this: **when you have a good system in place, delegating is easy.**

WORK AND PROJECT MANAGEMENT SHORTCUTS

Where most people get into trouble is trying to keep everything in their head. And then they get upset with themselves when they forget something using the infallible "mental note system."

The other ploy that has equally bad results is relying on countless written slips of paper on your desk, in your wallet and on your wall. The problem with paper slips is that they create clutter and stress in your life. They also tend to "slip" through the cracks and get lost—which is probably why they're called "slips" in the first place.

FORMS, CHECKLISTS AND CHARTS

It has been said that one person's form is another person's red tape. But a *well-designed* form is a clear, concise and useful summary of information at a glance. And contrary to popular belief, forms can actually help you *reduce* paperwork.

A good form *consolidates* information that is repetitive or might otherwise be scattered in many different places in your office or computer (or someone else's). A good form saves you time flipping through many pieces of paper (or through many different computer screens). Use forms to track such things as work flow, projects, responsibilities, schedules and personnel. Use forms to simplify communication.

A clean, well-designed form is not only pleasing to the eye but is more likely to insure a quicker response. Form phobia really sets in when clutter meets the eye or when poorly-designed forms keep asking for the same information over and over again.

We use the **program tracking form** in Figure 9-1 to record and consolidate important information and activities for each speaking engagement.

Create your own forms files in your file cabinet or on your computer. Collect samples of forms you like and those you often use. Make up a form to inventory all the forms you have in your office and when they're used. My husband designed such a form when he worked as a summer intern for the federal government. You may discover there are forms you should modify or eliminate altogether.

We keep most forms and form letters on computer. Our software programs let us easily create a special form letter called a **mail merge letter**, which merges information we select such as names and addresses or key phrases into our form letters.

Speaking of computers, watch as they continue to make paper forms obsolete. Electronic forms give you more control over and flexibility with information and are more responsive to our fast changing business environment. Paper forms are costly and wasteful; organizations have been spending $6 billion a year on pre-printed forms, one-third of which end up being thrown away before they're even used.

If you like and use forms, consider getting a **forms software** package. Forms software includes a variety of different programs. One type helps you design your own forms on screen and print them out on your printer. Another type helps you fill in preprinted forms that you use all the time, such as Federal Express forms, so that the information lines up correctly. More sophisticated forms software programs give you many options, including designing your own forms on screen, scanning an existing form into your computer, filling out preprinted forms and linking your databases with your forms. (See the Resource Guide for examples of popular products.)

Positively Organized!®

PROGRAM TRACKING FORM   Today's Date:

te/#_____ Time_____ Title_____

)e of PO! Program_____ Type of Mtg_____#____

э/Contract Terms_____

ne of **Organization**_____

y Contact/Title_____
                                          Off #   Home #
dress_____

ner Contacts/Numbers_____

cation of Prog/Mtg_____Mgr/#_____

tel Reservations at_____By Org____GLA_____

arest Airport_____Distance to Mtg/Hotel_____

ound Transp._____

avel: Drive/Fly Booked on_____w/_____

parture Date From City to City   At   ETA   Airline   #

parture Date From City to City   At   ETA   Airline   #

parture Date From City to City   At   ETA   Airline   #

adline for Ticketing_____ Receive Tickets by_____ Fare $_____

Program Checklist

nt to Client			Requested from Client	Date Rec'c
___ Contract	____	Intro	____ Signed Contract	_____
___ Photo	____	Invoice	____ Deposit of $____	_____
___ Bio	____	TU Note	____ Hotel Confirmation	_____
___ Blurb			____ Mtg brochure/map	_____
___ AV/Setup			____ Mtg agenda	_____
___ Handout for dup.			____ Trade pubs/bkg	_____
___ PR			____ Pre-program ques	_____
___ Pre-program Ques.			____ Fee/reim	_____
			____ Letter of Rec.	_____
			____ Referral	

Be Done   By Date   Date Completed
ite program_____
epare handout_____
epare/organize audio-visuals_____
nfirm a-v, setup, handouts one week before_____
ntact introducer/confirm has intro_____
ckout list/pack_____Wardrobe _____

igure 9-1. Program tracking form

The **checklist** is an example of a form. Checklists are old standbys that insure you won't forget something and often can be kept and referred to repeatedly. I have travel and seminar packing checklists that I use year after year, for instance.

Use a standardized checklist form to help you remember the repetitive tasks involved in similar projects. My program tracking form has a checklist at the bottom.

Charts provide the added dimension of a diagram or graph that shows relationships between different components. It is more of a visual picture of information, almost like a map.

The chart is a two-dimensional form that shows relationships visually and graphically. The chart maps out details and the big picture at the same time. It summarizes information at a glance. Sometimes a chart is large enough to go on a wall (as you'll soon see) or small enough to fit on a form.

Charts are also good at showing numerical information, which, according to research, helps produce quicker, easier decisions. When information is expressed in numbers rather than words, complex decisions can be made 20 percent faster. It's also easier to evaluate many more factors and options with numbers than with words. There's an added strain when making decisions with words alone.

In working with clients who have many ongoing projects where each project has most of the same tasks, I have developed the **checklist chart**. Figure 9-2 shows an example of the checklist chart I helped design for the office of professional speaker Danny Cox. The chart is a preprinted, 8½-by-11-inch form kept in a transparent plastic sleeve that sits conveniently on the desk of Tedi Patton, who uses it to coordinate all upcoming program details on a daily basis.

Since Cox travels so extensively, his office also uses a map of the United States that is dotted with his engagement locations. Self-adhesive dots indicate not only the location but the engagement dates. The map is a useful planning tool when the office gets calls from around the country asking when Cox will be "in their neighborhood."

Calendar or scheduling charts are a good way to show the relationship between periods of time and people, tasks or projects. Some scheduling charts list the months and weeks of the year. Such a chart can easily be turned into a **Gantt chart** or timeline that shows task start dates and deadlines and responsibilities. (Henry

PROGRAMS IN PROGRESS

CLIENT NAME	PROGRAM DATE	AGREEMENT SENT	AGREEMENT RETURNED	DEPOSIT RECEIVED	INTRO.	ROOM SET-UP	PHOTO	HANDOUT	AIRLINE RESERVATIONS	FINAL PROG. C/L	MONTH-OUT CHECK	TAPES PACKED / SENT

Figure 9-2. A checklist chart used by the office of speaker Danny Cox

Gantt invented this useful chart while working for the government during World War I.) Day-Timers makes a variety of scheduling charts and forms that adapt elements from highly acclaimed project management tools such as Gantt charts, PERT charts (*P*erformance *E*valuation and *R*eview *T*echnique) and CPM (*C*ritical *P*ath *M*ethod). These tools show the steps and sequence that must occur for a project to be completed. Figure 9-3 shows the Day-Timers Yearly Schedule form that functions as a Gantt chart.

If you're comparing prices and features for products (such as computers) or services from suppliers (such as print shops) consider developing a simple chart so you can record the information as you go. It's a lot easier than whipping out all those notes later on. Your chart keeps you on track by reminding you to ask the same questions of everyone. Leave some blank spaces for additional questions that come up as you do your research.

Use **quadrille** or **graph paper** to make your own charts. The "non-repro blue" lines will not photocopy but they will guide you in drawing your own lines. They come in many different styles and are available from your office supply store or catalog as well as a number of personal organizer companies, such as Day-Timers, Geodex and Time/Design (see Chapter 2 or the index).

If you need to track projects or personnel visually in such a way that you and/or other people can easily see the information, use **wall charts**. Also called **scheduling** or **visual control boards**, wall charts provide visibility to keep you on target. They're not the most attractive things in the world but if you have a work room or don't have to impress anyone with aesthetics, they are very functional.

Wall charts have an advantage over other systems because they crystallize your ideas, intentions and plans and make them visible. A wall chart gives you a visible game plan and very little escape. It's staring you straight in the face. Color coding works great for wall charts. You can code people, types of activities, progress and deadlines.

Use wall charts to track one complex project, several simultaneous projects, a production schedule, your master calendar, personnel schedules and marketing or fund-raising campaigns. They come in many different sizes, styles, configurations and materials. **Magnetic** wall charts have different components that you can move around. See Figure 9-4.

1990 YEARLY PROJECT SCHEDULE

(✓)	#	PROJECT	January					February				March			
		WK	1	2	3	4	5	6	7	8	9	10	11	12	13
	101	Smith Residence						S	—					R	—
		Foundation						S	—	F					
		Framing & Rough-ins									S	—		R	F
		Drywall													S
		Painting & Trim													
	102	Jones Residence									S	—			
		Foundation									S	—	F		
		Framing & Rough-ins											S	—	
		Drywall													
		Painting & Trim													
	103	Martin Residence													S
		Foundation													S
		Framing & Rough-ins													
		Drywall													
		Painting & Trim													
	104	Hamilton Residence													
	105	Kite Residence													
	106	Lanin Residence													
	107	Blaine Residence													
	108	Farrell Residence													

S = Start   R = Review   F = Finish

Notes _____

JANUARY								FEBRUARY								MARCH							
WK	S	M	T	W	T	F	S	WK	S	M	T	W	T	F	S	WK	S	M	T	W	T	F	S
01		1	2	3	4	5	6	05					1	2	3	09					1	2	3
02	7	8	9	10	11	12	13	06	4	5	6	7	8	9	10	10	4	5	6	7	8	9	10
03	14	15	16	17	18	19	20	07	11	12	13	14	15	16	17	11	11	12	13	14	15	16	17
04	21	22	23	24	25	26	27	08	18	19	20	21	22	23	24	12	18	19	20	21	22	23	24
05	28	29	30	31				09	25	26	27	28				13	25	26	27	28	29	30	31

*1987-1988, DAY-TIMERS, Inc. ALLENTOWN, PA • PRODUCT # 90684 • Printed in USA

Figure 9-3. A portion of the Day-Timer Yearly Project Schedule

Some people prefer the flexibility of a home-made chart such as the **action board** of psychiatrist and author Dr. David Viscott. With his system, you create the action board by putting up six or seven index cards on a wall or bulletin board. Each card stands for a different project and includes a key contact.

Figure 9-4. Magna Visual Work/Plan Visual Organizer Kit

Under each project card you put another index card that lists the next step to be taken on the project. Each project relates directly to your most important life goals.

If your work could benefit from charts that show either a *process* (such as a flowchart that maps out work flow or the steps needed to complete a project) or *structure* (such as an organization chart), consider using **diagramming software**. With single purpose or multipurpose diagramming software packages you can create such diagrams as flowcharts, process charts, organization (org) charts, floor plans and space plans. (See the Resource Guide for some examples.)

Don't let forms, checklists or charts scare you. They aren't straitjackets; rather they're guideposts to help you work through the maze of details in your office and your head.

Turn to the "Forms, Checklists and Charts" section in the chapter Resource Guide for more examples of tools and systems you can use.

CAPTURING AND HARNESSING CREATIVE IDEAS

There are many exciting ways to capture and harness all those creative ideas you (and others) may have in your head. One way is to chart them out.

Let me share with you one of the greatest and simplest tools I use to chart ideas whenever I begin a project or a writing task. It's called a **Mind Map** and it was originally developed in 1970 by Tony Buzan of the Brain Foundation in England. I first heard about it at a professional communications meeting devoted to "writer's block."

The Mind Map is an effective way to free up your mind and let your ideas flow. It's a combination brainstorming and outlining tool where you can see your ideas and thought patterns more graphically. The Mind Map is a great organizing tool for writing, speaking, project planning, meetings, training, negotiating, learning, memorizing and thinking. Figure 9-5 shows you an example of a Mind Map. For mind mapping books, tapes, videos and software products by Tony Buzan, contact The Buzan Centre of Palm Beach, Inc. at 800/Y MIND MAP or 407/881-0188, 415 Federal Highway, Lake Park, FL 33403.

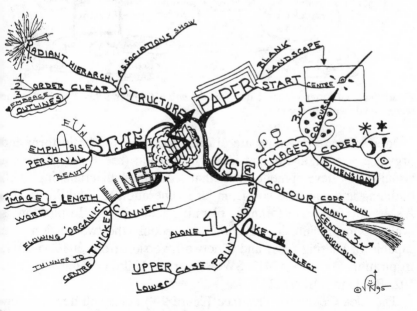

Figure 9-5. A Mind Map created by Vanda North to communicate the key Mind Map laws that include the use of paper, words, structure, images, colors and lines

Create the Life You Want! is a guidebook that shows how to apply Mind Maps to goal setting using the versatile SCAN/PLAN index card information systems. It's $14.95 from 800/SCANPLAN or 310/829-2888, SCAN/PLAN, Inc., PO Box 1662, Santa Monica, CA 90406.

I've also used **Clusters**, another idea organization tool. Clusters are described by Gabriele Rico in his book, *Writing the Natural Way*. You can see an example in Figure 9-6.

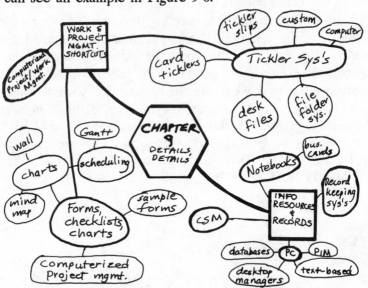

Figure 9-6. A Cluster outline I did before I wrote Chapter 9 (as it looked in the second edition of my book)

Idea software programs are offering more ways to brainstorm and organize your thoughts and ideas. Inspiration (see Figure 9-7) is a visual idea development tool that combines diagramming with outlining and can take you from idea generation to final document. It's useful for brainstorming, planning and writing. Inspiration is available in Macintosh and Windows versions (the two versions are capable of sharing files) and a network version from 503/245-9011, Inspiration Software, 7412 SW Beaverton Hillsdale Highway, Ste. 102, Portland, OR 97225.

The Idea Generator Plus (see Figure 9-8) helps you develop new solutions to tough problems by offering seven idea-generation techniques to help you brainstorm more ideas. These techniques are

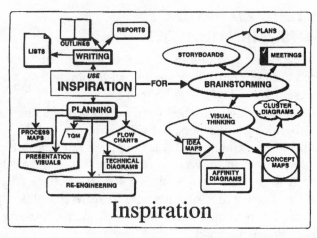

Figure 9-7. Here's an idea map that shows what Inspiration software can do.

easy to understand and apply and surprisingly effective in solving problems. It's available in a DOS version from 800/678-7008 or 510/644-0694, Experience in Software, 2000 Hearst Ave., Ste. 202, Berkeley, CA 94709-2176.

The Idea Generator(R) Plus

```
 MAIN MENU
 ────────

 Pro │   IDEA GENERATION TECHNIQUES  (highlight one or more)
     │   ──────────────────────────────────────────────
 Ide │    I1  Similar situations.
  ──>│    I2  Metaphors for your situation.
 Eva │    I3  Other perspectives.
     │    I4  Focus on your goals one by one.
 Rep │    I5  Reverse your goals.
     │    I6  Focus on the people involved.
 QUI │    I7  Make the most of your ideas.
     │
     │   ESC to MAIN MENU
     │
```

Figure 9-8. The seven idea generation techniques in Idea Generator Plus

COMPUTERIZED PROJECT
AND WORK MANAGEMENT

Think of computerized solutions as ways to extend your brain, giving you at once greater control, creativity and flexibility over your work and projects.

For project planning and scheduling, consider **project management software programs** for the personal computer.

These programs combine charts and reports that let you see project information in a variety of ways. You can easily make changes such as automatically updating schedules. Reports are easy to generate and distribute. And it's easy to store completed projects and schedules for reference later on—which means less reinventing of the wheel down the road.

Look for these features when you select a project management program: ease of learning (does it take a Ph.D. in computer sciences to grasp it?); ease of use; a good manual that's just the right size (if it's too hefty, forget it); good reviews by experts and/or people you know; and an easy-to-use tutorial. It's also a plus if the program can do both Gantt and PERT charts.

And here's a project planning tip: at the end of recurring projects summarize any steps or ideas that worked really well and any that didn't. Use the most recent summary as you begin planning the recurring project.

Management software, also called **MBA-ware** or **decision support software**, is a relatively new genre of software that draws upon business theory and management expertise to help with problem solving and the process of making complex decisions. Such software doesn't just manipulate data; it analyzes and advises, helping decision makers create uniform criteria and options. It's a mixture of project management programs, rules-based expert systems and forecasting software. It's particularly helpful for making personnel decisions.

Process management software is a new emerging category aimed at supporting the worldwide drive to improve business processes and help organizations remain competitive through programs such as Business Re-engineering, Business Process Improvement and Total Quality Management (TQM).

Such software helps you document process steps and estimate the duration of each step; define the information and materials that flow through the whole process; identify the people and materials used by the process; assign people and materials to each step in the process; and calculate the process performance via quantitative measures or simulation. The following are typical questions such software will help you ask and answer: 1) How long does the process take?, 2) Who needs to work on the process?, 3) How much does the process cost? and 4) Are there any bottlenecks? Process Charter is an example of process management software—see the Resource Guide.

Popular project management, decision support and process management programs are listed in the chapter Resource Guide under "Project and Work Management Software."

TOP TOOLS AND SYSTEMS TO MANAGE INFORMATION RESOURCES AND RECORDS

Each day as you're bombarded with more and more bits and pieces of information, it becomes a real challenge to organize all this information. Fortunately, you have many options.

DATABASE PROGRAMS

A **database management program** is one of the best ways to gain control over and access to many records and resources. A database program lets you not only store but *sort* and call up information based on criteria that you select. It's the sorting capability of a computerized database that provides real information power.

There are basically two different types of database management programs: **structured** and **unstructured** (also called **free-form**), although sometimes you can have a combination. In a structured database program, one **file** may contain dozens, hundreds or even thousands of **records**. Each record is an entry consisting of different items or **fields** of information. Let's suppose you create a file of all your clients. Each client would be a different record in the file. The client's name, address, phone number are three different fields in the record. The blank form that appears on your computer screen showing the different fields before they're completed is a **data-entry form**, because you use it to *enter data* or information for each field.

The simplest database programs function basically as computerized address books. Some come with PIMs (discussed in Chapter 2). Their functions will include storage of names, addresses and phone numbers and they may also print mailing labels.

These and other simple programs are often called **flat file databases**. As they add features and capabilities such as sorting, searching, reporting and **mail merge** (using your own word processor or a built-in word processor that prints form letters), expect to pay more money.

Contact management programs or **contact managers** are easy-to-use flat file database programs that were designed originally for those in sales but now are used universally by anyone who needs to stay in touch with at least 50 people on a regular basis. Such programs let you schedule and track calls, remind you with alarms when to do follow-up calls, encourage you to keep notes on calls and meetings with contacts and usually have an autodialer. It may also have other features such as scheduling, text search and mail merge. ACT! is an example of a contact manager.

Since the term "contact manager" has become more popular, you may see it used for simple address book style programs. You'll also see it used to describe programs that either are PIMs or have many PIM features. In other words, the line between contact managers and PIMs is blurring more and more.

Sales and telemarketing programs are specialized contact managers that are ideal for anyone who is managing a client database and/or is marketing products or services and wants to track these marketing efforts. Many of these programs combine features from other software such as database management, word processing, telecommunications and built-in follow-up. Consider these programs if you're in real estate, insurance, inside or outside sales, consulting, purchasing, financial services, association management, direct mail marketing, to name a few areas. You don't have to be in sales; you just need to deal with a large number of contacts on a regular basis.

The most sophisticated database management programs are the **relational databases**. Most of them are difficult to learn, some require a programmer and they tend to be expensive. What sets them apart besides these negatives, however, is their ability to work with more than one file at the same time. Relational databases can share related information between two or more files, keeping files up to date with just one entry of data. Relational databases are great for inventory control and billing, for example.

Many file managers are starting to adopt some of the more sophisticated features of "high-end" relational database programs, while still maintaining ease in learning and use.

Don't confuse databases that come on **CD-ROM**, such as PhoneDisc, with database *programs*. CD-ROM databases are for playing or reference only; you can not manipulate or add any data to them as you can to a hard disk or a floppy disk. CD-ROM stands for Compact Disc Read-Only Memory and each 4¾-inch plastic CD-ROM disc can store more than 600 megabytes of data, the equivalent of more than 250,000 pages of text or thousands of images. It can also store sound, in CD format, just like your CD music disc, from whose technology the CD-ROM developed.

According to most sources, PhoneDisc CD-ROM telephone directories provide the most complete and accurate listings available. (Don't expect 100 percent accuracy; PhoneDisc advertises 93 percent, however.) If you call directory assistance a lot for phone numbers or if you're involved in telemarketing, consider one of the PhoneDisc directories. Two of the most popular are PhoneDisc Business ($79), which contains 9.5 million U.S. businesses, and PhoneDisc PowerFinder ($249), which integrates 90 million residential and business listing with full reverse searching. PhoneDisc directories come with fast, search software to let you find information in a variety of ways. Contact info: 800/284-8353 or 301/657-8548, Digital Directory Assistance, Inc. (DDA), 6931 Arlington Rd., Ste. 405, Bethesda, MD 20814-5231.

When the resource information you want to store on computer isn't as structured as database records, you may prefer to use an **unstructured** or **free-form** database program, also called a **text-based management system** or a **text-based program**. Such a program is much more *free-form* in nature, generally without pre-defined fields and records, and includes **free-form text databases** and **outliners**. A text-based program may be ideal if the information you're managing resides in long documents.

Text-based programs give you more flexibility, although frequently less speed. You don't have to make your information conform to a database configuration. Search features are varied; some programs have you search on key words, others can search for "strings" of words or phrases.

SOME ORGANIZATION TIPS
FOR DESIGNING STRUCTURED DATABASES

I have use structured database files with fields for years. I spent time at the outset designing the data entry screens, thinking about naming and placement of field names. Careful design has helped me do fast searches and find the information I need.

I have found **codes** to be very useful. Let me give you an example. I have a field in most of my database files called "contact," in which I place codes that indicate the type of contact. I use the letter "c" for a consulting contact, the letter "s" for a speaking contact, "p" for professional and "f" for friend. I can then sort or do a report for all of my professional contacts, for example, or all of my speaking and consulting contacts.

Don't be afraid to reorganize database files. You may decide to split a large one into several smaller files. Conversely, you may decide to put several together in order to be able to sort by zip code. In either case, it will be easier it you've designed the fields in each file uniformly so that they have a one-to-one correspondence between the fields. Ideally, if you use two street address fields in one file, you'll not use three in another, especially if you ever plan to merge the files together at some time in the future.

DATA ACCESS AND SEARCH TOOLS

Accessing the information you need is becoming more challenging with increasingly larger and larger databases of information that you can store on your computer as well as those that are on-line. Fortunately, there are some products that can help. Most of these products focus on **keyword** searches and a handful focus on the underlying **concepts** or the linkages between data rather than on just keywords or phrases actually contained in the data. Both of these types of products are commonly known as "search engines."

PageKeeper retrieves information from virtually any source—word processing files, spreadsheets, faxes, e-mail, online downloads and scanned paper documents. PageKeeper reads and analyzes the content of your documents automatically as you describe what you want in your own words. It also includes built-in OmniPage OCR as well as electronic "sticky notes" you can attach to your documents. It even lets you launch the Windows application that created your document.

PageKeeper works by reading through each file, counting the number of times each of the words appears (bypassing common works such as "the"), noticing other words that appear nearby and then, based on all this information, determining the key concepts. Then, using statistical analysis, the concepts are compared to isolate those that are closely related. It costs $195, single user; $595, single user, network version; 5-users, network, $1,995; and ask about other volume pricing. Contact info is: 800/535-SCAN or 408/395-7000, Caere Corp., 100 Cooper Court, Los Gatos, CA 95030.

RECORD KEEPING SYSTEMS

Beyond the programs and products we've already discussed, a couple of other systems can help you track record keeping details. Let me tell you about a few of my favorites.

If you work with different clients or projects, the All-state Legal catalog has an easy manual system to keep track of billable time or expenses for clients or projects. No longer will you have to spend hours searching through your files, calendar, receipts and notes at billing time. (Although designed for attorneys, this system easily adapts to other professionals, such as consultants and writers.)

The system comes in two main styles: a time and service record system called Time Record and a system that tracks costs and expenses called Expense Record. Both are "one-write" systems that are designed to be used "as you go" (which is the ideal way to use a system anyway). Call 800/222-0510 for more information.

Let's see how the Expense Record works. You chronologically record expenses as they occur on the two-part Expense Record form, shown in Figure 9-9. As you write on the top sheet, a piece of carbon paper transfers your records to the second sheet. The preprinted top sheet is die-cut into 15 self-adhesive labels. When the sheet is full, each of these labels can be peeled off and attached to their respective project, case or client sheets known as "Client/Case Costs Record" forms, which can be kept in a handy notebook arranged either alphabetically or chronologically. Bills or statements

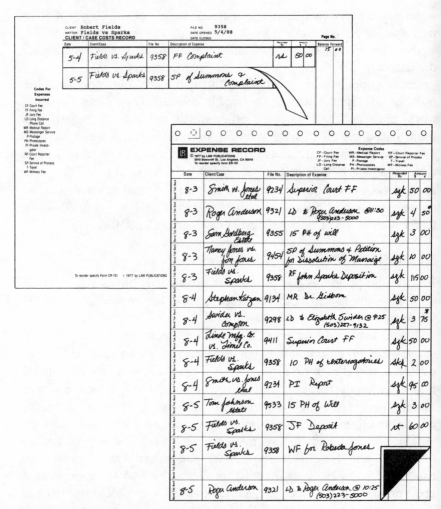

Figure 9-9. All-State Expense Record System

can be produced from these record forms. A carbon copy sheet under the preprinted 15-label sheet remains as a permanent, chronological backup copy.

The Time Record works the same way as the Expense Record. Some of my clients have selected one or the other, depending upon the type of records they need to keep the most. Others like having the two different systems.

For a builder/contractor client of mine, I recommended the Time Record to keep track of time and materials on building job sites. The Time Record form is attached to his clipboard, making for a convenient and portable system that's with him all the time.

Another "one-write" record keeping system that I recommend to clients is the Safeguard bookkeeping system (available in 200 formats). This is a simple-to-use manual system that is great for an entrepreneur or professional in private practice. We use it in our office. It actually makes bookkeeping *fun!*

The system comes with a "pegboard" or accounting board, imprinted checks in duplicate, journal sheets and sometimes special ledger sheets (depending on the style of system you select). First you set up your journal sheet (which is similar to an itemized check register).

When you write a check, the information is automatically transferred in one-write fashion to the duplicate check as well as the journal underneath. Then you simply write the amount of the check under the appropriate column. At the end of a monthly cycle (or when the journal fills up) use a calculator with a tape to add up all the columns vertically and horizontally to make sure you're in balance. The duplicate copy of the check is attached to the paid bill.

If you select a different one-write system, make sure the checks don't have a black carbon strip on the back, which can interfere with endorsements. Use one-write checks that provide high quality transfer of written information to journals, ledgers or duplicate copies beneath checks.

RESOURCE GUIDE

Note: See information on page 206 for abbreviations and software consumer tips. See this chapter, Chapters 2 and 11 and the index for other products.

FORMS, CHECKLISTS AND CHARTS

Abbot Office Systems (Figure 9-10) manufactures scheduling kits, boards and systems for projects, production, plant and office layout and applications for scheduling people and equipment. Free catalog.

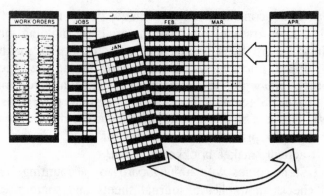

Figure 9-10. Abbot Office Systems Join-A-Panel lets you update your schedule by moving panels.

800/631-2233 or **908/938-6000**. Abbot Office Systems, 5012 Asbury Ave., Farmingdale, NJ 07727

ABC FlowCharter is an award-winning program that enables business people to clearly and quickly communicate ideas and information with ready-to-use diagrams such as flowcharts, timelines and network diagrams. This full-featured flowcharting program helps you graphically depict process flows in order to quickly analyze inefficiencies and bottlenecks in a process. Its breadth of diagramming functionality, along with its rich environment for customized application development, sets it apart from other diagramming tools. **Win.** $495. **800/676-3110** or 214/234-1769 Micro-grafx, 1303 E. Arapaho, Richardson, TX 75081

ABC SnapGraphics is an award-winning program that includes 21 templates to help business people easily create professional-looking presentation and business graphics such as popular business diagrams, basic flow charts, org charts, project timelines and network diagrams. **Win.** $495. **800/676-3110** or 214/234-1769 Micrografx

allCLEARIII for Windows is an award-winning, easy-to-use diagramming program that produces presentation-quality flowcharts, decisions trees and fishbone diagrams. This program gives you an optional script format that lets you focus more on the logic and content of your chart rather than on the actual graphical manipulation of the symbols. **Win.** $299. **800/338-1759** or 617/965-6755. CLEAR Software, Inc., 199 Wells Ave., Newton, MA 02159

Caddylak Tools for Time Management catalog offers a good selection of wall planning charts and boards. **800/523-8060** or **716/743-0500**. Cornerstone Direct Corp., 510 Fillmore Ave., Tonawanda, NY 14150

Day-Timers, Inc. offers a great selection of planning and scheduling forms as well as Marking Time dry-erase wall scheduling charts. **800/225-5005** or **610/266-9313**. Day-Timers, Inc., PO Box 27000, Lehigh Valley, PA 18003-9859

FastTrack Schedule lets you create and update presentation-quality Gantt chart schedules quickly and easily. **Mac** or **Win**. $299. **800/346-9413** or **703/450-1980**. AEC Software, 22611 Markey Court, Bldg. 113, Sterling, VA 20166

Magna Chart is a magnetic visual control board system that comes in different styles. **800/843-3399** or **314/843-9000**. Magna Visual, Inc., 9400 Watson Rd., St. Louis, MO 63126

Memindex Wall Planning Guides are write-on/wipe-off planners that come in a wide selection of styles. **800/828-5885** or **716/342-7890** Memindex, Inc., 149 Carter Street, Rochester, NY 14601

Delrina PerFORM for Windows is designed for users in small businesses, home offices and the corporate environment where forms are designed, filled in and printed. PerForm provides Delrina-Experts," which create professional-looking forms automatically. This award-winning easy-to-use product also includes on-line help demonstrations and the capability to enter and retain data directly in the forms. **Win** $129. **800/268-6082** or **408/363-2345**. Delrina Corporation, 6320 San Ignatio Avenue, San Jose, CA 95119-1209

PLANIT Board Systems Inc. makes a good selection of dry marker white boards. **800/222-7539** or **719/475-9500**. PLANIT Board Systems, Inc., 515 S. 25th St., Colorado Springs, CO 80904

Re-Markable boards are versatile, write-on-wipe-off wall charts. (See an example in Figure 9-11.) **201/784-0900**. Remarkable Products, Inc., 157 Veterans Drive, Northvale, NJ 07647

ROL-A-CHART visual control charts come in a dozen different models, all of which have a rotating sleeve that never runs out of space and allows for continuous scheduling. Different models are available to meet scheduling needs ranging from 13 weeks to two

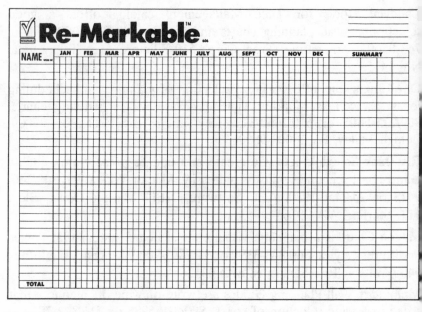

Figure 9-11. Project/Personnel Re-Markable board shows status of projects, assignments or personnel for the whole year on a weekly basis.

years. **800/824-0212** or 916/622-2437. ROL-A-CHART, PO Box 1810, Diamond Springs, CA 95619.

Static Images are white plastic easel pad sheets that cling to almost all walls. Use them as you would use a white board with dry-erase markers or with regular markers for permanent messages. They're made by Avery.

3M Post-it brand printed notes are handy forms that eliminate the need to write and rewrite requests for action. (You can also design and print your own custom Post-it messages—ask your printer.) Look, too, for the Post-it Designer Note Organizer to keep your Post-it notes handy, as well as your floppy disks.

TopDown Flowcharter is a highly-rated, easy-to-use, flexible program that creates flowcharts for a variety of business planning and documentation uses, including process flow and matrix diagrams, office procedure charts and network diagrams. Since it's cross-platform, you can share files on both Macintosh and Windows. **Mac** or **Win.** $199. **800/938-8900** or 713/298-1500. Kaetron Software Corp., 25211 Grogans Mill Rd., Ste. 260, The Woodlands, TX 77380

Visio is an award-winning, multipurpose diagramming program that lets you easily create flowcharts, org charts, network diagrams, space plans, marketing diagrams, technical schematics and more. It includes over 750 "SmartShapes," has OLE support and is customizable. **Win** and **Win 95**. $129. **800/446-3335** or 206/521-4500. Visio Corporation, 520 Pike St., Ste. 1800, Seattle, WA 98101.

PROJECT AND WORK MANAGEMENT SOFTWARE

Action Workflow Analyst helps managers to see and understand how work gets done, how long it takes, what it costs and who is involved. Managers can perform "what if" modeling by graphically mapping how the process works and making changes on screen to create alternatives. Through this process, they can see and evaluate the impact of changes before implementing them, saving time and money. In a recent *PC WORLD* article, medical director Dr. Edward Chaplin described how he and his "Process Action Team" used this software to greatly increase productivity in several key work processes. **Action Workflow Manager** and **Action Workflow Builder** further help you automate processes. **Win and DOS**. $495, Analyst; call for Manager and Builder pricing. **800/967-5356** or 510/521-6190. Action Technologies, 1301 Marina Village Parkway, Ste. 100, Alameda, CA 94501

AEC Information Manager is a project-oriented specialized database that allows you to schedule, organize and track project information and produce user-definable customized reports. **Mac**. $695. **800/346-9413** or 703/450-1980. AEC Software, 22611 Markey Court, Bldg. 113, Sterling, VA 20166

Business Insight is an MBA-ware, expert-system program that assists in developing and evaluating marketing strategies. It gathers information about the various factors in your business, your prospects, your product or service and your competition and then uses the knowledge of over 40 business and marketing experts to evaluate your activities. There are two versions—one for product-based businesses and one for service-based. **Win**. $495. **800/423-1228** or 512/251-7541. Business Resource Software, Inc., 2013 Wells Branch Pkwy., Ste. 305, Austin, TX 78728

CrossTies for Workgroups is a workgroup information manager that links pieces of information created on computer, such as a word processing document, an e-mail message or a spreadsheet, treats them as "objects" (which can be categorized and prioritized by type of project, activity, person or any other category) and lets you easily share these objects of information with coworkers. **Win.** $299, single user; $1800, 10 users. **214/407-9996.** CrossTies Software Corp.

DATA is a decision analysis program for analyzing, structuring and reporting on real-life business problems using graphical decisions trees and multi-attribute analysis. **Win and Mac.** $379. **800/254-1911** or 617/536-2128. TreeAge Software, PO Box 990207, Boston, MA 02199-0207

Decision Pad (see Figure 9-12) is an MBA-ware program that makes tough decisions clear and fast, whether you're dealing with a dozen criteria or a few hundred. It has special decision templates for such areas as purchasing, hiring, employee evaluations, vendor ratings and proposal prioritizing. **DOS.** $395; additional 5-user LAN Packs, $495 each. **800/237-4565** or 415/694-2900. Apian Software, PO Box 1224, Menlo Park, CA 94026-1224

```
(n)
  FILE  CRITERION  WEIGHT  ALTERNATIVE  EVALUATORS  DISPLAY  REPORT  QUIT
              ─Num Lock ON───────C:\GRAPHICS\COLLAT┌─────────────────────┐
                                Dell      Toshiba    G │ GRAPH SCORES       │
                              LiteNote  SuperBook   Pow│ THE BOTTOM LINE    │
                    WEIGHT                              │ PRINT MODEL        │
      Quoted Price    20        $1,599++   $3,999──    │ NOTES & RATINGS   ▲│
      Processor       15          386SX──   486DX++    │ INDIVIDUAL REPORT ■│
      Battery (hours) 15            4.5+      3.0       │ EXPERIMENTS        │
      Hard Disk (MB)  10           60.0─    120.0       │ WEIGHTING EFFECTS  │
      Weight (pounds) 10            3.8+      6.7       │ SCATTERPLOT        │
      Display Type    10      BW-Backlit-  CL-Active+ BW-│ FORMS            │
      Keyboard "Feel" 10          V-Good       ?       │ COVER NOTE      F7 │
  BASICS            ──    90        5.9    5.0-6.1      │ BRAINSTORM         │
      Trackball/Mouse  5           None   Built-in+  B │ MARGINS & CODES    │
      Internal Modem   5            NA-      Incl       └─────────────────────┘
  EXTRAS            ──    10        0.0     10.0         5.5       3.0
                        ══
  WGT TOTAL            100                                              ▼

  ┌─────────────────────────────────────────────────────────────────────┐
  │            score was:    5.3    4.8-5.8       5.6       5.7          │
  │            SCORE NOW:     5.3    5.5-6.5       5.6       5.7          │
  │            rank was:        3        3           2         1          │
  │            RANK IN 4:       4        1           3         2          │
  └─────────────────────────────────────────────────────────────────────┘
```

Figure 9-12. Using Decision Pad to help decide which notebook computer to buy

In Control is an award-winning Macintosh program that combines project outlining, scheduling and to-do-list management to help you plan, organize and track your projects, tasks and appointments. $84.95. **In Control for Workgroups** lets you and your team collaborate on group projects, tasks and activities by sharing outlines, calendars and to-do lists over networks. **Mac.** $149.95, single unit; $949.95, ten pack. **800/925-5615** or 617/776-1110. Attain Corp., 48 Grove St., Somerville, MA 02144

ManagePro for Windows is an MBA-ware best-seller that integrates goal and people management tools, a networked database and expert management advice. It provides a method of planning, delegating tasks and tracking business goals by promoting team collaboration. The latest version comes with helpful templates for different industries and also has workgroup features, including built-in e-mail. **Win.** Single, $199; volume pricing is available. **800/282-6867** or 510/654-4600. Avantos Performance Systems Inc., 5900 Hollis St., Ste. A, Emeryville, CA 94608

Microsoft Project is a sophisticated, yet easy-to-use, award-winning program that has workgroup capabilities and tight integration with Microsoft Office, Microsoft's suite of business applications. Cue Cards and Wizards provide lots of assistance. **Win** and **Mac.** $469. **800/426-9400** or 206/882-8080. Microsoft Corp., One Microsoft Way, Redmond, WA 98052-6399

PeopleScheduler is an award-winning program for managing employee schedules, profiles, attendance and time-away planning. It helps you schedule staff by availability and suitability, schedule breaks, be aware of conflicts, optimize work coverage and produce professional, printed schedules and reports. **Win.** $149. **800/598-1222** or 714/789-7300. Adaptiv Software Corp., 125 Pacifica, Ste. 250, Irvine, CA 92718-9601

Project KickStart is a project brainstorming and planning tool that asks key questions to help you conceptualize and organize a project from scratch. It links with major project management software programs. **DOS** and **Win.** $99.95. **800/678-7008** or 510/644-0694, Experience in Software, 2000 Hearst Ave., Ste. 202, Berkeley, CA 94709-2176.

Process Charter is "the flowcharter with brains"–both a flowcharting and process analysis tool. It's simple and flexible as a flowcharting package, yet will provide you with the intelligence you need to fully analyze your business processes. It will help you develop business process solutions. **Win.** $595. **800/549-9876** or 415/462-4200. Scitor Corp., 333 Middlefield Rd., Second Floor, Menlo Park, CA 94025

Project Scheduler is a good project management program that has its own graphical user interface, is easy to learn and use and gets high marks from computer magazine reviewers. **Win** and **Mac.** $695. **800/549-9876** or 415/462-4200. Scitor Corp., 333 Middlefield Rd., Second Floor, Menlo Park, CA 94025

TeamFlow (see Figure 9-13) provides an easy way for any manager or team leader to keep track of all the steps of a project as it relates (is "deployed") to members of the team. Worksheets can be multi-layered and as detailed as desired. Flowcharts can be easily edited. It includes Gantt and org charts. **Mac** and **Win.** $295. 800/647-1708 or 617/275-5258. CFM Inc., PO Box 353, Bedford, MA 01730. Internet: teamflow @ world.std.com

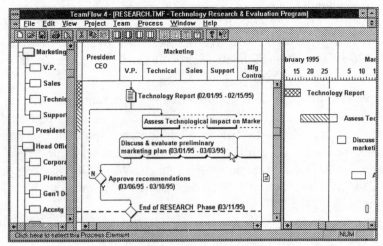

Figure 9-13. Three TeamFlow split windows showing an org chart (left), a flowchart of team members and their tasks and a project time line

Time Line is a comprehensive, award-winning project manager for planning and tracking multiple projects. **Win** and **DOS.** $699. **800/**

441-7234 or 408/253-9600. Symantec Corp., 10201 Torre Ave., Cupertino, CA 95014-2132

OTHER WORK MANAGEMENT TOOLS

AddressMate is an envelope printing program that grabs the inside address from a letter as it's being printed and sends the address to the printer, along with postal barcodes, to print the envelope. The Windows version can also do labels, name tags and business cards. **DOS and Win.** $29.95. **800/337-7460** or 510/237-7460. AddressMate Software, 6715 Canyon Trail, El Cerrito, CA 94530-1705

Crawford Slip Method (CSM) is a manual idea generator and organizing system that is great for people who like to physically manipulate, categorize and arrange ideas on slips of paper. CSM is particularly useful for assembling employee and procedure handbooks and manuals and can be used with groups of people whose ideas you want to tap. The CSM booklet and slip box are $3 each and the classification tray is $7. A book on CSM will be out soon. **213/740-0355** (USC School of Public Administration Business Office)

DAZzle Plus is an award-winning, easy-to-use envelope and label printing program. You can design and print mail pieces with graphics, text messages and barcodes using any Windows printer. It has a patented ZIP Code look-up feature you use with a modem that finds ZIP+4 codes and corrects addresses. **Win.** $79.95. **800/576-3279** or 415/321-2640. Envelope Manager Software, 247 High St., Palo Alto, CA 94301-1041.

FedEx Ship is a free, simple-to-use program that automates and simplifies the Federal Express shipping process, from printing air bills to locating packages. **Win and Mac.** Free! **800/463-3339**, Federal Express, Memphis, TN

PRD+ can help medical and legal transcriptionists as well as others who spend time typing double their typing speeds and production. PRD+ works with WordPerfect, WordStar, MS Word and practically every other word processing package. You type abbreviations instead of words, phrases or commands. Then, when you press the spacebar or punctuation key, the abbreviation is replaced with whatever it represents, up to 4,000 characters. PRD+ has been very favorably reviewed in *The New York Times*, *Fortune Magazine*, *PC Week* and many others. There are over 25 special editions of PRD+ for such applications as law, medicine, insurance and government. $349.95 to $579.95. 212/818-1144, Productivity Software International, Inc., 211 East 43rd Street, #2202, New York, NY 10017-4707

SCAN/PLAN's patented "QuickScan" technology using 3-by-5 or 5-by-8 cards plus 8½-by-11 pages allows the user to access information almost instantly. The system is perfect for organizing any information or activity, including projects, goals, records and tasks, as well as learning facts and skills. Other applications include writing, outlining speeches, notetaking and even creating company manuals. 800/SCANPLAN or 310/829-2888, SCAN/PLAN, Inc., PO Box 1662, Santa Monica, CA 90406

3M dispensers for Post-it brand notes are now available. Two handy dispensers permit easy, one-hand dispensing of special fan-folded Post-it notes. The Pop 'n Jot brand dispenser sits on the desktop. The C-300 Post-it brand pop-up note dispenser can be mounted anywhere, e.g., on your computer terminal or your filing cabinet.

3M Laser/Copier Labels, product number 7701, has one 8½-by-11-inch yellow label per sheet, which I use for presentations. The labels use repositionable adhesive. I print out presentation comments of any length, which were inputted in my computer, onto the label sheets. Then I cut up the comments and affix to them my presentation notes. What I have is the convenience of making my own customized, removable notes that can be moved easily from one presentation to the next. They're available in 25 label sheets per package from most office supply dealers.

3M tape products I couldn't live without: Post-it brand Correction and Cover-up Tape and Scotch brand Removable Magic Tape. Post-it Tape is a removable, opaque white tape for clean and quick copy blockout when making photocopies. Scotch brand Removable Tape is a transparent tape that attaches papers temporarily and removes easily without damaging the material it is attached to. You can write on it with ink, pencil or marker. Both tape products come in a variety of different widths.

ZIP+4 Diskette Coding is a one-time mailing list clean-up service offered by the U.S. Post Office. You can send up to 50,000 names from a mailing list on a diskette and they will convert the list to

tandard format, complete with nine-digit zip codes and corrected
treet and city names. Call **800/238-3150** and ask for the "ZIP+4
Diskette Coding program.

DATABASE PROGRAMS AND CONTACT MANAGERS

Address Book Plus is an easy-to-use, personal database manager that
organizes and prints quality pocket address books that fit many
organizers. **DOS. $38.95. 800/851-2917.** Misco Power Up! catalog

ACT! is a powerful, award-winning, easy-to-use contact management
program designed for sales and mobile professionals. It offers a
tightly integrated database, activities scheduler, word processor and
report generator. **Win, DOS, Mac, Net and HP 100LX.** $395; 4-
user network pack, $799. **800/441-7234** or 408/253-9600. Symantec
Corp., 10201 Torre Ave., Cupertino, CA 95014-2132

askSam is a highly-rated free-form database that combines database,
text-retrieval and word processing functions to manage both structured and free-form information. You can import information from
a variety of sources including e-mail and Internet or on-line research
and communications. You can easily search for any word or phrase
and generate database reports. An optional OCR module ($99) is
available for scanning directly into askSam. Network and electronic
publishing versions let you share and distribute information respectively. **Win, Net, Elec Pub.** $149.95; $1095 for five users; $995 for
Electronic Publisher. **800/800-1997** or 904/584-6590. askSam Systems,
PO Box 1428, Perry, FL 32347

GoldMine for Windows is an award-winning, comprehensive contact
manager for networks and remote users. This powerful enterprise-
wide business tool lets you automate common repetitive office tasks
with its "Automated Processes." Features include calendaring, e-mail,
mail merge letters, telemarketing, sales forecasting, lead tracking, fax/
merge, DDE links, wireless data synchronization, communication
server capability, sophisticated security, "remote transfer synchronization," report generator, user definable screens and fields and
unlimited additional contacts. **Win, Win 95 and Net.** $295 for single;
$895 for 5-user network version; site licenses available. **800/654-3526**
or 454-6800. Elan Software Corp., 17383 Sunset Blvd., Ste. 101,

Pacific Palisades, CA 90272. CompuServe Forum: GO: GOLDMINE BBS:310/459-3443.

INFO SELECT (formerly Tornado) is an award-winning, fast way to deal with notes, ideas, plans, contacts and all your random information. It's a personal information manager that is a free-form text database that lets you make miscellaneous notes on computer (instead of on paper slips) and search for them instantaneously. I you keep a lot of miscellaneous notes or ideas that are unrelated to each other or to particular projects or people, this could be a handy program. **Win** and **DOS.** $149.95. **800/342-5930** or 201/342-6518 Micro Logic Corp., PO Box 70, Hackensack, NJ 07602

Microsoft Access for Windows is an easy-to-use, fast relational database management system that's good for beginners, experienced users and even developers. More than 30 "wizards" simplify complex tasks and make routine tasks automatic. "Cue Cards" act as your own tutor. Workgroup features enable you to share information with others easily. **Win.** $339. **800/426-9400** or 206/882-8080. Microsoft Corp., One Microsoft Way, Redmond, WA 98052-6399

Now Contact is a full-featured contact manager that enables you to track your contacts and maintain a history of your interactions with them and can also be shared with colleagues. It integrates with Now Up-to-Date (see Chapter 2). **Mac and Net.** $69.95 (it's also bundled with Up-to-Date, $99.95). **800/237-2078** or 503/274-2800. Now Software, Inc., 921 S.W. Washington St., Ste. 500, Portland, OR 97205-2823.

Paradox is an award-winning, powerful, fast relational database program. **Win.** $795. 408/431-1000. Borland International, Inc., 100 Borland Way, Scotts Valley, CA 95066-3249

RECORD KEEPING SYSTEMS AND SOFTWARE

Acroprint Time Recorder Co. offers Badger 6000 and ATR 6000—an automated time keeping system that can tie into your computer for tracking and printing reports on time-and-attendance, labor distribution, job costing, payroll, overtime, tardiness, shift summaries and more. **DOS, Win and Net. 919/872-5800**, 5640 Departure Dr. Raleigh, NC 27604

BusinessWorks is an award-winning, easy-to-use-and-set-up, full-featured, modular accounting software system for small- to mid-sized companies. **DOS and Win.** $395 each for most modules. **800/854-3415** or 714/753-1222, State of the Art Accounting Software, 56 Technology, Irvine, CA 92718.

Kronos Time Accounting Systems link with your computer system to reduce time for payroll processing, increase payroll accuracy, improve payroll scheduling and control labor costs; they operate on most computer platforms. **800/225-1561** or 617/890-3232. Kronos Inc., 400 Fifth Ave., Waltham, MA 02154

Safeguard One-Write Bookkeeping System (available in 200 formats) is great for a private practice or a small office. With Safeguard, you keep a check journal and your tax records as you go. We've used this system for years. Safeguard also offers automated payroll services—Safepay (via telephone) and Safepay Connection (PC modem). Safeguard is also a major producer of business software computer forms and laser forms. 800/523-2422. Safeguard Business Systems, Inc. (Ft. Washington, PA)

Timeslips Deluxe for Windows is a top-rated time and billing system that helps any size company account for its time and expenses, produce customized billing and generate reports. The latest features include a Billing Assistant to reduce mistakes when producing bills; a customizable Navigator interface that provides quick, easy access to the program's functions and The Timeslips Connection for long distance telephone expense billing. **Timeslips Deluxe Remote** ($79.95) is for use in laptops, notebook and non-networked computers. **TimeSheet Professional** ($199.95) is a network-based time sheet system that links with project management software. From $179.95 to $699.95, **Windows** versions; **DOS** versions, $99 to $599; **Mac** versions, $299.95 to $699.95. **800/285-0999** or 214/248-9232. TIMESLIPS Corporation, 17950 Preston Rd., Ste. 800, Dallas, TX 75252

10

WORKING
WITH OTHERS

Quick Scan: If you have customers, co-workers or both, you need to read this chapter. Mastering the other chapters without mastering this one will leave you organized, but working in a vacuum. The real purpose of organization in today's competitive marketplace is to find better ways of working with others. The other chapters focused largely on you as an individual peppered with a few workgroup solutions. In this chapter you'll discover more ways to bring others into the fold by first building a philosophy of quality, service and teamwork.

The first nine chapters focused largely on what you as an individual can do in the work place. As a consultant and a trainer, I have found this is generally the best place to start. But for dramatic results, you need to spread the word so that everyone with whom you work has a chance to be their best and make exciting contributions toward helping your organization—whether it be your ffice, department, supplier base or company—reach its goals.

WHY EVERYONE YOU WORK WITH
IS YOUR CUSTOMER

ou have probably heard about the importance of customer service
nd customer satisfaction. You may not, however, realize the extent
o which it applies to you and your work. The point is, no matter
vhat kind of work you do or organization you work for, customer
ocus needs to be the bottom line.

To compete and be profitable in today's world economy, your
rganization can no longer be doing "business as usual." The old
naxim, "if it ain't broke, don't fix it," isn't true any more. Change
; the name of the game and to stay competitive in business, you
ieed to **improve continuously** in order to **provide quality goods or
services for your customers.**

Notice I've highlighted several key words. "Customers" need to be
our primary focus. There are two kinds of customers for every
rganization: **external** and **internal.** Some consider external custom-
rs to be the most important. They're the ones who are paying for
our goods or services. They're the ones you need to satisfy first to
tay in business.

Even the federal government now has customers. A friend of
nine who works for Social Security showed me a report written by
/ice President Al Gore called "From Red Tape to Results: Creating
 Government That Works Better and Costs Less" and the following
vords appear: "...we are going to make the federal government
ustomer friendly. A lot of people don't realize that the federal
overnment has customers. We have customers. The American
eople."

Internal customers are the team members with whom you work
o provide the goods or services for your external customers. They
ould be office co-workers, contacts in another department or
ivision or part of your supplier base.

For many, internal customers, are a close second. That's not so,
owever, for Hal Rosenbluth, CEO of the third largest travel man-
gement company in the world, Rosenbluth International, which was
eatured in *INC. Magazine* and was a Tom Peters Service Company

of the Year award winner. Rosenbluth, who calls his internal customers "associates," says, "We don't believe our customers can come first unless our associates come first. If we have happy people here, then they're free to concentrate only on our clients." Stated another way, if your internal customers aren't happy, chances are good your external customers won't be either.

Ralph Stayer, CEO for Johnsonville Foods Inc. in Sheboygan, Wisconsin, talks about employee happiness as a starting point.

> At Johnsonville, we want people to be happy, but never satisfied. We want people to see themselves becoming something. People should be continuously learning and striving to make something bigger and better of themselves. We try to make sure that happens. We aren't making just sausage here. I use the business to make great people. I don't use people to make a great business. If everyone is moving forward and working together, then the sausage will take care of itself.

So in a very real sense *everyone* with whom you work or interact is your customer. Even if you're a sole proprietor, you simply don't work in a vacuum. Once you recognize this fact, you've begun to get on board the quality revolution that is sweeping the globe.

"We are in the Quality Revolution and it's every bit as critical as the Industrial Revolution," so says Lloyd Dobyns, writer/narrator of the PBS program "Quality...or Else."

Even 99.9 percent quality isn't good enough; the following would result if organizations in the U.S. abided by only 99.9 percent quality: 1,314 phone calls would be misplaced in the next minute; 22,000 checks would be deducted from the wrong bank accounts in the next hour; 20,000 prescriptions would be written incorrectly this year; and 315 entries in *Webster's Third New International Dictionary* would be misspelled.

Focusing on quality products and/or services leads to and will increase customer satisfaction.

Quality, or more precisely **Total Quality Management**, is more than a buzz word or a fad; it's a way of doing business that permeates every aspect of a business. My colleague, Dr. Susan Resnick West, has summarized Total Quality Management as a comprehensive business strategy that 1) focuses on the customer, 2) focuses on

he work process and 3) develops the organization so that the first
wo are possible.

To **focus on the customer** means to provide service and quality
as the customer sees them. You stay close to your customers (both
external and internal) by listening to them, asking them questions
and working diligently to solve their problems. Customer focus
means following through, doing what you say—which all involves
good organizational skills and systems.

Oddly enough, some companies seem to provide just the opposite
of customer service and satisfaction, especially if a "problem" arises.
My husband just bought a new computer system by mail order
through a company he'd happily done business with before. It seems
they've grown a bit too much and aren't customer responsive anymore. The company made a mistake in fulfilling the order and my
husband was the one who had to pay for it in wasted time trying
to get the mistake corrected. The person who took the order
claimed he was unable, "given the way things work at this company,"
to resolve it, and so my husband was left scrambling to fix it himself.
I'm sure tempted to tell you the name of the company, as so many
angry customers will often do.)

What galled my husband even more was that not one person at
the company even empathized with an apology. "Service is Sometimes Saying You're Sorry" is the apt title of a consumer affairs article that I had clipped when researching this chapter. Not admitting
any wrongdoing coupled with no apology and no attempt to resolve
the problem is a good way to lose new and old customers.

And that brings us to the importance of **customer retention**. It
costs six times as much to attract new customers as to retain existing
ones. A study cited in the *Harvard Business Review* said that
customer retention has a substantial impact on profitability, with the
increase in dollar value of repeat customers ranging from 25 to 85
percent. Customer retention may, in fact, account for the biggest
source of future sales growth.

By the way, only 30 percent of customers with problems complain
they just take their business elsewhere) and only two to five percent of complaints ever get voiced to the headquarters level. I, for
one, have faxed this page to the president of the computer company
my husband just dealt with.

I like a sign that hangs at Ed Debevic's Restaurant which reads "At Ed's, we promise Friendly and Courteous Service at Reasonable Prices. If for any reason we fail to live up to this promise—please don't tell anyone."

Focus on the work process is the means by which you provide customer service. It's examining the effectiveness of your organizational skills, tools and systems to check whether they're the best means for providing goods and services on time, within budget and to the customer's satisfaction. Work process has been the main focus of this book.

My goal in faxing the computer company president was not to affix blame on anyone but rather to encourage the company to get to the root cause of the problem. The question the company needs to ask is, "What is it about the system (or the company) that allows this kind of problem to be handled in this fashion?"

Identify and eliminate inefficient work processes, especially those that stick out like a sore thumb. I remember many years ago standing endlessly in a hotel checkout line, while the woman ahead of me noticed one particularly inefficient hotel clerk. She commented, "He never gets anything right. And it takes him a long time to get it wrong." There has to be a better way of doing things such as hotel checkout (and of course, many hotels have finally innovated "express checkout" systems that save valuable customer time—both the internal and external customers' time).

Developing the organization involves upper and middle management's genuine commitment to quality and customer service as well as their support of all internal customers. An openness to change and continuous quality improvement is evident at *all* levels of such an organization. In a quality-conscious organization you'll see a driving emphasis on training, communication, innovation, flexibility, employee involvement and teamwork.

Nordstrom epitomizes such an organization and even their organization chart reflects it. Customers (external) appear at the *top*, followed by sales and sales support people (the internal customers who work closest to the external customers), then come the department managers, followed by the store managers, buyers and merchandise managers and finally the board of directors are at the bottom.

And according to a two-year Labor Department study, companies that train workers, involve them in decisions and give them a stake in the business are more profitable than those that do not. The Secretary of Labor said the study shows the "surest way to profits and productivity is to treat employees as assets to be developed rather than costs to be cut."

Look at where you work. See if there's at least a spark of *caring* about quality, service and external/internal customers. If so, you should be able to use at least a few of the ideas in the following sections to help develop your organization and create the right climate and context for customer-focused continuous improvement to occur.

DOWNSIZING DILEMMAS:
HOW TO DO MORE WITH LESS

Just how can you provide *more* customer service (or more of anything) when you have fewer people around and a shrunken budget? It's a challenge all right, but ironically we have the tools to make it work. All this quality stuff comes into play because it forces those who are left to seriously examine how they get things done and to eliminate unnecessary steps, tasks, activities and projects. Doing some serious work flow analysis is essential (refer to Chapter 9's Resource Guide for some flowcharting products that may help you). And the progressive companies, the ones that will survive, are doing it in cross-functional teams, in the "flattened hierarchies" that Tom Peters has been yelling about for years.

A flattened hierarchy brings internal and external customers closer together and problems come into the foreground faster and demand immediate attention. If you have team players around who accept change and are interested in solving problems, your organization will most likely survive. It's essential to have some team building, work process and group dynamics training and coaching either before, during and/or after downsizing.

The notion of "it's not my job" goes completely out the window, along with the concept of a "job." The term "work" is replacing the term "job," which harkens back to the Industrial Revolution, in which work was much more narrowly defined. So, you'll need to change your perception of your work—which, now will provide you more variety, less clarity and more opportunities than you may have time for!

According to author and management consultant William Bridges, many people simply don't have one job anymore; they have "portfolio careers" that consist of a mixture of part-time jobs or a full-time position supplemented with freelance work or self-employment. Portfolio careers are in large part the result of downsizing coupled with new technology.

Yes, there is more work with downsizing, but be careful about getting trapped into long work weeks. Avoid "face time," the assumption that you have to sit at your desk or be at work for longer hours, sometimes before as well as after work. Face time also assumes in some businesses that you would never leave the office before a certain time, say, 8:00 p.m. Face time can be devastating to not only one's personal life but to productivity as well.

I recently had the chance to visit a large corporate client of mine, post-downsizing. It was sad, on the one hand, to know that many of my former contacts and clients, were gone. But it was heartening, on the other, to see the teamwork and empowerment that was taking place. The work that I had begun before the downsizing, was being implemented and there was a hunger for more. My clients are now solving problems and making decisions that were previously reserved for higher levels in the company.

One *Wall Street Journal* story said it concisely: "Teamwork is in." The story went on to cite David Ehlen, the CEO of Wilson Learning in Eden Prairie, Minn., a management-training firm that has studied 4,500 teams in more than 500 companies. Ehlen indicated that advancement will be measured not only by your individual achievements but also by your ability to be a team player.

Team members must examine goals, priorities and work processes and become skilled at making decisions and implementing ideas. I think Speaker Francie Schwartz' definition of a "TEAM" sums up what we're after—Total Effectiveness of All Members.

SUREFIRE WAYS
TO INCREASE QUALITY AND TEAMWORK
WHETHER OR NOT YOU'RE THE BOSS

There's no great mystery to producing a winning team that offers quality goods or services. It takes a consistent, organized approach that addresses three key areas: communication, employee involvement and training.

Underlying these areas, however, should be a genuine foundation of *caring about people*. Without this foundation, many of the ideas in this section could be perceived as insincere and manipulative. It doesn't matter how many great, innovative ideas you introduce into your organization if an uncaring attitude exists. As the saying goes, "People don't care how much you know until they know how much you care."

COMMUNICATE WITH INTERNAL
AND EXTERNAL CUSTOMERS

People in the workplace often take communication for granted and assume that enough of it goes on. There's plenty of talking and memo writing every day. And just look at all the communication toys that they're using—from voice mail to electronic mail (e-mail). But the sheer quantity of communication that takes place doesn't insure quality in the communication.

Quality communication is a two-way street. First, **keep people informed**. As Thomas Jefferson observed, "When you don't keep people informed, you get one of three things: rumor, apathy or revolution." (And he ought to know.)

You may have noticed how infrequently people in workgroups really communicate with each other to keep one another informed—even of their simple comings and goings. It's especially important to keep a receptionist, assistant or office manager informed, particularly if they have any dealings with external customers. Lack of basic, up-to-date information about the availability of key personnel can create a credibility gap in the organization. Decide who needs to know what and how and when they will get that information. A simple in-out wall chart may do the trick or e-mail messages or the Day-Timer Message Center for a small office or a home office; whichever tool you choose for keeping tabs on people's whereabouts, use it consistently.

For any team that works closely together, such as a manager and an assistant, I almost always recommend a five- or ten-minute daily morning meeting. Sometimes it's not always possible to meet every day to go over things such as the day's or week's calendar, key projects, mail and messages but if the team makes a commitment to meet and does so more than half the time, there's all that much more communication taking place.

Communicate clearly, concisely and positively, whenever possible. Ask yourself as you begin any communication, what's the key question, its deadline and/or time frame–and be as specific as possible. Try to use numbers to add clarity to convey how much time you have ("I have three minutes to talk"), how much time you'll need, how many things you want to discuss, etc.

Don't forget to compliment key colleagues you work with, ideally at least once a day. But of course, you must be sincere. The power of a compliment can help transform a working (or personal) relationship. I have seen it happen in my consulting work.

Be positive and open about possibilities rather than negative and close-minded. Instead of saying, "I don't know" and leaving it at that, you might add, "But I'll find out." Instead of saying, "We can't do that" or "we never have done it that way," try "Let's see what we can do."

There may be times when you'll need to give some "constructive criticism" but even then, you can approach it positively as a way to help someone else grow and develop. Become aware, too, of different communication styles and preferences. Communications research indicates that people like to receive communication in the way they're most likely to deliver it. Male/female communication styles are useful to study and apply; Deborah Tannen has done some excellent work in this area (see her books *Talking From Nine to Five* and *You Just Don't Understand*).

Use multiple channels of communication but limit them, if possible. Multiple channels can make communication more interesting and less likely to fall prey to distortion or bias from information that's conveyed through only one channel or source. Such channels can include any of the following: mail, memos, meetings, faxes, company publications, co-workers, customers, bulletin boards, voice mail and e-mail.

Be on the lookout for communication channels that are innovative, creative or humorous. Use color-coding whenever possible to flag or categorize messages. Even the U.S. president is using color-coding on a "message calendar" that highlights key topics to discuss with his aides. You'll see different colored bars on each of the calendar's days: purple for foreign policy, orange for the economy, blue for social policy and green for government reform.

To avoid information overload, **beware of using too many channels or communication tools.** Most of my bigger corporate clients provide each employee with several means by which they can communicate with others inside and outside the company. The problem is workers spend a lot of time checking *all* of these communication channels. They may also try to use the preferred communication channel the receiver wants to receive messages. It gets very complicated and time-consuming. I developed a survey for a large corporate client in which I had all members of one department indicate their preferences, both when sending and receiving communications. Then I charted them all out so everyone could see one another's preferences. You could do such a survey with your workgroup, maybe even agreeing to reduce or eliminate certain communication channels.

Keeping people informed is only half of the communication story. To complete the story, **ask people what they think.** This needs to happen regularly for both internal and external customers. Be prepared, however, that once you ask people what they think, you really *listen*, take the information seriously and *act on it*.

Conducting a survey, such as the one I just described, is an excellent way to see what's on people's minds. Keep surveys as simple as possible. Design a major benefit into the survey–why should anyone want to take the time to complete it? Tell survey participants *what's in it for them*.

Companies are surveying both their external and internal customers. Some companies are involved in a "360-degree feedback" process to see how they're doing, which may include surveys by external customers, employee performance appraisals, "upward appraisals" (subordinates' evaluations of their superiors) and "peer appraisals." The latter are more typical of companies with a leaner flattened hierarchical structure.

Insurance agent Don Gambrell uses a clever, two-sided, Farmer. Insurance form/response letter to encourage customers to renew their policy and/or communicate with him about why they haven' done so. On the left half of the page is a brief, friendly letter called "This is My Side" asking for the customer to respond to the other half, called "This is Your Side," which has six different quick responses to check off. An SASE is also enclosed. He's used this form for over 20 years because it works.

"The President's Luncheon" is one way the Visions Federal Credit Union in Endicott, New York, asks employees what they think Every month, six or seven employees are chosen at random to have lunch with the president and discuss any topics they feel are important to them, to the credit union or to management.

The suggestion box can be a good way to get feedback but one department discovered a new twist. This was a busy mail and phone department, where phones rang off the hook and ten disgruntled employees didn't work well together. The department replaced the suggestion box with a "Gripe Box," and employees completed "Gripes and Complaints" cards anonymously. Though the Gripe Box sounds negative, it worked because it reflected how people were feeling and gave them a chance to vent those feelings. Gripes and complaints were handled openly at department meetings, solutions were generated and today everyone gets along very well.

One small business owner I know of offers an open dialogue for her employees every other month over pizza. She takes them out for pizza and then they meet for two hours. The first hour is an open gripes session about anything and anybody, including management. The second hour is spent on positive comments and solutions to gripes.

Just staying close to your customers and having your eyes and ears open can be a very effective way to find out what people think; convey that information back to your customers and you have real two-way communication. That's just what a local caterer-restaurant owner did. Zabie Vourvoulis published a beautiful, two-color brochure for her customers, in which she affirmed her "commitment to quality" and acknowledged customers' contributions.

We struggle constantly with the issue of service and how best to fill your needs. Many times, small suggestions or comments from you have led to big changes (paper biodegradable disposables for instance). We've also purchased new, more comfortable and sturdier stools, and we've developed an interesting, reasonably priced dinner menu...Your support has been wonderful. It's encouraging to know that effort and caring have a place in this fast-paced world of ours. We certainly appreciate yours and we hope that ours shows every day.

Standardize communication routines, whenever possible. See if you have any specific routines you're currently using in your own office, your workgroup and/or your company concerning communications—e.g, how the phone is answered, by whom and when calls are returned; how visitors are greeted and by whom; how faxes are handled and how often e-mail is checked. Do you have any procedures in writing? If not, now's a good time to start! Perhaps one person could put a draft on computer and the workgroup team members could modify it as necessary.

Develop and practice good listening skills. Listening is crucial to good communication skills and customer service. Yet recent studies show that 75 percent of what we hear is heard incorrectly and of the remaining 25 percent, we forget 75 percent of it within weeks or days. The average listener has an immediate retention level of only 50 percent; within 24 to 48 hours, the retention level drops to 25 percent. To be an "active listener," which is the most effective kind of listener, requires concentration and the ability to absorb information, restate accurately what you've heard, ask clarifying questions and evaluate the whole process objectively.

Personalize your communication, whenever possible. There are certain words people can't hear enough: their own names and "thank you." Take time to thank people for their thoughtfulness, hard work or good ideas. Sitting down to write a thank-you note is such a simple, but very powerful method of communication. It shows that the recipient is worth your time and you're organized enough to make time for it. Writing quick, two- or three-sentence notes on personalized note cards can be accomplished easily during spare moments, such as waiting in a doctor's office or sitting on a plane.

(By the way, it's more effective to send a note right away but better to send a note late than not at all.)

Learning and using people's names can have a big impact on opening up communication. I recently had a dramatic example of seeing that it's "all in a name." Around 4:30 every afternoon, a postal carrier makes the last pick-up at several boxes near our office. Occasionally, I will go out to the boxes right at 4:30, when the postal truck arrives and hand my mail to the carrier.

Over the years, there have been several carriers, each of whom was very friendly. This year a new carrier assumed the route but he seemed very different. He was very serious and wouldn't look up when you handed him mail. He appeared almost upset that you were breaking his routine. He seemed, in a word, anti-social. Normally, I would have introduced myself and made small talk but I figured that was a real waste of time with this guy.

Weeks went by and I avoided making any contact with the carrier. Being normally a very outgoing individual, I decided one day to simply introduce myself. Much to my surprise, when I told him my name and learned his was Richard, he really lit up and began to talk. Every time I see him now, he calls me by name and has something pleasant to say.

Richard is an internal customer who is part of my supplier base. The service he provides makes it possible for me to be of service to my external customers. Because he's a part of my team, it's important to be able to communicate with him.

ACTIVELY INVOLVE EMPLOYEES

Once you've begun implementing effective communication strategies, you've opened the door to employee involvement, the secret to quality and teamwork. Research indicates a direct correlation between high employee involvement and motivation, quality, productivity and profitability. Let's look at some ways for you and all employees to get involved.

Start by zeroing in on the **mission of your company or organization.** Everybody should have a copy of the company mission statement, as well as the company's guiding values. Mission and values statements are often buried in long-range planning documents that the upper management team may have generated. Progressive companies distribute copies of these statements to all employees, reprint them in company publications and may even make special posters that appear around the company. You should also share your mission and values with external customers. See Figure 10-1 for an example of the mission statement and guiding values for PDQ, a personnel agency in Los Angeles.

Figure 10-1. PDQ PERSONNEL SERVICES, INC. MISSION AND VALUES

Mission:

We serve the business community in a sincere and thorough manner by providing timely, cost effective results in meeting their regular, temporary and long-term staffing needs. We continually invest our talents to establish and maintain long-term relationships with both our clients and employees. Through innovation and education we strive to maintain the competitive edge.

Values:

Heritage of Excellence—We maintain the highest levels of professionalism to be the best we can.

Customer Service—We provide all of our customers with quality personnel services by treating each of their staffing needs as if it were our own.

Employee Responsiveness—We treat people in all positions with fairness and dignity. We provide opportunities for earned growth to reach their potential both inside and outside the organization. Our people are proud of their high standards and are equitably rewarded.

Civic Spirit—The community benefits from both our individual and company commitments to continually participate in the community's growth. Our people are educated and enriched through community involvement.

Adaptability—We test and try new concepts and services. We understand that one key strength in maintaining the competitive edge is our ability to identify and benefit from change.

Teamwork—We communicate openly and with trust in mutually pursuing opportunities and meeting challenges. Each person plays an integral role in the success of the PDQ team.

If your company has no written mission statement or guiding values, suggest that a committee or action team be formed to develop them. This group could have representatives from all different levels or departments in the company. This is a great way to build participation in the company and co-ownership of the mission statement and values. And ideally, the mission statement and guiding values will include the importance of employee involvement.

THE SPECIAL ROLE OF MANAGERS

If you're a manager or you work for one, recognize that the role of the manager today must be that of **team leader, teacher and coach** who facilitates employee participation. Old, autocratic, traditional management styles of "do it my way" no longer work. Interesting enough, a recent study showed that women more naturally exhibit the kind of nontraditional traits needed in today's managers—the ability to share information and power, encourage employee participation and demonstrate how both individual, personal goals may be reached while attaining organizational goals.

Today's managers and leaders would do well to embrace the following statement by John McDonnell, chairman of McDonnell Douglas, about operating with a "fundamental belief that everyone wants to do a good job and that overall performance will be greatly enhanced if people are assisted, coached, trained and supported rather than controlled."

According to management consultant and author Lee Cheaney, today's managers should also "manage on the behavior of 95 percent of employees and not on the five percent who cause problems." He suggests dealing with that five percent promptly and fairly, spending the bulk of your time developing your team.

To develop the 95 percent, today's manager needs to help form work teams that have real authority to make decisions and to act. One General Mills cereal plant has given such authority to its work teams and has realized a 40 percent higher productivity rate compared with traditionally managed groups.

We're seeing this kind of shift taking place in manufacturing circles as well as in service areas and in the office. Research indicates that workers are happier, too, with more involvement. Studies indicate that workers want much more than a paycheck and when ranking job factors, the "money" comes after such things as honesty and ethical behavior of management, open communications, the opportunity to develop skills, being able to contribute, the nature of the work, the desire to have their work and contributions recognized, work schedule flexibility and the effect of the job on one's personal/family life.

Managers today have the opportunity to address these factors through open communications and a participative management style that gives more responsibility to workers and work teams.

Participatory managers encourage their people to make decisions nd come up with solutions of their own. Sun Microsystems CEO 'cott G. McNealy jokes, "When our people have difficulty making decision, then I threaten to make the decision. That notion gets 'eople scared enough to make the right decision themselves."

When I presented a seminar to a credit union group in Portland, 'ne manager shared his policy, "Don't come to me with a problem 'nless you have at least two solutions."

In today's business climate, effective managers need to become 'eaders. They need to be proactive, embrace change and innovation, 'e passionate about their work, provide training and development 'pportunities and genuinely care about their people.

TEAM MEETINGS

Traditional meetings, as someone once put it, are all too often a 'lace where minutes are taken and hours are lost. They've also been place where, according to one recent survey, many participants 'eel uncomfortable freely sharing their opinions and believe that 'nost meetings are dominated by hidden agendas.

Participatory team meetings are an important way for workers to 'evelop their skills and make contributions. They're also important 'or dealing with problems, making decisions by consensus, promoting 'ommunication, developing leadership, building commitment, sharing 'nformation, setting goals and improving operations.

To improve your meetings, why not have a meeting on meetings? Have your work team come prepared to share at least one idea on how to make more productive, participatory meetings.

Consider having a training session on meetings. I recently conducted such a session for one company and used an entertaining, informative video called "Meetings, Bloody Meetings" starring English actor/comedian John Clease (available from Video Arts, 800/553-0091).

In a nutshell, here are the ten tips I teach about effective meetings:

1. **Every meeting should have a stated purpose or goal** that is determined in advance of the meeting and that is defined in a **prepared agenda** to which participants have had a chance to contribute. The agenda should be distributed far enough in

advance so participants can prepare. Each agenda item should
be as specific as possible, should ideally include the individual
who's introducing it and should cite the purpose of the item at
the meeting, e.g, "For Discussion," "For Information" or "For
Decision." One company I know distributes a memo/survey
before each staff meeting that solicits two agenda items. It
reads in part, "Please write down two things that you would
like to hear talked about, questions that need answering, topics
of interest, etc.," and participants are asked to leave the
completed sheet in a specific person's in box.

2. **Limit the size of the group.** Include only those who need to
   be there. Four to seven people is an ideal number of people
   for a planning or problem-solving meeting. A training session
   or informational meeting could handle many more.

3. Ideally **arrange participants in a circle to encourage more
   participation** and provide refreshments to set a more informal
   atmosphere.

4. **List start and end times for the meeting on the agenda and
   stick to them.** It may be helpful to use a countdown timer to
   stay on schedule.

5. Each meeting should **have a facilitator who keeps the meeting
   moving,** clarifies and summarizes key points, acknowledges
   contributions of participants by name and ends the meeting on
   time. The facilitator can provide a quick verbal summary at the
   end, reviewing the goals of the meeting and how participants
   contributed to reaching those goals. To build leadership, use a
   "rotating facilitator," a different person from the work team to
   lead each meeting.

6. **Have a recorder take minutes** that reflect key points, decisions,
   action items and the responsible participants. Minutes should
   be prepared and distributed to attendees within a few days of
   the meeting. Underline action items, deadlines and names of
   responsible individuals so that they stand out. Have a different
   recorder at each meeting.

7. Have either the facilitator or someone else **use a flip chart,
   overhead projector or a computer with a large screen to record
   key ideas** and make them visible to everyone at the meeting.
   Such an ongoing record serves as a "group memory," is useful
   reference for the recorder when preparing minutes and can be

used at future meetings. Visual tools also can help improve retention of the information by 50 percent. 3M Post-it Easel Pads offer all the benefits of Post-it notes in a large size that lets you easily and safely post and remove these sheets; this product also doubles as a flip chart pad that attaches to most easel stands and transports easily with a convenient built-in handle. The Paper Direct catalog (800/A-PAPERS) has some handy meeting and presentation tools and accessories for visuals—The Cobra Overhead Projector, Casio Board Copy (a portable copier that photographs such things as white boards and prints black and white copies), Flip Frame Overhead Protectors and preprinted overhead transparencies and matching handouts.

8. Include several **standing agenda items** that appear at each meeting. **Action items, decisions and delegations listed in the minutes** should be brought forward to appear **on the next meeting's agenda** for a status report follow-up. Always include time on the agenda for **successes and accomplishments** that have occurred since the last meeting.

9. **Be flexible and creative** with your meetings and **use different formats** that are appropriate. For manager/assistant teams I recommend **short, but frequent daily meetings** that take no more than five to ten minutes. Certainly a formal agenda for such meetings would be inappropriate but a "standing agenda," that covers routine items, such as the day's schedule, correspondence, telephone calls and certain ongoing clients, would be a good way to standardize and streamline this business meeting.

10. **Keep meetings confidential.** Confidentiality breeds trust and encourages participants to open up more fully.

To solve problems and build teamwork, **use "Quality Circle" meetings**, also called "brainstorming sessions" and "Nominal Group Technique." Such meetings (and parts within the meetings) have a time limit and typically include four parts: 1) identification and definition of the problem (because as Charles Kettering once said, "A problem well-stated is a problem half-solved"); 2) in round-robin fashion, contribution by each participant of brainstorming suggestions, alternatives and solutions without discussion; 3) discussion and evaluation of the brainstormed ideas; and 4) selection of one to three ideas for implementation. Number 4 can be done by a simple show of hands but a more effective way is to use a preprinted voting card that includes a place to indicate your choice, as well as your priority ranking or the weight you assign to your choice. For example, you might vote for idea D and give it a priority ranking of only 2 (on a scale of 1 to 5, where 5 is high) because you don't feel so strongly about this particular idea.

Another way to do a problem-solving meeting is to have each participant zero in on one key problem area and generate some solutions *before* the meeting. Use a simple survey with three questions: 1) In the coming year (or any other designated period of time), what would you most like to see changed here at this company (or substitute department or other workgroup designation)?; 2) Describe how that change can come about by listing specific solutions and steps that need to be taken; 3) How much time will you contribute to make this change happen and what *exactly* will you do to help bring about this change?

A solutions-orientation to any meeting keeps the energy on a more positive and focused level. You may even want to avoid using the word "problem," substituting instead the word "item," "idea" or "challenge." Try to encourage participants to state comments, ideas or questions as positively as possible and discourage negativity or criticism. It's an effective way to run a meeting.

Consider using graphics whenever possible in your meetings. One Wharton School of Business study showed that the average business meeting with graphics was 28 percent shorter than those without graphics. Maybe a picture is indeed worth a thousand words.

As a professional speaker, I pay close attention to meeting room logistics. I avoid long, narrow rooms and cavernous rooms. I love well-lit spaces. I always find out where the heating and air-conditioning controls are in advance (or who is responsible for controlling them). Whenever possible I place myself opposite the entrance to the room. I prefer a round table but if I get stuck with a long, rectangular one, I place myself at the head if I wish to present more of an authoritarian, expert position and in the middle on one side, if it's a more informal, participatory meeting.

OTHER EMPLOYEE INVOLVEMENT PROGRAMS

Many companies today have a whole variety of **employee incentive** or **employee recognition programs** that encourage and reward employee-generated, innovative, cost-saving ideas; a superior work effort; surpassed performance goals; and employee longevity.

Forms of recognition vary widely from certificates of appreciation (University of California, San Diego Medical Center has a Pride-O-Gram) to cash and prize incentive awards. After 61 years of offering cash incentives to employees for cost-saving ideas, Florida Power & Light (FPL) discovered employees overwhelmingly preferred premiums; a staggering 52 percent of FPL's 15,000 employees participated in its new premium program the first year compared to a two percent participation rate while using cash incentives.

There is a difference between "recognition" and "incentive" programs and the types of items that are given to employees. An incentive program is designed specifically to motivate employees, whereas a recognition program shows appreciation and recognizes achievement after the fact. In your organization, it may be more appropriate to use one type of program alone or to use a combination.

Some companies, one newspaper story reported, are rewarding employee risk-taking even to the extent of doing things wrong because such companies are encouraging employees to *think* for themselves and try to solve company problems. Esso Resources Canada has an "Order of the Duck" award consisting of a wooden duck's head mounted on a plunger; the duck's head symbolizes vision and the plunger represents sticking your neck out. The award goes to an employee who challenges management or does something without the boss's approval.

Some employee recognition programs are more successful than others. The sincerity and caring on behalf of management may have much to do with how these programs are perceived and hence, their success. In addition, the programs should reflect the mission and values of the company.

These programs need to be spiced up from time to time as they can become old hat in a hurry. And what works well in one company may not work well in yours.

Survey employees to see what they think of such programs and the program awards and what changes they'd like to make. (You may find, for example, that employees rate a trip to Hawaii for two as a much greater incentive than an equivalent cash award.)

If you're a manager who wants to keep track of the various ways you recognize good work from your employees, consider keeping a chart form like the one manager Susan Steven keeps for her 150 employees (see Figure 10-2). It's also a good way to spot outstanding personnel at a glance.

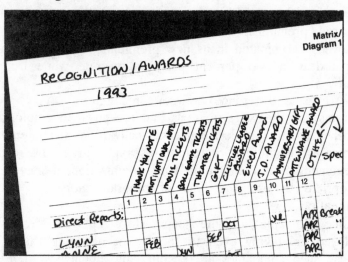

Figure 10-2. One manager's use of the Time/Design matrix diagram form to keep track of the ways she recognizes her employees' good work each year

Performance management in which employees set and evaluate their own performance objectives is an important way to involve employees. Be sure to build in recognition and reward for good and/or improved performance.

As a part of their performance management process, the Tennessee Teachers Credit Union in Nashville has each employee complete a thought-provoking, two-page, self-evaluation form for past and future performance. The form asks employees to list their performance objectives for the coming 12 months, any necessary behavior changes they'll need to make and significant achievements during the past 12 months. In addition, employees are asked to "stretch" themselves—to make a special effort to accomplish omething in the next 12 months and identify what that effort will e. There is also a chart for listing strengths, weaknesses, problems nd opportunities.

Finally, beware of too much employee involvement, especially uring the cold and flu season. One story in the *Wall Street Journal* ad this humorous title, "Boss, You Look Ill (What We Mean Is: Beat It, Phlegm Boy)," which was about sick workaholic bosses who von't stay home and instead help spread illness at the office. It's o laughing matter that "office buildings can be incubators for nfectious disease," according to occupational medicine expert Rupert Burtan. He suggests telling ill workaholics that it's simply "inefficient" or everyone in the office to get sick.

THE BENEFITS OF CAMARADERIE

Building camaraderie is a fun way to encourage employee articipation, teamwork and creativity. Many companies are finding hat the group that plays together, stays together. Odetics, Inc., an lectronics company in Anaheim, California, that was featured in the ook *The 100 Best Companies to Work for in America*, even has a Fun Committee." Joel Slutzky, Odetics chairman and CEO, notes hat since people spend more time at work than anywhere else, it nakes sense to encourage them to look forward to coming to work. Besides low absenteeism, his company has a very low turnover rate nd low medical costs for his industry. He also believes his mployees are more innovative.

Slutzky emphasizes that fun events don't have to cost a lot but hould be creative and different and go beyond the typical company icnic. Past events have included a 50s party; a "couch potato" ontest that included miniature golf and paper airplane activities for mployees "who wanted to get into fitness without working up a weat"; plays put on by the company repertoire theater; a surprise ash to celebrate the company's 20th birthday; and a Secretaries Day celebration that had managers dress up as waiters and serve unch to company secretaries in the cafeteria.

Every year, Payday, a payroll company in San Francisco, invites mployees' children in for a visit. The children play games, have unch with their parents and watch their parents work. A side enefit is that employees get to discover something personal about heir co-workers.

You may spend at least eight hours a day at work, yet know very little about your co-workers. The Tennessee Teachers Credit Union has a voluntary Employee Profile form that asks about such areas as hobbies, outside interests, children and background. These forms are compiled and published periodically in an employee directory that helps employees become better acquainted.

I developed my own profile form when I was president of the Los Angeles chapter of NAPO (the National Association of Professional Organizers). It was a useful tool for board members to get to know one another. I included such items as, "family members or significant others," "pets," "education/Alma Mater(s)," "activities, hobbies, interests, charities, etc." and "special goals, dreams, aspirations." I encouraged my board members to answer any of the items that felt comfortable or appropriate for them.

TRAIN TO SEE A REAL GAIN

To maintain a quality-oriented team that focuses on continuous improvement, you'll need an ongoing, quality training program. Such a program results from meeting needs identified through excellent communication with customers (both internal and external) and a high level of employee involvement.

It also requires the support of top management and should reflect a continuous improvement, growth philosophy of your company. Unfortunately, in all too many businesses, training is perceived as an unnecessary frill. But top companies, who seek to attain and maintain the competitive edge, recognize that training is an integral essential part.

Get involved in your own training. Assess areas where you could use some additional training. Progressive companies frequently conduct needs assessment surveys for employees and their managers to identify training areas. Some training departments have identified and organized skill areas by category and by level or position and invite all employees to evaluate their own skill strengths and weaknesses. Training programs and materials are developed or brought in-house, based on these identified needs.

Notice whenever you feel uncomfortable in doing new work or taking on a new responsibility. Don't pretend you know something when you don't. Don't worry about feeling inadequate. Let it be a

ignal that it's time for you to learn something new, and whenever
ou do, there's usually some feeling of discomfort that's natural.

This feeling often occurs when someone delegates something new
o you. You may remember the four steps to delegation discussed in
Chapter 3. The second one had to do with training. It's your
esponsibility to make sure you get the necessary training to do the
elegated task. In a larger sense, it's your responsibility to make sure
ou get the necessary training to do all your work. Of course, it's
asier in a corporate culture that actively supports training. But it's
till your responsibility.

CAPITALIZE ON CROSS TRAINING

One way to get training, aside from a formal training department, is
o take advantage of **cross training**. This kind of training lets you
ee, and in some cases lets you do, other people's jobs. There are
many advantages to this kind of training. First, you have a chance to
earn new skills or new aspects of your company. Learning additional
kills could add to your marketing and career potential. Second, it
an be helpful from an operations standpoint to have someone else
ill in for you if you're out sick or on vacation.

Third, when you can see what procedures are followed by other
people or departments, you have a chance to see why these
procedures are necessary. You may be more cooperative when you're
asked to fill out a form, for example, because you've seen firsthand,
ust how important it is to another department.

Building a real sense of cooperation is a major reason to cross
rain. Teledyne Systems Company in Northridge, California, has a
chart that reads:

YOUR PROBLEM
Cooperation is spelled with two letters: "WE."

Cross-functional teams take cross-training even further, in which
people from different "departments" or workgroups come together
o work as a team on a specific project or problem. The notion of
re-engineering" also describes this phenomenon of breaking down
barriers between people who work in different workgroups,
departments and even different companies. More and more teams

and "partnerships" are flourishing than ever before and creating som
impressive collaborative efforts.

DESCRIBE WHAT YOU DO AND HOW YOU DO IT

Your department or office should develop its own **training manu:**
that describes all of the different positions and responsibilities i
detail. You (and everyone) should write a description of you
responsibilities, functions and processes. All of the informatio
should be checked, tested and updated from time to time. Writin;
the manual on a computer makes updates easy.

Normally, training for a new position is handled by one othe
person, often a predecessor. When the training isn't in some writte
format, vital items can become omitted.

It's important to document in a manual all that you do in you
position. Such documentation might even justify why you need a
assistant (or a raise!). Plus it's a real help when you train someon
else to do your work—temporarily, when you go on vacation, o
permanently, when you get that promotion.

TEAM BUILDING THROUGH RECYCLING

Implementing a recycling program where you work is an easy wa
to build teamwork that extends beyond your organization to you
community, country and indeed, the world. It involves *everyone*, is a
"easy sell" because of all the national media publicity on recycling
offers financial rewards for companies and makes people feel goo
about participating. It's a real "win-win" kind of operation, where th
benefits are plainly visible.

The following are sample actions to take and products to use i
your recycling program (see how many you're already doing o
using):

- Whenever possible, avoid disposable cups, plates, utensils
  Americans supposedly toss out enough of this stuff to circle the
  equator 300 times. (Once would be too much.) Let's go back tc
  using ceramic mugs.
- Whenever possible, try to buy and use **recycled** and **recyclable**
  products. Recycled products contain a certain percentage of usec
  materials (for example, recycled office paper has to have at leas
  50 percent recovered material). Recyclable means the produc

has the *potential* to be recycled. Look for 3M Post-it brand recycled paper notes (3M also has a list of recyclers nationwide that will accept the notes as recyclable office waste–you can write 3M at 3M Commercial Office Supply Division, 3M Center Bldg. 223-3S-03, St. Paul, MN 55144-1000); recycled file folders such as Esselte Pendaflex's EarthWise brand (which contain the highest percentage of post-consumer content available today) and those in the Quill catalog described in Chapter 7; Perma Products EcoSafe record storage boxes made from 100 percent recycled corrugated fiberboard, which are 100 percent recyclable; 100 percent recycled bond paper and envelopes for letterhead and ruled writing pads through the All-state Legal catalog (800/222-0510).

- Cut the copier habit, whenever possible, or if you must, try to use scratch paper or copy on both sides of paper; if each copier in the U.S. used five fewer copies every business day, we could save up to 17.5 million reams of paper, which would save lots of trees and landfill space. (Check with your copier manufacturer to see if this will harm your machine.)
- Form a recycling committee and designate a coordinator in your office, department or better yet, company.
- Design a recycling program that: identifies which materials will be recycled and which recycled materials will be purchased; provides a collection and storage system; offers ways to deal with confidential material; and develops an employee education and suggestion program.
- Consider using a non-profit organization to help you with your recycling program. Datco, a division of the Autistic Treatment Center, has received the Environmental Vision Award from the city of Dallas for its model program.
- Consider recycling these materials: aluminum cans, glass containers, paper (computer paper is the most valuable), envelopes and cardboard.
- Try to reuse items such as file folders and boxes.
- The Resource Guide to Recyled Products and Programs contains environmentally-friendly products from over 70 companies. It's $20 from the Business Products Industry Assn. (800/542-6672).
- Use paper clips instead of staples. Paper clips can be reused and staples interfere with paper recycling.

- Use paper shredders not only for controlling access to sensitive material but also to help you in your recycling program. Shredded paper makes great packing material or you can sell shredded paper directly to recycling houses.
- Use specially marked recycling containers such as those made by Rubbermaid Office Products Inc.

HOW TO ORGANIZE OTHERS

A question I'm often asked by well-organized individuals is how they can organize a boss or a co-worker. Impossible as it may seem, there are a number of steps you can take.

Broaden your definition of "organize." Make sure it goes well beyond clean desks to incorporate the importance of goal setting, prioritizing, working more effectively and the notion of process improvement. Make sure it also complements your "corporate culture" or the philosophy and mission of your organization as a whole.

In addition, recognize that organizing others is a communication issue and a training issue. The communication issue focuses on how to *motivate* someone to *want* to be better organized. The main way to motivate anyone is to ask yourself, "What's in it for them?" There have to be real benefits for them in terms of power, prestige, profits or whatever is a real motivator. They have to clearly see a connection between getting organized and any benefits that are motivators.

Once you can show a positive connection, you have a good shot at helping them begin the organizing training process. As with most training, this is a process that takes place over time. There are skills to learn and habits to practice. If you yourself are organized and are a patient teacher, who acknowledges and reinforces small successes, you have a chance to see some exciting results. If you're a team player, not a dictator, you could even transform your entire organization.

But even after all your efforts, you may at times need to recognize the limitations of certain individuals who just can't seem to grasp certain "basic" organizational skills. In those situations, you may need to just take more control, insist on a daily meeting (in person or by phone) and intercept certain details or papers that simply shouldn't end up in that person's office.

Let's see how Linda was able to apply these techniques to solve a paper organization problem that she faced with co-workers.

PREVENTING THE DUMP-IT-ON-THE-DESK SYNDROME

Linda, an administrative assistant for a small but successful public relations firm, had a problem. Everyone would feed work to her by dumping it in the middle of her desk. They also had the habit of interrupting her from other work to explain what they wanted done.

Together Linda and I devised a special daily paperwork system that helps Linda better control interruptions and incoming paperwork. She now uses colored, two-pocket presentation folders, a different color for each person. She puts mail in the right-hand pocket and staff members feed back work to her in the left-hand pocket once a day. If a special project or deadline comes up during the day, she has a red folder on her desk to handle these top priorities.

Designing the system was only half the story, since her system involved the other staff members who needed to "buy into it." So I suggested she make a presentation at a staff meeting to introduce the system and ask for everyone's support in *trying it out* for a week. Then everyone was to get together at the following week's meeting to evaluate this new *office* system (not Linda's system). The system is still working well several years later.

It's very important to get everyone's agreement and support whenever one person introduces a new system. Otherwise, the office staff may be resistant to a system that appears to be imposed upon them.

When introducing a system such as Linda's presentation folders, remember that good communication and training skills come into play here. First, communicate the benefits to everyone. Second, clearly train people in how you see the system functioning. Be open to reasonable modifications at this point. Encourage people to be involved in this initial discussion (which is really a training session). Give up ownership of the system—it's no longer "my" system, it's "ours."

MANAGING MULTIPLE BOSSES, PROJECTS OR PRIORITIES

It's a real challenge trying to work with multiple bosses or co-workers and juggle different projects and priorities. The key word here is "priorities" because that's where you'll need to start.

Begin by setting up a work priority system. First, define priority levels, get agreement on these levels from co-workers and bosses and incorporate these levels onto a work priority slip (you could have your printer print up these levels onto Post-it Notes). Here are some suggested priorities that may work for you:

A-1 Drop everything–this requires immediate attention!
A-2 This is a hot priority to be done ASAP.
A-3 Handle this by the end of the day.
B-1 Complete by the end of the next work day.
B-2 Complete by a specified day, from two to seven days out.
B-3 This is an important but long-term project, due in more than a week's time up to several months.

Note that priorities can and will change; what was a B-1 yesterday may become an A-3 today, unless, of course, the task is reprioritized.

You also need to set up some guidelines along with any agreed-upon priorities. One guideline could be to work on all urgent priorities before going on to the next level. Another should offer suggestions on conflicting priorities (it's best to do this before the actual conflicts arise). Still another should provide for setting aside set blocks of time every day or week to work on long-term projects. Ideally, work as much out on paper (or computer) as possible and then have your team meet and work out the final details.

You could use different colored pre-printed Post-it Notes or Tape Flags for different priorities. Color has a way of really jumping out, especially with some of the new, bright colors that are now available. Another alternative, if you want to keep track of work you delegate, is to use the tickler slip system described in Chapter 2, in which you keep a copy of any delegated work and file it in your tickler system to make sure it gets done.

~HE TEAM WITH A TEMP

At some point in time you may have the opportunity to either select and/or work with a "temp." If the temp reports to you, these ideas may be particularly useful.

I've found most temps to be friendly and interested in doing a good job. For some, the temporary position is a foot in the door of a company and they end up being hired for full-time employment. For others, they enjoy the ability to do a good job and not get caught up in office politics. Often, it's a good mutual "test" to see if the chemistry is there for something more permanent.

Consequently, the attitude is usually open and receptive, which is a good place to start because you'll need to do some important training. Here are some guidelines I recommend:

- Take all of these suggestions, and any others you think of, and write them down (preferably on computer so you can more easily make revisions) and keep your list in front of you as you go over each item. (Or at the very least, photocopy the items here in my book.)
- Give temps an overview of your position, your responsibilities and your priorities, as well as a tour of the office and any other key facilities. Introduce key people with whom they may interact frequently.
- Provide an overview of temp priorities and responsibilities.
- Since communications most likely will be a good part of temp responsibilities, go into some detail about your phone system, voice mail, e-mail, fax machine and copier; train on both the mechanics as well as the policies and procedures you follow. Emphasize attention to detail, e.g., correct phone numbers and spelling of names.
- Encourage open, two-way communication with you and indicate the best times and methods you like to communicate–ask temps if they have any preferences; encourage questions.
- Keep assignments or projects small in number and complexity, especially at first; be sure to detail all the necessary steps.
- Never assume anything and communicate that you don't assume anything and to please excuse you for going over anything that is rudimentary.

- Carefully evaluate delegated tasks in terms of training tim required, how long the temp will be with you, a temp's ski level; in other words, is the return on investment of time an energy worth it to you for any given delegation?
- Communicate any things you *don't* want your temp to do.
- At the very least, have five- to 10-minute, daily mornin meetings.
- Communicate clearly, concisely and positively.

TRAINING AND LEADING BY ORGANIZING

As an organized member of your work group, you have a speci ability to lead, if you are excited about organization and can trai others in this vital area. Another way to say it is, "As you organiz so shall you lead."

As an organized person, you're a doer but you can also be leader if you master the art of delegation, which has an importar training component. (Review Chapter 3 for a discussion of deleg tion.) When you're organized, *Positively Organized!*, you have a goo view of both the macro and the micro—the big picture as well as th details. You can see more clearly what needs to be done, when an how.

Getting involved in training others requires you to look for an apply a variety of approaches, depending on the needs of th individuals involved. Look for books, videos, cassettes, trainin classes and seminars and consultants to teach organizational skil and processes. In some cases, you can be the trainer yourself, if yo take various tasks and activities, write out the steps involved ahea of time and then teach those steps to someone else.

Review this chapter, as well as the rest of the book. Look fc ways to improve how you and your co-workers can get things don Sometimes it's the little things that can make a big difference. suggest, for example, that a manager/assistant team take five to 1 minutes daily to meet and discuss the day's schedule, projects an priorities. Or use a well-designed work request form to help organiz and prioritize work flow. Such a form should have a checklist sectio for routine work, the time frame or deadline for completion and "special instructions" area for writing additional comment: requirements or notes.

If you're not in management, don't be afraid you won't have enough impact. An organized person with vision, creativity and drive can accomplish miracles. But don't do it alone. Look for other like-minded individuals who are open to change, quality improvement and innovation.

If you *are* in management, you have a special responsibility to influence and inspire others. That does not mean, however, having others do it *your* way. It means facilitating change, teamwork and an exchange of ideas and information.

RESOURCE GUIDE

READING AND REFERENCE

American Productivity & Quality Center is a nonprofit organization that works with business, labor, government and academia to improve productivity, quality and quality of work life. It issues a variety of publications, conducts courses and conferences and offers research, reference and individualized services. It's the co-administrator of the Malcolm Baldrige National Quality Award. 713/681-4020. 123 N. Post Oak Lane, Houston, TX 77024

The Business Bible: Ten New Commandments for Creating an Ethical Workplace by Wayne Dosick (HarperBusiness, 1994) uses contemporary examples and ancient parables to back the importance of an ethics-based workplace.

The Deming Management Method by Mary Walton (New York: Putnam Publishing Group, 1986). This book summarizes the 14 quality management principles of quality guru W. Edwards Deming and shows how they have been applied in American industry. $10.95

50 Simple Things Your Business Can Do to Save the Earth by Earthworks Press. Like its predecessor best-seller, this book includes some great, easy-to-apply reusing and recycling ideas with some convincing rationales for doing so.

The HUMOResources catalog is filled with books, videos, audiotapes, games, software and other items dealing with humor and creativity in the work place (as well as in your personal life).

800/600-4242 or 518/587-8770. The Humor Project, Inc., 110 Spring St., Saratoga Springs, NY 12866

Midland City by Robert Schwarz is a delightful book written as a novel combined with how-to text and instructional appendices that show how to bring growth and prosperity to any community with a declining economy. Incorporating quality principles into real-life business situations, the book is as inspiring as it is informative. $36.95. **800/952-6587** or 414/272-8575. Quality Press, American Society for Quality Control, 310 West Wisconsin Avenue, Milwaukee, WI 53203

Out of the Crisis by W. Edwards Deming (Cambridge, MA: MIT Center for Advanced Engineering Study). This is Deming's famous textbook on quality. $60. It's available by contacting 617/253-7444, MIT Center for Advanced Engineering Study, 77 Mass. Ave., Rm. 9-234, Cambridge, MA 02139.

Quality is Free and **Quality Without Tears** by Philip Crosby (New York: McGraw-Hill, 1979 and 1984, respectively). These books by quality guru Crosby are important resources for your quality library.

Quality Press is the publishing arm of the American Society for Quality Control and has a complete catalog of their publications as well as those by other publishers, all dealing with quality principles and processes. (See address above under *Midland City*.)

Resources & Solutions is a business resource center that researches, recommends and ships human resource training and development books, tapes and other employee development materials. **404/756-0757**. JEL Enterprises, PO Box 42578, Atlanta, GA 30311-0578

The Training Store is a catalog for trainers and other human resource professionals. It features resources such as full training programs, books, videos, slides and accessories—all under $500 and most under $100. **800/222-9909** or 717/652-6300. Five South Miller Road, Harrisburg, PA 17109

SPECIAL PRODUCTS FOR SPECIAL NEEDS

Abledata is an ADA (Americans with Disabilities Act) database of assistive devices. **800/346-2742.**

AT&T Special Needs Access Program offers ADA consulting and installation services and education about assistive devices. 800/762-7123.

Goodwill Industries contract services divisions recruit and train disabled or economically disadvantaged people, providing them with job skills and experience while also helping local business owners. Contact your local Goodwill office.

Job Accommodation Network is a free ADA consulting service for employers and disabled employees. 800/232-9675.

Office Systems for the Visually or Physically Impaired is a resource of technology resellers and consultants. 800/253-4391.

TRAINING SEMINARS

American Management Association provides educational forums worldwide where members and their colleagues learn superior, practical business skills and explore best practices of world-class organizations through interaction with each other and expert training practitioners. Look for three-hour satellite updates, six hour one-day seminars in your area, multi-day programs presented in major cities, national conferences, and customized on-site training. AMA's publishing program provides tools individuals can use to extend learning beyond the classroom in a process of life-long professional growth and development. 800/255-4141 or 913/451-2700. American Management Association, 11221 Roe Avenue, Leawood KS 66211

SkillPath Seminars present more than 8,000 seminars on 30 topics throughout North America and the Pacific Rim. The seminar leaders are a select group of trainers at the top of their profession—skilled teachers with a tremendous depth of knowledge in their respective topic areas. 800/873-7545 or 913/362-3900, SkillPath Seminars, 6900 Squibb Road, Ste. 300, Mission, KS 66201-2768

11

USING COMPUTERS AND TECHNOLOGY TO IMPROVE COMMUNICATIONS AND QUALITY

Quick Scan: Read this chapter if you want to maximize your voice mail, telephone, fax system, e-mail and "workgroup computing" in order to improve your communications, your effectiveness in working with other people and ultimately, your products or services. You'll find specific computer and technology tips and tools to improve how you and others work together.

Technology is here to stay. The trick today is to make the most of it and to determine which forms of it you really need in your work and how you'll use them.

Don't ask yourself the best way a task can be done but rather the best way *you* (or your workgroup) can do the task. There's a difference. Yes, a task could perhaps be automated at great expense of time and energy but it may be more effective to do the task manually. It's easy to get sucked into the notion of automating everything, but always come back to the question: What's the best way for us (yourself plus internal or external customers) to do a task?

Before you take advantage of technology, computers and automation, make sure you evaluate your existing work process. There may be steps that shouldn't be done at all. Get involved with **work simplification** if possible. For example, one major American auto maker developed an automated system to track sales, inventory and production because of a complex system that gave consumers options in some 40,000 possible combinations. A foreign manufacturer, on the other hand, didn't need such a complex automated system, because it created only 32 possible combinations. Try to eliminate the problems that require a complex automated system in the first place.

But what about customer service? Some might argue that 40,000 combinations give the customer more choice; others would argue that having too many choices overwhelms most people. Look for a balance between serving the external and internal customers.

If you do determine a task or process is necessary, see if it needs to be automated or not. For some size processes or businesses, the "return on investment" may not be worth the time nor money.

On the other hand, you may not have the luxury of a choice. If all your suppliers are using e-mail, you may need to switch over, whether of not you're using e-mail with others.

Computers and technology in a larger sense are changing the ways we work. Sheer numbers indicate that more than 100 million personal computers now exist. More than 50 percent of office workers in the U.S. use computers. Computer columnist Michael Miller writes that a personal computer used to be primarily for word and number processing and now it's becoming a major communications tool.

Since 1989, personal computer networks have exploded in popularity. About half of the personal computers in the U.S. are connected to networks. In this chapter you'll see **workgroup computing** and **groupware** software products, which are networked applications designed to help people in business communicate, share information, collaborate and work together in some new and exciting ways. Such products are changing the amount as well as the flow of information. With information no longer in the hands of a few individuals and with the trend toward **re-engineering**, which breaks down barriers between departments, companies and organizations we're seeing new teamwork possibilities where people can come together on-line to solve problems and create new business opportunities.

Along with all this technology comes a sense of urgency and a expectancy of working quickly. We have instant communications that are leaving many people breathless. One recent *Wall Street Journal* story was entitled "Pushing the Pace: The Latest Big Thing at Many Companies is Speed, Speed, Speed" and another story outlined the "multitasking" occupational hazards that Type A personalities develop in using technology—they're using several different communication tools at the same time. As a consultant, I'm terribly concerned about these aspects of technology that are producing a pressure-cooker workplace. That's why it's so important to select technological tools carefully and conservatively and to identify and use specific guidelines and habits that spell out how and when to use these tools.

VALUE YOUR VOICE MAIL AND
TAP YOUR TELEPHONE'S POTENTIAL

Voice mail has become a valuable, timesaving telecommunications tool. Its many advantages include: reducing telephone tag (but don't fall into "voice mail tag"!); screening calls during critical work projects; not having to return a call if a caller's message is complete enough and/or requires no response; receiving private, usually more accurate messages; and you can access messages at your convenience.

Yet, if you value voice mail itself over the needs of your customers, you can quickly lose the advantages this automated system machine has to offer. (For the purposes of this section, the term "voice mail" includes multi-user, computer-driven answering systems, of course, but I'm also including the automated answering systems found in stand-alone answering machines.)

The trick is learning how to make it serve your external as well as your internal customers. I encourage you to evaluate your system and follow the following guidelines:

1. Focus first on serving your external customer. Determine if all the options and directions of your voice mail maze encourage

or discourage contact. Regularly check out the system yourself (or better yet, by a friend who hasn't used your system), for any bugs and survey your customers' reactions.

2. Always give your caller the option to speak to a real live person. (But make sure that the referral's voice mail isn't on, though!) Not having this option is sometimes called "voice mail jail."

3. Limit, if possible, the number of options to no more than three. Too many choices can be confusing and impersonal. Design your "automated attendant" or "electronic menuing" feature to keep the menu simple and avoid layers of menus and choices.

4. Ideally, have a well-trained receptionist handle your company's main phone number. So few companies do anymore that you'll really stand out. (I almost always tell such receptionists how nice it is to speak with a real person and I'm often told they've heard that from other people as well.)

5. Your outgoing message should be inviting, personable and have a "smiling voice" quality. Avoid generic, nonspecific messages, if possible, and give the caller specific information about your availability and other options for more immediate assistance. Give your name, job title, department, division or any pertinent information. (How many times have you been transferred to someone who supposedly can solve your problem and you have no idea what that person does and whether you'll get a return call.) Also, be sure to change your message in a timely fashion (it doesn't sound very organized nor instill a lot of confidence if you have an old outgoing message.) You may want to make a note in your planner to change it. Be sure to tell the caller how long they have to speak, especially if it's less than a minute.

6. On your outgoing message always ask callers to leave the best time(s) to call them back to prevent telephone tag. Assure callers that their call is important and will be handled in a timely fashion.

7. Make sure your system has an electronic telephone directory so that callers can easily get a person's extension number, even after business hours.

8. Your system should let callers speed up or bypass messages and enter the extension number or correct code to move quickly through the system. It's great, too, if you include the option of dialing "O" for a real-life operator–or at least provide some other option of speaking with a person. I like systems that after a few minutes, will give the caller an option of remaining on hold or leaving a message.

9. Periodically offer short training sessions on your telephone/ voice mail system. Rarely does anyone ever read the manual and people generally need more than an initial orientation. It's time well spent to continue learning about some of the timesaving features your system just may have. Since you may have some turnover, there will probably be some new people who are depending most likely on other employees who received a brief introduction and never read the manual!

When calling someone else's voice mail system, be sure to leave your name and number and a brief message that indicates the purpose of your call and any action you may need from the person you're calling and when you need it. You may even want to leave your phone number twice–once at the beginning and once at the end of your message. Let them know the best times to reach you. Also speak slowly and distinctly, especially when giving your name and number. Be complete and concise, yet friendly, with good, appreciative etiquette, and somehow convey what's in it for them to return your call (recognize that only one in four calls are indeed returned). Always write down an individual's extension or direct dial number for future reference so you can bypass the company wide system. (Also, if you've called a company system and you can tell you're entering a layered menu system, immediately press "O" and hope you can escape!)

Telecommunications are important to the bottom line. Poor telephone contact, live or voice mail, can affect customer retention. A Rockefeller Institute study found that of the eight to 15 percent of a company's annual client loss, 68 percent was due to poor telephone treatment.

EIGHT ANNOYING TELECOMMUNICATIONS PROBLEMS AND WHAT TO DO ABOUT THEM

Here are eight challenging problems, along with some solutions:

1. Being put on hold for too long. **Solutions:** Get a telephone headset or use your speaker phone and do what my husband does—accumulate things to do when you're left on hold, which for him is all too frequently; but be sure they're quiet things if you use speaker phone. If you've been on hold for at least 10 minutes, fax or write a note on your letterhead to the head of the organization and write simply, "I've been on hold for _ minutes today and thought you'd like to know. I'm a current, prospective, former, customer of yours." (Use the appropriate words.)

2. If you're ever cut off in the middle of leaving a voice mail message, then you've experienced **talk-off**, the inadvertent activation of telephone voice mail system functions that's triggered by frequencies in a person's voice that match the very Touch-Tone frequencies that activate certain functions. Besides the inadvertent ending of a message, the most common signs of talk-off are when a caller is transferred out of the system or messages are unintentionally marked "urgent." **Solution:** I've read that a product called the ToneMate Voice Filter by Mytech Systems Corp. can solve the problem and is simply installed between a phone user's handset and telephone, using no tools and taking about 10 seconds.

3. I'd like a dime every time someone has a dialed a fax number instead of a phone number off of a business card or a piece of letterhead. **Solution:** Put your phone number in boldface type. (For someone else's card or letterhead, use a highlighter pen to make the phone number stand out).

4. Major cities now often have several area codes for phone numbers alone and if you don't know a city well, it may be hard to get a correct phone number. **Solution:** Ask your information operator to "go full book."

5. A record 14 new telephone area codes changed in 1995 alone in North America (and look for a total of 640 new ones in the coming years). **Solutions:** Be aware that PBX automated

switchboards weren't designed to handle area codes with middle digits other than 0 or 1 and may involve some expense for companies to adapt their equipment. It may also be difficult to reach some companies that have these new area codes. Automated switchboards purchased after 1992 can be reprogrammed to call the new codes fairly easily and cheaply. Reprogramming or an upgrade can be costly for older switch-boards. Here's a habit to cultivate for frequent nationwide calling: give your city or state when you leave a message, and when you receive a message, jot that information down next to the phone number so you can return a call appropriately for a given time zone.

6. Someone's automatic fax machine keeps calling your phone line. **Solution:** When the fax call beeps on the line, dial any seven-digit number once or twice and hopefully the tones generated will signal the fax that it has reached a wrong number and cancel the redial function.

7. If you switch long distance telephone carriers, your current plan will not be automatically cancelled. **Solution:** Find out what you have to do to cancel an existing program.

8. You have call waiting but you want to temporarily disable it because you're about to make an important call or you're making a call with you modem (call waiting's beep can disrupt a modem transmission). **Solution:** Call your local phone company to see if they offer a call waiting disabling service, for which you will probably have to pay extra. You then enter a code, such as *71 or *70 to disable call waiting prior to a call. It's possible to add the code to your modem setup screen. Call waiting is reactivated when the call is complete.

HOW TO MAX YOUR FAX

It's amazing how in a very short period of time the facsimile (fax) machine has become almost as indispensable as the copy machine. In some offices, however, the fax machine (like the copy machine) is used too much; we don't just max the fax, we overtax it.

We now have about 25 million fax machines. And we've come a long way from the fax machines back in 1960, which weighed in at

0 pounds and transmitted only 10 pages per hour and you needed ne machine to send transmissions and another one to receive them.

By the way, when you're shopping for fax machines and omparing speeds between them, you'll want to ask about and ompare the "transmission" time, which is the only speed that varies. The "handshake," getting set up with the other machine, and the scanning" time do not vary.

Today, some of us rely not only on fax machines but also on ersonal computers, **fax software** and **fax modems** (also called "fax oards" if they're internal modems) in order to fax electronic locuments from one computer to another. This is a more efficient vay to go if you primarily fax documents created on computer by a vord processor, for example, or receive electronic documents. It also aves paper and lets the receiving party use the information more eadily. Software and a modem should also cost less than a stand-lone fax machine. (Most modems sold today have built-in fax apabilities; even a non-fax modem, called a data modem, could let ou send a fax using an Internet fax service or one of the ommercial on-line services.)

Computer-based fax software helps you store, organize, retrieve, rchive, recycle and keyword-search your faxes, as well as design ustom cover pages. There are two types: 1) **desktop** stand-alone oftware for faxing from your computer and 2) **network,** which unctions as a **fax server** that allows other computers called **clients** o share its resources such as fax boards and phone lines. Some of he more highly rated desktop software programs include: WinFax RO by Delrina Corp. (800/268-6082 or 408/363-2345); FaxWorks RO by SofNet, Inc. (800/329-9675 or 404/984-8088); and for the 1etwork, Object Fax Advanced by Traffic Software (800/840-0708 or 107/995-5282).

Every office needs to develop suggested guidelines or a policy egarding fax use. Here are several I've developed for fax machines 1nd computer-based faxing that may apply to your office:

1. As a general rule, I advise not having your fax number printed on your business card, unless the fax is specifically designated for a purpose, such as taking orders, or unless you prefer receiving them to another mode of communication such as phone calls. Putting a fax number on a card makes it too easy

for others to send you unsolicited, unwanted faxes. Also it may encourage others to overtax your fax. If you do need to include your fax number on your business card or letterhead, make the phone number larger or in bold face to differentiate it from your fax number (unless you do prefer to emphasize the fax number).

2. To fax or not to fax—make fax decisions based on urgency, length of document and preference of the receiver, not simply because it's easier and more convenient for you to fax than mail. Faxes are no longer a novelty that grab attention; instead of getting attention they just get lost.

3. Faxing may seem like it saves time and money, but consider the cost of fax paper (the thermal type isn't even biodegradable) plus the cost of photocopies you may have to make if you don't have a plain paper fax machine. Then, too, if the fax machine is being overtaxed on your end or your recipient's, you may find it takes many attempts to get through. And if you've ever experienced difficulty with your "automatic" document feeder, in which papers don't feed correctly, you know how labor intensive it can be at times.

4. Limit the number of pages to be faxed—*before* they're faxed to you. Find out how many pages will be coming. You may decide on another method. As a courtesy to someone *you* fax, let them know how many pages you'll be faxing and see if that is acceptable.

5. Number pages to be faxed.

6. Don't send unsolicited faxes. I broke my own rule when contacting the manufacturers for this edition and let me tell you, it doesn't work! Call and get permission first. It will confirm that the recipient is indeed the right person and alert them in advance.

7. Make sure your fax machine has enough memory to store a message in case your machine runs out of paper. and check the paper supply, especially if you receive many incoming faxes. In fact, make sure your fax is automatic enough for your business—that besides memory, it has such features as an automatic document feeder, an automatic document cutter, delayed transmission (to take advantage of lower phone rates), on-hook dialing, automatic dialing and activity report (printout

of the date, time and phone number of each fax that's sent and received—this reporting feature may also be used if you only receive part of a fax and want the fax number of the sender to let them know you only received a partial fax).

8. Get a fax modem for your personal computer if you receive and send mostly electronic computer documents, you prefer getting confidential fax messages, want the option to print them out or not and you want to automate the process of sending multiple faxes.

9. When designing your own fax transmission forms, include a section called "Method/Urgency of Delivery," that has four boxes: one for "Urgent...Notify Recipient as Soon as Possible"; one for "Confidential"; one for "Regular Interoffice Mail Delivery"; and another marked "Other" (Specify). You may also want to include a section called "Response Needed" and include these four options: 1) Urgently, by the close of business day, 2) Tomorrow will be OK, 3) Please respond within 3 days and 4) Prefer response on or by_____. Also include the following: the sender's name and telephone and fax numbers; the company name and address; date and time sent; recipient's name, company and fax number; number of pages, including the cover sheet; subject or "RE:" section; a "Special Instructions" section that lists options to check, e.g., "Please reply," "For Your Information" and "As You Requested"; and space for a "Message" section for a hand-written or typed message.

10. To save time and money, use Post-it brand Fax Notes, which measure 1½ by 4 inches and attach to a corner of the original document to be transmitted. Eliminating a separate transmittal cover sheet saves paper costs as well as telephone transmission charges. See Figure 11-1.

11. If a document doesn't need a cover sheet, type or print "Sent via fax" on the document along with the page number on each page, e.g., Page 1 of 2 and Page 2 of 2. Make sure your phone and fax numbers on your letterhead will fax legibly; better yet, be sure to include them clearly on the first page.

12. For plain paper fax machines, put light yellow paper in the receiving tray of your fax to alert recipients to faxes that have come in and use it for incoming faxes only. This is a good way

Post-It™ brand fax transmittal memo 7671 | # of pages ►

To	From
Co.	Co.
Dept.	Phone #
Fax #	Fax #

Figure 11-1. Post-it brand Fax Notes

to separate faxes, which may be more urgent, from other papers. Avoid other colors, especially pink or darker shades that aren't good if you'll need to photocopy any faxes; these colors will produce a muddied, gray shadow on copies. A light blue or green could also work; test it out on your photocopier first.

13. If a fax is confidential and you need to send it via a fax machine, call right before faxing so the recipient can pick it up right away.

14. Double check any fax number you key into a fax machine or on your computer; if you make an error, it's unlikely the incorrect recipient will bother to call you.

15. Avoid unattended faxes. If you fax a phone number by mistake and it reaches an answering machine, it could rack up a hefty phone bill.

16. If you delegate your faxing, use a fax request slip that says, "Please send this fax within the next ___hour(s) or the next ___minutes." It's fast and easy to write in the correct number by either hours or minutes.

ENERGIZE YOUR E-MAIL

The fastest growing communication tool is undoubtedly e-mail. Estimates are that more than 25 billion e-mail messages will be sent this year alone—that's more than twice as many that were sent two years ago. About 1 billion messages a month are sent via the

Internet. One prediction is that e-mail will replace at least half of all corporate first-class mail.

An e-mail address is equivalent to an electronic post office box that receives messages from a variety of people and places. Some people have several e-mail addresses, which makes it even more complicated for those individuals—but more about that later (see Chapter 13).

I attribute the popularity of e-mail to several factors. First, it's easy to use. Second, it's an effective communication tool that can be quicker and/or clearer than other methods. Third, it's versatile and flexible—you can send a message to one or more individuals, with or without an electronic document attachment, you can do it whether you're in the office or on the road, you can easily reply to a message and you can often confirm that a recipient actually read your message. Fourth, it's usually less expensive to use e-mail to communicate with people in other time zones (if you use an on-line service, it will cost you a local call). Fifth, there is greater connectivity now than ever before between e-mail users of all types—those on corporate networks, commercial on-line services and the Internet.

E-mail has also become the foundation for all kinds of workgroup computing products—document sharing, group scheduling, electronic-forms routing, workflow automation and discussion databases to name a few. E-mail is becoming central to how many of us now work and communicate.

HOW TO DEAL WITH THE DOWN SIDE OF E-MAIL

Unfortunately, all is not rosy with e-mail. Some people have been known to abuse this communication tool by sending downright nasty messages or by clogging up mailboxes with junk e-mail. Security and privacy, too, are issues that have to be addressed. E-mail messages can accumulate very quickly and wind up taking up too much space on computers or backup tapes if they aren't properly cleaned out. Finally, what many are facing today is a problem known as **e-mail overload**, which can be very time-consuming.

Fortunately, there are solutions available that can help.

Start by establishing some well publicized policies in your company or at least in your immediate workgroup. One policy should strongly advise participants to exercise the same restraint that they would show when writing memos or letters. The policy should further remind them that anything they put in writing, even on computer, could have legal ramifications and even be used against them in a court of law. I read a newspaper story about "electronic data detectives" who now make their living searching for incriminating e-mail messages on computers and backup media.

To save computer and storage facilities space, another policy should limit the number of e-mail messages that can be saved and for how long. Such a policy could well relate to your organization's overall records and document retention policies. Some experts recommend, however, that e-mail messages should be erased every two weeks.

A third policy should warn employees to exercise caution before forwarding any message internally or externally.

Let's face it—e-mail is not as secure nor as private as other communication methods. Perhaps you need two addresses, one public and the other a private, more restricted address. And it's a good idea to reemphasize your e-mail policies at frequent intervals; it's very easy to fall into a false sense of privacy and end up writing "personal" notes and politically sensitive messages.

Encryption, though, may be the best solution. ViaCrypt is military-grade encryption software, supposedly too tough for any intelligence service to crack. The freeware version, called PGP for "Pretty Good Privacy," is available for personal, not commercial use, through MIT's Internet location. It's also become available on CompuServe and some bulletin-board systems. Check the Resource Guide for Viacrypt PGP, the commercial version.

The **electronic** or **digital signature** is another valuable security tool. It tells the recipient who "signed" the document with certainty and guarantees that nothing was changed. The electronic signature is a feature of an encryption program such as Viacrypt PGP.

The use of **passwords** may be useful to limit access by others to your computer or an on-line service. Password protection is an option in many software programs. Security experts suggest your chosen password should contain at least eight characters but not many more in order to prevent typing errors. Don't share your password with anyone and change it every two months. It should be a phrase, not a single word, and shouldn't be related to your name, birth date or anything personal. A good password contains letters (in upper and lower case), numbers and symbols. It's recommended you use a different one for each of your activities that requires a password but I personally think that's too much of an organizational challenge. Here are some examples that were included in a *Wall Street Journal* story: 2b/orNOT2b% and Alfred!E!Newman7. As an organizer, I would recommend a secret hiding place in your house or office to keep track of your password(s).

If you receive an onslaught of messages (you think *you* have it bad—our U.S. vice president gets 600 a week!), you will probably want to install special software to help you manage them. A good program will have a **text editor** that works much like your word processor. Most importantly, the program should be **rules-based**. A **rules** feature lets you set up all kinds of operational parameters that can be real timesavers. It can guide you in setting up **filters** to accept or block messages from certain people or on certain topics. Or you could decide you want your e-mail system to perform certain tasks if certain events occur. You might tell the system to notify you with an alarm if you get a message from your boss for instance.

A rules-based program can help you with electronic filing. Your system could automatically archive messages that are older than a certain designated date or file different types of messages into separate folders.

A rules-based program can help you better prioritize your messages and deal with the most important ones in a timely manner. BeyondMail is an e-mail software program that pioneered rules and supports Windows and DOS (617/229-0006)

If you have several different mail services look at the highly-touted E-Mail Connection from ConnectSoft (800/ 234-9497), which will coordinate mail from different services and also give you excellent rules-based management; they also have KidMail, which is a great way to introduce your kids to e-mail.

E-MAIL ORGANIZATION TIPS

If you think organizing your paperwork is challenging, e-mail could be more so if you use it extensively. The bigger your e-mail overload, the more organizational thought and habits you need to build into your system.

Know when to use it over another communication method. It can take a few seconds or up to a day and a half to transmit over the Internet. The phone is faster, but that's assuming the person on the other end is there or regularly picks up their messages. If possible send e-mail messages to those who prefer that method and if you have time to wait for delivery of your message and a response. Research studies indicate that e-mail can be less personal and more task-oriented, but forces a better use of language and often clearer communication. Writing anything (including e-mail messages) tends to require more thoughtful reflection than say a phone conversation. Research also indicates that e-mail is particularly well suited for long-term projects that don't need to be rushed.

Use it to streamline your telephone messaging system. Attorney David Hirsch replaced telephone message slips with e-mail telephone messages in his Iowa law firm to transcribe live and voice mail messages onto an e-mail template that resembles a "While You Were Out" slip. (Many e-mail packages have such a template built in.) The big advantage is that such a system lets you sort and search messages in a variety of ways.

Create an "E-mail Message Management System" with electronic folders for storing and organizing messages (just as you created a "Daily Paperwork System" with paper folders for your every day mail and paperwork described in Chapter 4). Your e-mail program may come with several generic folders and will also let you create your own. Remember to work the system at least once a day and be sure to regularly clean out old messages.

Set up a clearly-defined message priority system. When you use priority terms on your messages, such as "Urgent," "Regular" or "Special Attention," make sure you and your e-mail correspondents have determined in advance what these terms mean. Another option is to include a deadline date or response needed date. (See the "Response Needed" priority system described earlier in the "Max Your Fax" section or the work priority system described in Chapter 10.)

Study your e-mail software. Discover the shortcuts that are built in and design ways to customize the software for you and/or your workgroup(s).

Resist the urge to copy others, ad nauseam. Just because it's easy to send e-mail copies to others, stop and think about whether the recipients really need or want the information.

Program your e-mail interruptions to match your work style or workload. There may be times when you want your e-mail delivered right away but you may routinely prefer to turn it off and have mail delivery only at specified times of the day. This is all part of your time management planning and prioritizing—give it some thought.

E-MAIL WRITING TIPS

You'll notice that many of the following tips will also apply to business writing in general. E-mail is doing much, in fact, to revive the art of writing as well as well develop clearer thinking and decision-making—all important professional and personal skills.

1. **Determine the recipient(s) of your message in advance.** Decide who really needs the message. Knowing your audience will help you better frame the message.
2. **Be very careful what you write**—any number of others could see it, without your even knowing it. See if your e-mail program has an "Unsend" feature, too.
3. **Write a subject line that gets noticed.** It's useful to build in some kind of action and/or deadline that's required.
4. **Include the most important information right up front.**
5. **Use subheads, numbers and bullets** to break up long messages and to guide your reader through your message.
6. **Be careful about conveying negative information through e-mail.**
7. **Limit the use of capital letters.** Besides being difficult to read, overuse of caps is the equivalent of screaming at someone. Don't scream on-line.
8. **Check the tone and emotional content** of your messages. Avoid jokes and sarcasm unless you've clearly indicated you're joking. It may be fine to use **"emoticons,"** the use of standard keyboard symbols as graphics to indicate emotion, but I'm not sure how universal they are and whether they will be understood. (Here are two common emoticons: (: stands for a happy face and <g> signifies a grin.)

9. **Avoid sending long messages** unless you've cleared it in advance with the recipient(s). Remote users will be particularly appreciative.
10. **Read carefully.** This goes for rereading a message you've written *before* sending it and well as reading messages you've received in their entirety.
11. **When responding to a message, clearly refer to the original message you received,** if it's not included in the reply.

E-MAIL AND INTERNET CONNECTIONS

Just what *is* the Internet? It's a federation of 3.2 million computers in 48,000 networks around the world. It was originally developed by the Pentagon in the 70s as a communications network deliberately designed without a center (which could have been attacked) and is theoretically without limits. Over the years, various colleges and universities, libraries, corporations and other organizations have joined these interconnected networks, which are like train tracks that bring us to different communication stations around the world.

You may have wondered just how to send e-mail to people on other Internet networks. Let's look at some options.

If you're using **LAN-based e-mail** (LAN stands for Local Area Network and such e-mail is used by companies that want to improve employee communications), you'll need an **Internet gateway**, which is software that connects an installed LAN-based mail system to the Internet. With such a gateway, companies can send mail outside the LAN but won't be adding an additional mail system. Such gateways are provided by LAN-based e-mail or third-party vendors. (Lotus's cc:Mail, Microsoft Mail and Novell's GroupWise are examples of software products that send and receive messages across a LAN.)

If you're on a LAN-based e-mail system and want to have two-way communications with others via the Internet or other sites within your company, then you could use an **Internet front end**, which is software that lets you send and receive messages across the Internet. (An Internet front end is also useful if you aren't on a LAN.) Eudora and Z-Mail for Windows are examples of Internet front end programs (see the Resource Guide for more information.)

If you or your company wish to communicate via e-mail with users outside your company, you may prefer either a **commercial on-**

line service (such as CompuServe, America Online or Prodigy) or a business communications service (such as networkMCI Business or Business Network). The latter type offers many services besides e-mail, including fax, news and information. Both of these services send and receive messages via built-in gateways from the service itself to other mail systems, including the Internet. (You'll need on-line service front-end software, a modem and an optional connection via a gateway. (See Chapter 13 for examples of such software.) By the way, computer columnist John Dvorak calls E-Mail Connection the best general-purpose e-mail front end, which you could use with an on-line service—it's available from ConnectSoft at 206/827-6467.

INTEGRATED COMMUNICATIONS

Despite (or maybe because of) the complexity of today's communications, the trend is to simplify and consolidate whenever possible. We're going to see more and more of this in the years to come.

Personal computer-based voice mail has been available for a few years. Now you can manage both voice mail and faxing. VoiceFX by Orion Telecom (800/669-8088 or 214/416-3720) is a highly-rated package that can handle up to four phone lines, offers auto-attendant capabilities and has high-performance fax handling, including fax-on-demand features. You will have to dedicate a PC, however, as the message center.

Fax-communications software integrates data and fax communications. You should look for the following data communications features: easy fill-in-the-blank scripts for dialing in to on-line services and bulletin board systems (BBSs), an off-line e-mail manager (to save you money), phone book and e-mail organization. On the fax side, look for basic fax operations, annotation tools, auto-forwarding, cover page design capabilities, OCR (optical character recognition) software that turns incoming faxes into editable text, a fax-back or "fax-on-demand" feature and binary file transfer (BFT) that lets you send files in an editable format so the recipient doesn't have to use OCR.

A recent issue of *PC WORLD* gave two "Best Buy" awards in the fax-communications category, one to Delrina Communications Suite ($179), which has powerful fax tools and an Internet mail manager (by Delrina, 800/268-6082), and the other to Procomm Plus for Windows ($179), which features shared resources for both data and fax communications and an integrated phone book (by Datastorm Technologies, 314/443-3282).

Look for the convergence of the personal computer and the telephone and new **universal in-box** products. Such products will let you manage voice mail, fax and e-mail from your personal computer. Novell's GroupWise may well be worth checking for its in-box features.

Look, also, to **Modern Office Technology**, an excellent monthly magazine that gives you the latest in automation, technology and communication systems for your office (216/696-7000, 1100 Superior Avenue, Cleveland, OH 44114-2518).

WORKGROUP COMPUTING

One of the hottest trends today is the push to use computers and technology to improve how people work together. More and more software programs either have built-in workgroup features or are designed specifically as **groupware** or **workgroup software** to work over a network.

Whenever you mention "groupware," Lotus Notes immediately comes to mind because Notes pioneered this category. Notes is not an application but rather the leading workgroup application **platform** used for building and delivering a wide range of applications. Programmers and other highly technical people can use Lotus Notes directly to build custom, corporate, groupware applications.

But there are also "off-the-shelf" packages now that can provide specific workgroup solutions. We're going to look at the types of workgroup software packages that are now available.

In general these packages help work group(s) do one or more of the following: a) communicate with each other, b) share information and c) automate the work process(es) for better collaboration. In a larger sense, they all help reorganize and coordinate the ways people work together in order to produce quality products or services that satisfy customers. They also reflect and enhance the newer, more flexible ways people are working in teams that we discussed in Chapter 10.

Suites combine several different software programs, such as word processing, spreadsheet, presentation graphics and database. Look for them to become increasingly workgroup oriented with e-mail, calendaring and group scheduling. The most popular PC suites are Lotus SmartSuite (look also at the new Lotus NotesSuite), Microsoft Office and Novell's PerfectOffice. The latter, as of this writing, has received top praise for its integration and workgroup features. ClarisWorks is the highly-rated and best-selling suite for Macintosh users and now offers cross-platform compatibility for Windows and Mac.

E-mail is central to workgroup computing and can also be the foundation of other workgroup products such as **group schedulers**. CaLANdar by Microsystems (508/879-9000) is a good group scheduler. (Also check out Chapter 2 for group scheduling features in some of the PIMs; some of the suites offer group scheduling, too.)

Document management software is offering ways to store and synchronize electronic files (keep versions of files straight); retrieve them; and share documents and collaborate on them. Keyfile and Common Ground are two top-rated document management products (see them in the Resource Guide). **Electronic publishing** products, such as Novell's Envoy, let you electronically distribute documents, no matter what program they were created in, across platforms so that they can be viewed and even annotated. **Document conferencing** programs let you view and annotate documents in real time.

Conferencing software (sometimes called **whiteboard software**) lets you have discussion forums, brainstorms and meetings on different computers using a topic or a document as the basis for dialogue. Of course, you may already to able to do some of this now if you have access to a **bulletin board system** (BBS) through your e-mail or groupware package(s) that allows multiple users to have a discussion at the same time. (One BBS vendor, SoftArc, has received some good publicity for its FirstClass group communications product 905/415-7000.) But good conferencing software better manages a **discussion thread**, the progress of the topic(s) and the "postings" (comments, replies, questions and documents that are added or posted to the discussion). Threads can then be collected into **forums**. Conferencing software can also maintain indexes to speed up searches for words or phrases. Attachmate Corp.'s OpenMind (and

Crosstalk for the Mac) are award-winning examples (800/348-3221 or 404/475-8380) as are Collabra Share by Collabra Software (800/474-7427) and Trax Softwork's TeamTalk (310/649-5800).

Electronic meeting support software is conferencing software that helps you conduct either same-time, same-place or different-time, different-place meetings via the computer and offers a highly structured approach to conferencing. Ventana's GroupSystems V (800/368-6338 or 602/325-8228) and Eden Systems Corp.'s The Meeting Room (800/779-6338 or 317/848-9600) are examples.

The most sophisticated conferencing software is called **desktop or personal videoconferencing**, which provides a multimedia approach using video on a personal computer that lets people "meet," share information and collaborate in real time in different locations. Companies can save a lot of money on travel, overnight mail and faxing expenses. But research or review any necessary hardware you'll need to use with such software. Look for increasingly better video quality and for prices to continue to decline. Among the best products to date are PictureTel's Live PCS 50 (800/716-6000, 508/762-5367 and see Resource Guide) and AT&T Vistium Personal Video 1200 or 1300 (800/225-5627 or 513/445-5000).

Finally, **workflow automation software** uses rules-based logic to move information within your workgroup(s) and to automate and coordinate your business processes. Information can be structured and **text-based**, such as that contained in forms, or **image-based**. Delrina FormFlow (800/268-6082) and KeyFile (603/883-3800) are good examples (see their listings in the Resource Guide). The award-winning ActionWorkflow System (Builder and Manager components) by Action Technologies (800/967-5356 or 510/521-6190) runs on top of Lotus Notes (see the Chapter 9 Resource Guide).

RESOURCE GUIDE

Note: Always check with vendors for the latest version of software products and the compatibility with your existing hardware and software. "Suggested retail prices" are used; for most products look for lower "street" and special marketing prices. The following abbreviations are used and are in boldface for easy reference: **Win**=Windows; **Mac**=Macintosh; **Net**=network; **DOS**=MS-DOS or PC-DOS; and **OS/2**=OS/2 Warp. Many of the software products are widely available through computer dealers and software stores or can be ordered directly by calling the listed number. See this chapter and the index for other products. **See also the earlier portions of Chapter 11 and the index for other products.**

E-MAIL, FAX AND TELEPHONE

Delrina WinFax PRO is popular PC fax software that allows users to send, receive and manage faxes in any Windows application. It's easy to use and has many advanced features including: powerful phone books with links to most of the popular PIMs and contact management software; a cover page designer with over 100 predesigned cover pages; the ability to annotate and mark up faxes and the ability to convert faxes into editable text (OCR). It can be used standalone or on a network with **WinFax PRO for Networks.** Look for a Windows 95 version. **800/268-6082** or 408/363-2345. Delrina Corporation, 6320 San Ignatio Ave., San Jose, CA 95119

Eclipse FAX V lets you prepare, send, receive, print, edit and organize faxes. Its fast, accurate OCR easily and reliably converts faxed documents into usable, editable text. The new "Fax Assistant" feature automatically remembers what to do every time a fax is sent to or received from a particular person—a real timesaver. **Win.** $84.95. **800/452-0120** or 312/541-0260. Phoenix Technologies Ltd., Three First National Plaza, Ste. 1616, Chicago, IL 60602

Eudora allows users to send, receive, sort and manage e-mail over TCP/IP (Transmission Control Protocol/Internet Protocol) networks. It interacts seamlessly with existing e-mail packages without the need for specialized gateways. Regardless of platform, users can communicate with remote offices, distribute such things as formatted spreadsheets and documents and hold electronic meetings with other individuals and organizations in virtually any location. **Win or Mac.** $65. **800/2-Eudora** or 619/658-1291. Qualcomm Inc., 5545 Morehouse Blvd., Ste. 210, San Diego, CA 92121

FreeMail is a full-featured, easy-to-use unique mail program that allows users to exchange messages and files over phone lines using standard modems. FreeMail allows users to create their own private network without purchasing expensive networking hardware or subscribing to a commercial bulletin board service. The network is created by FreeMail's proprietary self-replicating feature, that lets you make program disks and give them to anyone to include in the network. FreeMail is cross-platform compatible, allowing direct PC and Mac communication, and also includes voice messaging. **Win, Win NT, Win 95 and Mac.** From $74.95 to $595.95. **406/586-4200** or FreeMail@aol.com. FreeMail Inc., PO Box 1656, Bozeman, MT 59771-1656

Personal-E Mailbox is software that allows any two or more PCs to automatically send or receive e-mail person-to-person direct over ordinary phone lines without interfering with voice calls on the same line. It requires no special hardware, fees or subscriptions. **Win and DOS.** $49.95. **503/531-2880.** AmerCom Inc., 1100 NW Compton Dr., Ste. 302, Beaverton, OR 97006

Tele-Tips is a rate survey that compares the major carriers' long-distance calling plans. It's conducted and produced by a 25-year-old consumer advocacy group. The residential guide is $3; the small-business guide is $5. Send a self-addressed stamped envelope and a check to the Telecommunications Research and Action Center, PO Box 12038, Washington, DC 20005.

ViaCrypt PGP (Pretty Good Privacy) is the most popular and trusted software program that will completely protect the privacy of your files and e-mail messages. Digitally signed messages authenticate the sender and detect tampering. Powerful encryption ensures that only your intended receiver can decipher your message. ViaCrypt PGP is ideal for individuals, small businesses and large corporations—anyone with proprietary or sensitive data. Fully interoperable versions are available for **Win, DOS, Mac and Unix.** $99.98 to $149.98, depending on the operating system. **800/536-2664** or 602/944-0773. ViaCrypt, 9033 N. 24th Ave., Ste. 7, Phoenix, AZ 85021-2847

Z-Mail for Windows is an award-winning program that provides complete cross-platform messaging. It supports virtually any version of Unix, Windows and Macintosh operating systems, as well as character-based terminals. **Win, Mac and Unix.** **415/898-8649** or e-mail: info@z-code.com. NCD, Z-Code Division, 101 Rowland Way, Ste. 300, Novato, CA 94945

ON-LINE/BUSINESS COMMUNICATION SERVICES

CompuServe Information Service is an award-winning, on-line service with 2.8 million members who access the service from more than 150 countries. The service offers global e-mail, the industry's first CD-ROM supplement, libraries of free software, selected 28.8kbps (kilobytes per second, a high modem speed), and worldwide Internet services. It's on-line newsstand features more than 200 general interest and niche publications, dozens of syndicated columnists and more than 900 entertainment, hobby, games and personal computer forums. You have unlimited access to more than 120 services including daily worldwide news, weather and sports reports. CompuServe offers networking, e-mail and business information services to major corporations worldwide. **Win, DOS and Mac.** $9.95 per month. **800/848-8199.** CompuServe Inc., PO Box 20212 Columbus, OH 43220-0212

Dow Jones News/Retrieval provides on-line business and financial information, including 1,900 publications and over 300 other sources of business and financial data. It's the only on-line service to offer same-day access to the full text of *The Wall Street Journal*, the New York Times News Service and the *Los Angeles Times*. Additional, optional services include your own customized electronic newspaper for *The Wall Street Journal*, CustomClips (selected from 1,600 world news sources and Ask Dow Jones for immediate research on companies, industries or topics of interest. **Win and Mac.** Call for pricing. **800/522-3567** or 609/520-4000. Dow Jones & Company, Inc., PO Box 300, Princeton, NJ 08543-0300

networkMCI Business was the top-rated business communication service in a recent *PC Magazine* article very close to press time for my book. Powerful and easy to use, networkMCI Business offers e-mail (customized versions of MCI Mail and ConnectSoft's E-Mail Connection), fax, news, personalized information retrieval, document sharing, videoconferencing services, Internet access and electronic shopping. **Win.** Call for pricing. **800/955-5210 or 800/955-6505** or e-mail, 690.5444@mcimail.com. MCI Telecommunications Corp., Business Markets Division, 3 Ravinia Dr., Atlanta, GA 30346

WORKGROUP COMPUTING

CaLANdar schedules appointments and tasks, both personal and group, for people and resources. Additionally, CaLANdar includes a telephone message center, a note pad facility and an in/out of the office "pegboard" system. An award-winning program, CaLANdar offers unilateral support for Windows, Macintosh and DOS. 800/489-2001 or 508/879-9000. Microsystems Software, Inc., 600 Worcester Rd., Framingham, MA 01701

Common Ground is an award-winning document management and sharing program that lets you share documents in their exact form, no matter which applications or fonts were used, across networks with others. It includes powerful indexing, search and retrieval. Because Common Ground isn't dependent on operating systems or specific fonts, it's ideal for cross-platform compatibility. **Win or Mac.** $189. 800/598-3821 or 415/802-5800. Common Ground Software, 1301 Shoreway Rd., Ste. 220, Belmont, CA 94002

Delrina FormFlow allows users with little or no programming experience to quickly create sophisticated forms applications with conditional routing and deploy them across their organization using their e-mail systems. Delrina FormFlow has extensive database connectivity, including native support for databases such as Oracle, Paradox, Microsoft SQL Server and many more. It has multi-platform support. The FormFlow starter kit includes a designer, two fillers, "Crystal Reports," a video, full documentation and 12 sample applications. **Win and net.** $399. 800/268-6082 or 408/363-2345. Delrina Corporation, 6320 San Ignatio Ave., San Jose, CA 95119

Keyfile is award-winning, full function, client/server-based document management and workflow software for automating business processes. Keyfile enables users to electronically handle every office document, both paper and electronic, by providing a complete tool for filing, retrieving, sharing, distributing and automating document management. **Win and OS/2.** Call for pricing. 603/883-3800. Keyfile Corp., 22 Cotton Rd., Nashua, NH 03063

12

THE TRAVELING OFFICE: HOW TO GET THINGS DONE ON THE ROAD OR AT HOME AND TRAVEL SMARTER

Quick Scan: If you travel a good portion of the time or you're a telecommuter with a home office or you have multiple offices, you need special time management techniques and office tools to handle work responsibilities. Discover how to master paperwork and communications from afar. Discover high-tech telecommunications options that are now available. Read about specific tips and tricks that other professionals use when they're in the air, on the road or just on the go.

More people today have the challenge of a "traveling office," of working in at least one non-traditional office—be it a car, a corner at home, a hotel room or the cramped quarters of an airplane seat. It's estimated that 25 million people now work outside the office on a regular basis and that figure is expected to jump by 25 percent in the next five years. We're seeing more "telecommuting" (that term, by the way was coined by futurist Jack Nilles in 1973 when he was a professor at USC). More and more people are setting up home offices (by the year 2000, more than 40 percent of adults will work out of their homes at least part of the time).

We're also seeing the mobile **virtual office**, which "nomad" workers can locate almost anywhere–their home, a hotel, their car or their customer's place of business. A virtual office is equipped with laptop computer, cellular phone, pager and other mobile telecommunication tools and is easy to relocate whenever the need arises. Just as Chapter 10 talked about how the term "job" is changing and is being replaced by the notion of "work," so, too, the traditional office where we used to do much of our work is changing, too.

Whether you "travel" 8 or 80 percent of the time for business keeping up with all your responsibilities in multiple, mobile offices can be quite a challenge. As one executive admitted, keeping up is difficult even when you're *not* traveling. The tools, tips and techniques in this chapter could make the difference for you between exhaustion and exhilaration.

For some business people, traveling, particularly by plane represents the opportunity to finally get some real work done without all the constant interruptions. Airplane travel time can be a precious respite from the more demanding everyday routine. One association executive told me a number of years ago, "The airplane is the best place to read, think and write because you're away from the telephone." That may not be as true today, what with phones on most planes and other telecommunications tools available; but many people choose not to use these tools during travel time.

WORKING ON THE ROAD

Make special use of your travel time.

While on a plane, Bill Butler, president of BCG Consulting, likes to make use of "creative thinking time." He'll take a sheet of paper and jot down ideas in the form of mind maps (visual idea outlines) and decision trees (pros and cons) for two or three of his current projects.

When Mike Welch was an association executive who had a secretary, he would bring along his portable Dictaphone recorder the size of a pager) and some pre-stamped "Jiffy" envelopes when he traveled. He would mail back the tapes in the padded envelopes. He said, "The *letters* weren't waiting for my signature; what was waiting for me when I returned was the *reply*."

For urgent dictation, Welch dialed into his desk dictation machine, which was on 24 hours a day. And since his secretary was "super sharp," if a change had occurred since he last dictated (e.g, a certain report had already come in), she would automatically update and correct the final letter.

If you use dictation, then you may want to use a **digital dictation machine**, which records the voice electronically to a computer hard drive or other mass storage medium. The big advantage to digitized technology is you can use it over phone lines and dictate from any type of phone from any location. You can key in simple codes to label your dictation and indicate its priority; high priority dictation gets transcribed first. You can dictate at any speed and transcribers can set the playback to match their typing speed without distorting the tone of the voice. Perhaps the biggest advantage is the ability to edit–to insert new material at any point. Another big plus is the ability to search quickly via random access rather than having to search laboriously through a tape. (For digital dictation systems contact the following companies: Dictaphone Straight Talk at 800/447-7749, Lanier Information Systems at 800/708-7088, PC Dart Digital Systems at 800/263-9947 and Philips Dictation systems at 800/445-8255.)

You can make good use of your commuting time by dictating, making calls on your cellular phone or listening to tapes. Encoders Inc. in Alexandria, Virginia (800/334-5771 or 703/548-3800) publishes "Newstrack Executive Tape Service," a biweekly tape cassette series that summarizes newspapers and magazine articles. (Try listening to tapes such as Newstrack on a plane, too.)

Accomplish as much as you can in the allotted time by **consolidating activities** when you travel. Plan ahead all the meetings you want to have and the people you want to see in a particular location. Consolidate similar activities–for example, group together all your writing work. Because space is at a premium, you're almost forced to work in this linear way. It's harder to jump from one thing to another when you can't spread out all your "stuff." (And if you're one of those people who accomplishes more when you travel, perhaps you should incorporate this one-thing-at-a-time work style into your back-at-the-ranch office, too.)

KEEPING UP WITH CALLS WHILE AWAY

"I stay flexible about which telephone I use—I don't have to be in a hotel room. I use pay phones when I can to keep the cost down but it's nice to use a cellular phone occasionally for convenience," says Betsy Kovacs, Deputy Director of the Center for Applied Public Health, Columbia University School of Public Health.

On a more philosophical note, Kovacs says that the telephone helps her "maintain the rhythm of life," no matter where she is. Besides telephoning for business, Kovacs will place "stay-in-touch" phone calls. "The telephone works from out of town. The other person doesn't really care where you are when you're calling to wish a happy birthday." She adds that personal telephoning also helps make travel less jolting.

Most business travelers will call in at least once a day for messages and try to return calls the same day. Derrick Crandall, president of the American Recreation Coalition, says, "I'm a big believer in telephone services on the road." Crandall, with a staff of five, feels a need to stay in touch with his office so he calls in two or three times a day. He also calls the office's voice-mail after business hours to leave or receive messages pertaining to staff.

Other business travelers rely more heavily on their staff or may use other communication channels, such as e-mail or faxing.

HANDLING PAPERWORK ON THE ROAD

Planning is the secret to handling paperwork when you travel. When you book your hotel reservation, for example, make sure the room has the basic paperwork necessities: a flat writing surface (or desk) with a light, a telephone and close access to phone and electrical outlets. (Isn't it inconvenient when the telephone is on the night table when you have a lot of phoning to do?) See if any in-room PCs, printers or fax machines are available. Here are some other ways to plan ahead for paperwork.

SET UP A PORTABLE OFFICE SYSTEM

You'll need to plan a system to organize your paperwork and office supplies. As with everything else, there's no one right way to organize this system. But having a regular system in place, with the right tools and routines for you, can guarantee a more productive trip.

Select practical accessories to hold and transport paperwork and supplies. Butler carries an expandable, leather document case that contains different colored folders. He also takes along a standard manila folder to store materials collected during the trip. Butler carries a lightweight tote bag filled with reading material; when empty, the bag can be folded inside the document case. He also has a plastic folder that holds thank you notes, sympathy cards, get well cards, stamps, number 10 envelopes and letterhead.

Categorize different types of papers. Welch organizes his reading material for a trip into three categories. One category he calls "First Priority," which includes all of the material related to a meeting. Another category is "Fun Stuff" such as the daily paper, *USA Today* and the *Wall Street Journal*, which he says are good sources of conversation starters. A third category is "Business Reading," such as lengthy reports, industry newsletters and selected articles.

Derrick Crandall travels with a very heavy briefcase containing project files, his long-term projects list and a trip file that has a trip sheet on top and other related material underneath. To keep up with correspondence, he also carries three or four number ten envelopes with stamps for one and two ounces of postage as well as one large envelope with three dollars of postage.

Take pertinent resource material with you in a concise, easy-to-carry format. One regional sales manager created an alphabetical notebook system that he takes with him when he travels. He says, "I'm not at my desk that often so I can't carry the whole file cabinet with me." So instead he carries a three-ring notebook with alphabetical tabs and reinforced paper sheets that contain summaries of clients and prospects, the latest meetings and the types of programs his company is offering. He uses single word phrases, "buzz words" he calls them, so he can see information at a glance. Typical information would include people profile facts such as key contacts, spouse's name and special interests, and buzz word summaries of problems and solutions that would instantly remind him of next actions to be taken. If a client calls when he is on the road, he is prepared to talk intelligently, armed with up-to-date information. When he's in the office, he uses the book there, too, because it saves him the motion of filing.

A **loose-leaf personal notebook organizer** is an invaluable tool for carrying information you collect on a particular trip. Many organizers come with special expense envelopes that are great for keeping all your records and receipts together in one place. These envelopes make it easy to compile expense reports when you return from your trip.

Portable file boxes may work for you if your office is in your car trunk or you have many files to take with you on a business trip. File boxes come in all shapes and sizes and can accommodate legal and letter files and hanging file folders. Check your office supply catalog under "file boxes" or "storage files." (See "Portable Office Products" in the chapter Resource Guide.)

If you're working at your airplane seat and you need some additional space to put your paperwork besides the tiny tray table, the SkyDesk ($14.85) gives you an additional ledge that you hang onto the back of the seat in front of you. It also has a stretch band that keeps books, magazines and papers in place while you work.

Kathryn Johnson, president/CEO of The Healthcare Forum in San Francisco, carries what she calls her "portable office," containing transparent plastic folders, supplies, dictation tapes and an Express Mail envelope. (Look, too, for the transparent, pastel colored plastic envelopes that let you see contents quickly and color code at the same time—the Paper Direct catalog has them, 800/A-PAPERS.)

PROCESS PAPERWORK IN TWO PLACES AT ONCE

If Johnson is away for more than three days, she takes work with her, completes it on the plane and mails it back to her office in the Express Mail envelope. She also mails back dictation tapes.

One executive has mail and important reading material sent to *him* via Federal Express when on an extended trip. Backup copies of written correspondence remain in the office. He says, "Nothing is more depressing than returning from a trip to a stack of papers. When I come back, rarely do I have anything on my desk."

If you're lucky enough to have an assistant, have your paperwork filed into active project folders or at the very least, into two colored folders, say, red for "urgent" and blue for "not urgent." When you return, check these folders in order of their priority.

As for the piles of papers that accumulate on any trip, organizing consultant Barbara Hemphill, author of *Taming the Paper Tiger*, offers several suggestions. She says the time to handle those papers is during the trip *before* you get home. Throw out what you can; sort the rest into file folders. (See Chapter 4 for file folders in your daily paperwork system, which can be adapted for your traveling office.)

One of Hemphill's folders has her secretary's name. She puts papers that her secretary will handle in this folder. Then she takes out her Dictaphone recorder and dictates instructions for each paper. This saves Hemphill time when she returns from her trip and gives her secretary some control over when she processes this paperwork.

If you're uncomfortable with dictating machines, you could use Post-it Notes. Use different colored Post-it Notes to distinguish paperwork with different priorities or to categorize different types of work.

As for all those business cards you collect, here are some tips to try, which are especially useful at trade shows and conferences. I jot down either an "A," "B" or "C" at the top to indicate how I view the importance of this contact. If a card doesn't rate one of these letters, it gets tossed as soon as possible. I also write the date and event or place where we met. If I need to write more background or followup information, I'll write "over" on the front and jot it on the back. (If you learn any personal tidbit, for example, names and ages of kids, write that down, too.) "A" cards usually are ones that will need some immediate followup and are grouped together, as are Bs and Cs. If you should ever use the back of your card to write someone else's name and address (because they don't have a card) be sure to cross out the front of your card so that you don't accidentally give it to someone else.

Finally, it really *is* possible to process paperwork in two places at once, particularly if it's electronic paperwork. See the upcoming Traveling Technology section for some exciting ways to reduce real paper and work collaboratively on electronic documents and information. (Chapter 11 also has some good ideas for you.)

And here's a tip if you ever plan to use the hotel fax machine:

check the cost first. Hotels sometimes assess high service charges—a flat rate $25 service charge per message or per-page fees of up to $10 for the first page and $1 for each additional page. An overnight mail service could be cheaper and the hotel may even have a daily pickup and delivery by such a service, which in many cases is Federal Express. (For other options see the section "More Traveling Technology" later in this chapter.)

TRAVELING TECHNOLOGY

Today's high-tech telecommunications make traveling and staying in touch easier than ever. **Rule Number One is how much and even whether you need to communicate at all** in any given instance. Just because you *can* do it (and in exciting high-tech ways) doesn't mean you *should* do it. Many people become too busy doing things they shouldn't be doing in the first place. Many are also making too many routine things urgent—not a very effective use of time. Too many people are communicating just too much of the time so that they have no down time, no private time, they're always working. Prioritizing is more important than ever before. Good organizational skills let you first see the big picture and then choose your system—the right habits and tools.

Another big problem is trying to decide which tools (or toys) to use. I did some seminar work for one Fortune 500 firm that had a problem with too many telecommunications toys. Many employees had to check five or six systems several times a day just to make sure they received all their messages. Pity those employees who were less than positively organized and forgot to check their computer's electronic mail box or the computerized message center. The more tools and systems you have, the more likely it is that something will slip through the cracks.

In addition, the company, through its strong emphasis on individualism, encouraged people to use communication channels that best fit them. This is a nice idea in theory, but when you have to remember how all of your colleagues like best to communicate and those colleagues are scattered across the country, your communications difficulties can easily multiply.

Rule Number Two is use the right telecommunications tools for you and keep them simple but effective for your applications. Cost

f the tools you select is a consideration, but be sure you measure
st in terms of time and energy savings as well as actual dollars.
se technology where it really counts.

ELEPHONY TOOLS

et's look at some voice communication tools, which fall under an
portant area of telecommunications, **telephony** (accent goes on the
cond syllable, pronounced as you would say "telepathy"). According
the dictionary, telephony is the technology of electrical sound
ansmission between distant points. It includes tools such as
swering machines, voice mail, cellular phones and pagers.

Telephone answering machines or **voice mail systems** can work
eat when you're out of your office. (Why is it you always seem to
t even more calls when you're away?) Of course if you have a
achine, you'll have one with remote access where you dial a code
retrieve messages. If you have a voice mail system or service, find
it if you can arrange to have it beep you via a pager. When you're
the road, you should change your message to encourage callers
leave a short, concise, message (and their phone number, which
ou might not have with you) and/or to direct them to other
mmunication tools—your e-mail, your pager or a cellular phone, if
asible. (And of course, a voice mail or "voice messaging" system is
r preferable to an answering machine because it lets several callers
ave messages at the same time, especially important if you receive
any calls and don't want to risk the chance of losing a call
henever your answering machine is handling another call
multaneously.)

Here's a timesaving voice mail tip if you're traveling and are
rtunate enough to have an assistant. Have your assistant listen to
d transcribe your voice mail and then summarize important
essages for you by leaving one message on your voice mail (or e-
ail.)

Many hotels now have their own voice messaging systems for
ests but be careful when using them because they don't offer as
uch privacy as other tools. It's best not to discuss any sensitive,
nfidential or personal matters on hotel voice mail (or on an
coming hotel telephone line for that matter). Call back on an
tgoing line to discuss such matters; you'll hear a beeping sound if
third party is on an outgoing line. It's possible for a hotel

employee or anyone familiar with a given hotel's system to be ab[
to listen to messages of any guest. If the hotel voice mail syste[
uses a code (such as your room number and the first four letters [
your last name), ask if you can change the code. You could opt n[
to use the system at all and revert back to written telephor
messages; that will discourage callers from leaving private message

We're seeing more uses for voice mail besides telephor
messages. Novell includes its Telephone Access Server feature [
part of its GroupWise software, which lets you *listen* to your e-ma
and scheduling/calendaring information. (You probably wouldn't wa[
to use your cellular phone for this, which could be quite costly.)

Sign up for a **call forwarding** service through your phor
company if you want to be able to forward some or *all* your calls

If you use your car frequently in your work or have a lo[
commute, a **cellular telephone** is a must. Stuart Crump, editor of th
Cellular Sales and Marketing newsletter says to look for these fo[
features: hands-free speaker phone, memory dialing, voice-activate
dialing and a car adaptor so it can be used safely in the car.

Crump says that 90 percent of all cellular phones are used in th
car. Consequently, it's essential to have hands-free operation. Ca
cellular phone dealers to see what devices they recommend for you
particular phone. Some phones come with an earphone. In *The Wa
Street Journal* I read about one investment manager who uses a str[
of Velcro tape on the back of his phone and another strip
attached to the earpiece of an inexpensive plastic headset that h
"wears" when he's using his phone.

Selecting a cellular phone can be a challenge. There are abo[
a dozen major manufacturers, each of which makes about three [
four models—giving you about 40 models from which to choose. I'[
used an AT&T phone and GE is also a solid brand.

My personal favorite brand is Motorola, which pioneered th
cellular phone starting in the 70s, and is known for its line of "Fl[
Phones." I have used the state-of-the-art Motorola MicroTAC Eli[
personal cellular phone (see Figure 12-1 for the digital version
which is a "totally cool" phone that even offers a built-in digit[
answering machine. Motorola now offers a "wallet on a string" that
ideal for carrying any size or style Motorola Flip Phone (see Figu[
12-2).

Figure 12-1. The Motorola Micro Digital Elite is a light (6.6 ounces), advanced digital pocket phone that includes a vibration alert mode feature (call 800/331-6456 for Motorola's Cellular Information Center).

Figure 12-2. Two views of the handy Motorola Purse PAK "wallet on a string." There's an expanding pocket to accommodate different size batteries on the Motorola Flip Phones; an interior section has space for driver's license, cards, money, checkbook and other small personal items.

Type of use should also be a prime factor to help you select an appropriate model. For example, if you only plan to use your phone in your car, then select a permanently installed "mobile" **car** phone, which has a high-powered (three-watt) transmitter. (Car phones typically offer hands-free operation by featuring a speakerphone and sometimes a voice-activated feature that lets you say someone's name and the phone automatically dials the person's number.) However if you need more flexibility, consider a **transportable** phone. A transportable is a briefcase-size model that has its own battery pack and weighs in at about 10 pounds; it's useful if you want to use the phone away from your car at another location. A transportable offers similar power to a mobile phone's.

For the greatest flexibility, use a light **handheld** or **pocket** phone—the most popular cellular phone today. A handheld is light (under two pounds) and therefore very portable, but it isn't as powerful as the other models (about a half-watt). You may lose some reception at times, and since it's battery-operated, you'll have to recharge occasionally. But the fact that it can easily be carried in a briefcase or purse has led to its current popularity—that plus a continual decline in price.

It's also possible to slip your portable into a car adapter bracket equipped with an external antenna, which will improve its performance inside the car dramatically. Some adapters will also let you operate and charge the phone directly off the car battery, saving your portable's batteries for use outside the car.

The new **digital** networks will be able to handle a greater number of calls than the older **analog** technology, ensuring that your call will go through the first time. Digital technology usually provides clearer sound, better reception and greater privacy (digital impulses are hard to tap). Plus, cellular modems are more reliable with digital technology. All digital cellular phones are "dual-mode" (analog/digital).

Choosing the hardware is only half the story; you'll also need to select a **carrier** or service provider. There are usually just two choices in a given area. Find out what each provider can offer in terms of coverage area, quality of customer service, clarity of sound, a convenient location and rates. Make sure there are no hidden costs in your purchase or even your monthly service—find out what all the fees are or *could* be. Typically, a cellular phone costs $60 to $70 a month.

You'll also want to choose a carrier that most closely matches the areas you travel. When you travel outside your carrier's territory you'll have to pay an expensive "roaming" fee. If you use an outside area frequently, consider having an additional carrier for that area as well. Or you could get a "Follow Me Roaming" service, where callers can easily call you outside your carrier's area without having to dial an access code for the area you're in.

Ask a carrier about any other special "custom calling" services that are offered, such as call waiting, call forwarding, no-answer transfer, conferencing and voice mail.

Here's one important cellular tip, especially if you're using analog technology with your cellular phone and you have confidential information to discuss—don't do it! Be up front and share your concerns about cellular security and privacy and reschedule, if possible, any confidential conversation for another time. Or try the cellular encryption technology that SafeCall of Boston (800/222-2395) sells to its customers (mostly lawyers) who simply must use the cellular phone for their confidential calls (it costs 62 to 75 cents a minute for this technology).

Many people prefer **pagers** (which are small radio receivers) to or in combination with cellular phones. Pagers have a number of advantages. They're smaller and lighter to carry, much less expensive (typically $8 to $10 per month for basic service), can reach inside buildings, have great battery life, work nationwide (if you have a nationwide pager) and in many other countries and are becoming more and more versatile. A **PCMCIA pager** connects to either your laptop or a palmtop, such as the HP 100LX, and works great for e-mail because you have your computer there to display the message in its entirety (for more about PCMCIA pagers and cards, see the upcoming section, "More Traveling Technology"). Some paging companies provide software to let PCs and Macs send text messages or you can buy one such highly rated software program called WinBEEP or its networking cousin, WANbeep (see the Resource Guide or call 810/362-2288).

Alphanumeric pagers have been around for more than a decade. They can provide both numeric and text messages; sometimes an instant concise message from such a pager is sufficient, eliminating the need to call someone back. Alphanumeric pagers can also now receive e-mail (or at least the message header and a line or two at a time). The Motorola Memo Express can receive and display messages of up to 120 letters or numbers. Motorola's newest pager, the ADVISOR Pro (Figure 12-3), lets you receive up to 20 text or numeric characters a line and scrolls down to handle up to 1800

Figure 12-3. The Motorola ADVISOR Pro alphanumeric pager features a two-line, high-contrast display that can scroll down to include up to 1800 characters per message. (For its full line of pagers reach Motorola at 800/548-9954.)

characters per message.

If you send a lot of pages or have several pagers going in your office, look at the Motorola WordSender, a combination phone/alphanumeric pager. This device offers 20-number speed-dial, a redial feature, pager information storage, a timer and a handy help screen.

An alphanumeric pager (and its paging service) costs more than the more common **numeric** type, which provides only a digital readout of the phone number of the person calling you. Also, paging companies charge by the byte, so you will want to limit your e-mail-to-alphanumeric-paging routine or have people send you shorter messages! One other word of caution: pagers can drop characters when they're used in airplanes, tunnels, trains and buildings with a lot of steel.

If you need a cross between a pager and an answering machine, consider getting the Motorola Spirit tone and voice pager. According to Barbara and Jim Suitor, who manage the Holiday Hills Resort in Eddyville, Kentucky, this pager lets someone call you on the phone and leave a 15-second live, audible message.

Look, too, for **wrist watch pagers** such as the Seiko MessageWatch, which is pioneering the FM radio broadcast infrastructure to transmit paging and information services data. The MessageWatch is currently activated in select cities and is expected to be in major U.S. markets within the next two years. For more information about this exciting new product call 800/456-5600.

Check to see how many messages/numbers your pager will hold.

ow-cost pagers (about $40) will hold up to five, which may be fine
 you don't get many calls and/or you can call people back right
way. For another $20 you can get a pager that will hold 16 or
1ore. Look for pagers with the choice of a beep or a vibration (the
atter is handy in public places, where you don't want to call
ttention to the beeper or disturb others).

There are many nationwide paging services. Two of the biggest
re SkyTel (Mobile Telecommunications Corp.) at 800/456-3333
which also has links to MCI Mail and other e-mail services) and
1obileComm. Also ask your local paging company to help you get
onnected to a nationwide service.

Here's a tip: don't tell everyone you carry a pager. Some people
ill abuse your time and expect you to call back right away, perhaps
ven at night or weekends, which may be too invasive, depending of
ourse upon your work and/or lifestyle.

Many mobile professionals will combine several different
elecommunications tools such as a cellular phone with a pager and
oice mail. You may be able to program your voice mail to beep you
henever you receive a voice mail message or simply for urgent
alls. And then you can promptly return the calls you choose with
our cellular phone.

1ORE TRAVELING TECHNOLOGY

A laptop computer is central to most people's traveling office,
hether you have telecommunications requirements or you just need
o get some work done while on the road. In fact, laptops are often
alled simply "notebooks." Some models are as thin as a notebook
nd weigh under four or five pounds—and are called "subnotebooks."
Jnfortunately, most subnotebooks have smaller keyboards and
creens and lack some other notebook features. Expect to see more
nprovements that bring the weight down to no more than four
ounds and maintain standard keyboard and screen sizes and
sability. The keyboard design and screen are essential features,
specially if your laptop is a serious business tool you use every day.
IBM's ThinkPad and Apple's PowerBook series of notebook
omputers have received some excellent reviews.)

A laptop computer can be an invaluable tool if you're in outside
ales, giving you a real customer service edge. That's the case for

salespeople who work for one food distributor. Armed with laptop and order-taking software, the 35 sales reps call on restaurants hospitals and other institutions. Sales reps save customers time an money by providing on-site analyses and up-to-the-minute dollar an supply figures, transmitting and verifying orders on the spot an printing out the final order for the customer (sales reps also carr portable printers). Using technology in this way can transform you relationship with customers; you become more like partners i business.

A number of products and accessories will help to make you laptop more productive. Be sure yours comes equipped with battery that has a long life—ideally at least six hours long, the tim of roughly one transcontinental flight. (Or plan to bring along spare battery, which is a good idea in any event.)

If you use your laptop on your lap you'll appreciate the Noteboo Wrist Perch/Lap Cat Combo (Figure 12-4) made of lightweigh medical-grade foam that keeps your laptop securely in place an comfortably supports your wrists. It also provides extra padding whe you pack up your laptop. (It costs $27.98; call 800/487-0781 to orde or for store information.)

Figure 12-4. The Notebook Wrist Perch/Lap Cat Combo lets you comfortably us your laptop where it was designed to be used, your lap. You can adjust the slope c the keyboard for even more comfortable typing as shown in the picture on right.

Take care of your laptop on the road. Make sure its travel case has plenty of padding, to protect your computer if it's accidentally dropped. (Kensington makes a great line of cases called the NoteBook Traveler, 800/535-4242 or 415/572-2700 as does Targus (714/523-5429). Avoid temperature extremes and fluctuations in temperature. For example, don't leave your laptop in a hot trunk, which can cook components and screens. An icy cold environment could crack a screen. Use antiviral software to protect against viruses. Deter laptop theft with the Kensington MicroSaver cable and locking system.

It's convenient to use **PCMCIA cards**, also called "PC cards," which are credit-card-sized cards that expand the capability of your laptop. You can get different PCMCIA cards for such things as paging, to use as modems, to provide "flash memory," to use for sound and to use for additional portable hard disk storage. PCMCIA, by the way, stands for Personal Computer Memory Card International Association, a group that set an important standard for "plug and play" operations using these cards, which today are more standardized. Most notebooks provide a dual socket that can usually take two PCMCIA cards.

Here's another very important tip to follow when using a PCMCIA card modem: **don't plug into a digital or PBX phone jack** (usually located in the wall), because the high current can destroy your modem. If you don't know whether a line is analog or digital, you'll want to get the IBM Modem Saver, a simple, penlike test instrument that's $29 (800/388-7080). If it turns out to be digital, you can use the Konexx Konnector Model 111 ($159) by Unlimited Systems Corp. (800/275-6354 or 619/622-1400) to connect your modem and communicate over the digital or PBX phone.

A **connector** is especially handy in a hotel room when you want to connect your modem-equipped laptop computer (or compact fax machine) into the hotel room's telephone system. Two good brands for connectors are Unlimited Systems Corp. (800/275-6354 or 619/622-1400) or TeleAdapt, which provides 24-hour international customer service, (408/370-5105).

A **docking station** and/or a **port replicator** let you more easily and quickly connect your laptop to your desktop system or turn it into one.

Here are three more tips for traveling laptops. First, make sure your laptop is covered by your insurance, no matter where your laptop happens to be (think up all the various scenarios you can). Second, if possible get 24-hour on-site service and/or replacement for your laptop. Third, take your overnight delivery service number with you (and any of their forms).

If you plan to send or receive many faxes, you have several options. Using your laptop (with either an internal modem or external PCMCIA fax/modem card), you could send and receive faxes via your computer. (Check out Angia Communications' award-winning SafeJack PCMCIA data/fax modems, 800/877-9159 or 801/371-0488; Practical Peripherals ProClass 288, 800/442-4774; and Megahertz XJ2288, 800/517-8677.) You'll need some software to help you, of course, such as WinFAX Pro by Delrina Corp. (800/268-6082 or 408/363-2345) and FaxWorks PRO by SofNet, Inc. (800/329-9675 or 404/984-8088). It's probably more convenient to put the software on your desktop computer and then dial in for your faxes from your laptop.

Since faxes can take up a lot disk space on your computer, you may also need a **fax mailbox**, which holds faxes until they are retrieved or forwarded. You can receive faxes into your computer or send them to other destinations—another computer or fax machine. Delrina Fax MailBox is one such service. A business communications service such as networkMCI Business also offers a fax mailbox, as does Mobile Telecommunications (Mtel), which offers SkyFax in addition to its nationwide paging service, SkyTel (800/759-1911). A fax mail service (also called a fax mail network) may have other features such as automatic redialing, delay and send, "polling" (asking another machine if it has any messages) and sending one document to many different recipients.

If you need a hard copy fax, you can print out any fax stored in your modem-equipped computer via a hotel fax machine or at a **public fax station**, located at a quick printer or commercial mail station.

If you do heavy faxing when traveling, consider getting a **portable fax machine**. Some of the latest models are very compact and relatively light (five to 10 pounds) and can work with cellular phones. A **portable printer**, which weighs less than five pounds, may be a better option.

Look at more options. If you're staying in a hotel, look for one that caters to business travelers with either special business floors or special equipment in the rooms. (Start with Marriott and Hyatt, which are becoming more business friendly.) By the way, if you're planning to do extensive work from your hotel room, check the status of their telephone system and rooms before you get there. Find out if there's a business center on site, available equipment, hours of operation and fees; if there's no business center, find out what the hotel charges for printing, copying and faxing and availability, as well as any special services. Some hotels have faxes sent to an electronic fax mailbox, which guests can retrieve at the nearest fax machine. Some hotels may offer a service that delivers faxes via guest-room TV sets; using a remote control, a guest can either order the fax they see or have it deleted. Some airlines now have phones with fax capabilities.

If you have a lot of detailed information to transmit that would be cumbersome in fax form, such as lengthy documents, databases or computer programs, e-mail may be the way to go. You can send and receive messages and/or attachments (separate files) as well as have access to e-mail networks and systems, which in turn integrate with other telecommunications channels. E-mail subscribers also have access to a variety of on-line databases and information services. E-mail is also useful for international business travelers who must communicate between vastly different time zones–the power of global e-mail systems is awesome.

There are three basic types of programs that connect laptops with desktop computers (some of the mentioned programs may overlap with one another). If you're on the road with your laptop and you want to use files and applications that are on your desktop computer, a **remote control program** will let you do so. The applications and files remain on your desktop computer, although you can see file changes on your laptop. (Just as you have a remote control to turn on your TV, your laptop and modem act as a remote control device to work your desktop computer.) If you have a powerful laptop with a fast modem that can handle applications itself, you may need a program that also provides **remote access.** Highly rated remote control programs are Close-up ($199) by Norton-Lambert (805/964-6767) and Norton pcAnywhere by Symantec (800/441-7234, 503/334-6054); for remote access there's WanderLink, 800/828-4146.

A **file transfer program**, such as Traveling Software's award-winning LapLink, lets you easily and quickly copy files from one machine to another, also called "downloading" or "uploading" files (800/343-8080 or 206/483-8088). You could use LapLink to back up your notebook computer every day to a special directory on your desktop computer called "notebook." A good communications program, such as Procomm Plus by Datastorm Technologies (800/ 315-3282 or 314/443-3282) also offers remote file-transfer capabilities.

Finally, a **file synchronization program** helps you keep the latest most up-to-date versions of files on laptop and desktop machines. Same<>Same is a simple program you can use by DPM Computer Solutions (800/242-4775 or 619/693-4162) as is FileRunner for Windows by MBS Technologies (800/860-8700 or 412/941-9076). PowerMerge by Leader Technologies is highly-rated Macintosh file synchronization and on-line backup software that works via network or removable media (it's widely available from resellers).

If you don't need the price nor capabilities of a laptop, but would like automatic access to a phone and address database, calendar, scheduler, calculator and other handy features, get yourself a **palmtop** or an **electronic organizer**. Some of these products can exchange information with a personal computer. (See Chapter 2 for more information about these and other personal information manager products.)

Finally, be on the lookout for more and more **wireless technology**. Of course, we've already talked about the popularity of pagers and cellular phones—but there's more.

Using Traveling Software's LapLink Wireless software, you can network two computers at distances of 30 to 40 feet (you could connect two desktops, a desktop and a laptop or two laptops, for example). This program lets you do easy file transfers and file synchronization, as well as share a printer. It's also great for setting up a new machine and backing up onto a different computer. LapLink Wireless (800/343-8080 or 206/483-8088) works with a radio-frequency technology that uses tiny transmitter/receivers connected to your machines' serial ports. It's not super fast, though, transmitting at only 115 kps (half as fast as a floppy).

Personal digital assistants (PDAs) are evolving handheld wireless communicators that can connect you to all kinds of information and communication services. The operative word here is "evolving" because these devices aren't quite there yet, nor are the wireless networks over which they will ultimately travel. A PDA has both 'oice and data capability and will eventually make use of "electronic ¡gents" that will be able to do remote searching, matching and :ompiling for you to pinpoint products or services that fit your :riteria. You could put out a Request for Proposal (RFP) for a >roduct or a service and the PDA's agent would search networks for 'ou, download appropriate information and beep you when it found his information.

Two-way wireless communications is a reality today (although not ¡s fully developed as it will be one day). Two main wireless networks ≥xist (Ardis and RAM Mobile Data) but only for data ::ommunications and these networks are limited to metropolitan areas (although more than 90 percent of U.S. business locations are :overed). Wireless networks are also known as "packet radio networks" and are more secure than cellular ones.

RadioMail (415/286-7800) is a nationwide, two-way wireless communications service that operates through an Internet gateway. It lets you send e-mail and faxes; provides news headlines and customized stock quotes; offers a voice-message service (for callers who don't have e-mail) that lets them call a toll-free operator who takes their voice message and converts it into an e-mail message that is then forwarded; and offers 24-hour customer service. RadioMail works on a wide range of platforms. RadioMail has been nicknamed "fast mail" because messages are sent and received instantly if your modem is on; if not, messages are stored in a box and as soon as your modem is on, messages are sent automatically, instantly.

Wynd Communications (805/545-5174) is another wireless communications service that focuses largely on e-mail. It has excellent customer service.

The hardware you'll need to work with a wireless communications service requires a wireless modem plus a device. The following are hardware examples: Ericsson GE's Mobidem, a battery-operated wireless modem that you'd use with your desktop computer; IBM's OEM Wireless Modem (model no. 29H3880) that is used with a notebook computer; a Motorola PCMCIA wireless modem card with a keyboard-based palmtop PDA (such as Hewlett Packard's 200LX or the Sharp Zaurus); and a pen-based PDA, which already has the wireless modem built in (Motorola's Envoy and Marco are examples).

Look, too, for wireless software that lets you easily access computer files and information. GoldMine Wireless, for example gives you easy access to database information and works with Mobidem and PCMCIA cards.

SEVEN TRAVEL TIPS
YOU NEED TO KNOW

Let's face it: traveling is time consuming and energy draining particularly when you're out several days at a time, working feverishly with all of your high-tech tools and you're crossing different time zones. All the more so if you tend toward disorganization. So part of maintaining an effective traveling office and staying physically effective yourself is learning to handle the logistics of travel. Here are seven travel tips that will make your trips less hectic and maybe even pleasurable.

ONE: TAKE TIME TO PREPARE

You are only as organized as you are prepared. "I pack my suitcase, my briefcase and my mind for each trip," says Mike Welch. "I really think it through. Like great athletes who picture themselves leaping over the bar, I picture myself at the business meeting." In addition to packing all the pertinent meeting materials, Welch commits to memory all the important details concerning the agenda.

Bill Butler advises, "Read any briefing papers or material pertaining to your trip *before* you leave. State Department research indicates information is not absorbed and retained as well when you're in a travel mode."

Take time to prepare your clients or customers when you're leaving them to go on a trip. Trish Lester, president of a business communications company, writes her clients three weeks before she leaves for an extended period of time. She encourages them to call her before she departs, but also assures them they have the option of leaving messages on her voice mail while she's away.

If you're planning to meet someone at an airport, hotel or restaurant, be sure you each have a backup plan. Having prearranged contacts, such as secretaries, at each respective office, can help with any last minute change in plans.

Find out in advance about any timesaving services offered by your car rental agency and hotels, such as **counter-bypass programs,** to avoid standing in line and otherwise wasting your valuable time. Be sure to check all travel benefits, including rental car discounts, that are available to you through your company or any professional association memberships. Always ask about special deals, such as a "corporate rate," but don't assume that's the best deal. A discount through an association may be better.

As for hotel accommodations, you may not be aware just how much influence you can have in that area, too. For starters, you should **negotiate your room rate.** Did you know that many hotels have more than 30 different rates for each guest room? Ask about any specials—such as corporate, weekend or midweek rates or if there are any special ads or coupons running in the local paper. Some hotels offer their own clubs and extend special discounts to members. Never use a hotel chain's toll-free 800 number if you plan to negotiate. Call the hotel directly.

Be sure to **spell out important room preferences** you may have—non-smoking, quiet and proximity to an elevator. If you need to do a lot of work from your room, find out what the setup is regarding work space, access to the phone and outlets, whether there is a data line in the room for a modem and any telecommunications equipment and services the hotel provides for business people. Marriott and Hyatt, by the way, are offering special rooms for business people. Call ahead to see if a hair dryer or other items are automatically provided so you don't have to pack them. If you're traveling in Europe, you may also want to request a room on a lower floor for safety reasons, as fire alarm systems are nonexistent in many foreign countries.

If you have an agent, make sure yours is organized and routinely remembers to handle all the details, such as crediting mileage to your frequent flyer club. This is one item that is typically missed. One agency uses a quality checklist that is printed on the front cover of a special jacket that holds airline tickets and itinerary. As a customer, you can see at a glance that indeed all those details have been handled.

The ideal agent will ask for and keep up-to-date travel information regarding your frequent flyer numbers, your billing procedures (perhaps you use two different credit cards, one for

business and the other for personal travel, which is a good idea) and
your travel preferences (such as airline seating, rental cars and hotel
rooms). If you have to start from scratch for each trip, your agent
just isn't organized enough.

Your agent should routinely provide you with seat assignments
and boarding passes so that you don't have to wait in line at the
airport.

For flight times to avoid, Bill Butler comments, "I look with a
jaundiced eye at the first flight out, which is often a very popular
flight for business. I will usually avoid it because it's too crowded
and hectic." Also avoid, if possible, booking the last flight out
especially if you have a speaking engagement or a critical meeting.
It's far better to spend extra time at your destination than arriving
a day late because of a cancelled flight.

While you may not want the first flight out, do travel early in
the day, if you can. You have more options if a flight is cancelled.
Avoid connecting flights but if you must schedule them, leave
enough time between them—at least double what the airline tells
you. If you must book a connecting flight, try to do so through a
smaller airport. Also avoid traveling during holidays.

Many business travelers prefer aisle seats because they offer a
little more leg room and are less confining. But not just any aisle
seat will do. Derrick Crandall likes an aisle seat close to the
boarding ramp since he carries on luggage rather than checking it in.

Mike Welch's seat preference is a no-smoking, aisle seat. His
preference is so strong that he jokes, "I'll sit on the wing rather than
sit anywhere else."

Some people prefer the "bulkhead," which has seats with the most
leg room—more leg room than aisle seats. The disadvantages are that
you have no underseat storage and you'll have to move if you want
to see the movie screen.

If you're safety conscious, you may prefer to take the advice of
most air safety experts who recommend an aisle seat next to the
rearmost overwing exit. On the subject of safety, also read the
emergency card in the seat pocket to find out how to open the
various door and window exits and to locate the four exits that are
closest to your seat. Also recommended is counting the rows of seats
to each exit; you might not be able to see the exit signs in an
emergency but you could still feel and count the seats.

Before you leave for the airport, always call the airline to make sure your flight is on time. For return flights, it's also a good idea to call the day before to reconfirm your flight, even if you are ticketed.

Allow plenty of time to get to the airport and your gate, especially for larger airports. You should get to the gate at least 30 minutes to an hour before a domestic flight; you can lose your seat assignment if you don't. If you get there less than 10 to 15 minutes before the flight, you could lose your reservation altogether.

As for hotels, avoid checking in with your MasterCard or Visa, which the hotel will use to pre-approve and set aside a dollar amount to cover your expected expenses. This pre-approval actually reduces your current credit limit. Instead, check in with a card without any credit limit such as an American Express, a Diners Club or a Carte Blanche card, even if you later decide to pay with a MasterCard or Visa.

TWO: ORGANIZE YOUR TRAVEL INFO

The more you travel, the more you need to stay current on travel trends, topics and your own travel information.

Butler stays current on flight information by subscribing to the pocket-size *OAG Pocket Flight Guide* (North American edition), which is updated monthly and available by subscription from Official Airline Guides (OAG), Reed Travel Group Airline Division, 2000 Clearwater Drive, Oak Brook, IL 60521-8806, 800/DIAL-OAG (708/574-6000). Carry the "OAG" when you travel; if your flight is canceled, you could find an alternate on your own more quickly using it. And then to avoid waiting in line, go to a pay phone and call the airline directly yourself.

If you have a personal wireless communicator, such as Envoy, you can access OAG's FlightLine, an on-line OAG; if you have your laptop with you and you have an on-line service, you could subscribe to Electronic Edition Travel Services (EETS), which provides not only flight information but the ability to book the reservations directly (EETS is available through OAG or through services such as CompuServe and Dow Jones). Other OAG products include FlightFAX, which allows you to call into the OAG on-line system requesting available flights, pricing and seating and within minutes, the requested information, including the lowest fare, is faxed back to you. FlightDisk provides monthly updated flight information giving you access to hundreds of thousands of flights across the country and around the world, as well as to ground information.

Eaasy Sabre is another on-line travel reservation service available through CompuServe and other on-line services.

Butler stays current, also, by following industry reports included in the *New York Times* travel section. He has learned, for example, that Atlanta often shows extra delays because of a big problem with early morning ground fog. On the other hand, Memphis, which has Federal Express' major terminal, is considered the "all weather airport." Butler points out Chicago is noted for lots of traffic so you need to allow extra time between connecting flights.

Butler used to travel 50 to 60 percent of the time; he now travels 30 to 40 percent. With such a heavy travel schedule, it makes good sense to have fingertip travel information. Butler maintains files on major cities he visits frequently, such as New York and Washington, D.C., and he subscribes to *New York* and *Washingtonian* magazines.

Butler also keeps his own travel notebook, which is arranged by client and location. The notebook contains directions, places to stay, ground transportation, how long it takes to get to the airport at various times of day, the "leading food adventures to the locals," restaurants to avoid and hotel history, in particular his room preferences. (Nonsmokers may also want to request and note for future reference which hotel rooms and floors are smoke-free.)

Organized travelers have a trip form they carry with them that lists their itinerary, transportation, lodging, key contacts and phone numbers. They also leave at least one copy of their trip sheet with a staff member, as well as with their family. Butler has an expense report printed on the back of his form, which makes for a convenient system.

Mike Welch uses a sheet that lists such things as the airlines and types of planes he'll be flying, seat assignments, who confirmed his reservations, rental car arrangements and who will pick him up. Along with this sheet, Welch also brings photocopies of airline guide pages he may need. He carries these items in his pockets, which have been specially organized for travel so that he doesn't have to look in a million places. Having a simple and dependable system, even when it comes to organizing your pockets, can make a big difference when traveling.

THREE: HOW TO SELECT TRAVEL CLOTHING

"Keep it simple" is the best advice when it comes to selecting clothes for a trip.

Betsy Kovacs buys clothing that doesn't wrinkle. She says, "If they are wrinkled on the rack, you know they will wrinkle on the road." (Anything with wool travels great, as well as knits and polyester blends.) She also wears (never packs) one all-purpose coat appropriate for a particular trip.

Bill Butler simplifies his travel wardrobe. Butler packs black shoes and socks, makes sure shirts go with all suits and relies on neckties to provide color. Designer Bill Blass, I understand, limits his travel wardrobe to two basic "colors"—black and white.

Image consultant Jill Sprengel, of Redondo Beach, California, suggests women stick with solid colors and separates. Use accessories such as belts, print scarves or necklaces to add variety and choose ones that bring up the bottom color from your skirt or pair of slacks. Some handy items to include are a dressy blouse and belt to go out in the evening and a tweed jacket that has many colors. Sprengel advises you to take no more than three pairs of shoes—one for walking or sports (such as tennis shoes), a pair of flats and low heels that match your hair or skin color. Have at least one belt to match the main pair of shoes you'll be wearing.

Wear the right clothing when you're flying. Several layers of light-colored, well-fitting (but not tight) clothing are best. From a safety perspective, select clothes made of wool, a naturally flame retardant fabric. It's better than most materials, especially synthetics and leather, which should be avoided. (A good way to test flammability is to snip off a small piece of fabric and set it afire. If it melts rather than chars, don't wear it.) Also avoid high-heeled shoes.

FOUR: HOW TO CHOOSE AND USE LUGGAGE ON THE GO

When it comes to luggage, I recommend a small suitcase with built-in wheels that you can roll through the terminal and right down a plane aisle. I recommend and use the Travelpro Rollaboard line, which pioneered the concept of a suitcase with wheels and a retractable handle. I prefer taking luggage on board so as to avoid the hassles of lost, stolen or misdirected luggage. (It also saves you time waiting for luggage at baggage claim.) But FAA (Federal Aviation Administration) guidelines may put a crimp in this practice, if you must pack a lot of stuff.

The guidelines advise that passengers carry on no more than two pieces of baggage. Here are three options from which to choose:

- an underseat piece that is 9 by 14 by 22 inches maximum
- an overhead bin item that is 10 by 14 by 36 inches maximum
- a cabin closet hanging piece that is 4 by 23 by 45 inches.

Fortunately, personal items such as purses, coats, hats, umbrellas and cameras don't count as carry-on luggage; unfortunately, briefcases do.

Apparently, there may be some variation in how the guidelines are administered by different airlines, depending on factors such as aircraft size and the number of passengers on a flight.

I always recommend carrying luggage on board. I never check luggage on my way to any destination if I can help it; occasionally, coming back I will, however, depending on my own energy level or if I have a particularly heavy load. Even if you check most of your luggage, be sure to pack toiletries, prescriptions, underwear, a change of clothing, important documents, valuables and any other critical items in a carry-on bag.

By the way, the maximum a domestic airline will pay for lost luggage is $1,250 per paying passenger; it's much less for international flights—only $9 per pound. Since airlines try avoiding responsibility for valuables such as electronic equipment, cameras and jewelry, you may want to obtain some additional insurance coverage.

I enjoy using my Travelpro Rollaboard Suit Carrier and the Portfolio Case that attaches to a special clip (see Figure 12-5). The Suit Carrier has a special section for packing suits and dresses in a wrinkle-free fashion. The Portfolio Case is great for holding a laptop as well as my own portable office system. (The Travelpro system sure beats the garment bag, tote and luggage carrier I previously have used.) There are all kinds of zippered pockets and compartments that I label with round colored key tags (you can get

Figure 12-5. The Travelpro Suit Carrier and Portfolio Case make a great duo.

them in stationery stores). Tags tells the types of articles contained in each pocket or compartment. Having all those pockets can be a blessing if you stay consistent and always keep certain items in them—develop a good system. With compartments, you don't have to open up the main sections, which is difficult to do in cramped airplane seating. (The Travelpro line is widely available in luggage stores and catalogs or call Travelpro USA, 305/426-5996.)

If you're carrying around an expensive laptop and you're going to be out in public quite a bit, try using a backpack bookbag to look more inconspicuous. That's what project manager Sue McGinty does. She securely packs the computer in the bag, surrounding it with manuals (you could use towels), puts peripherals such as a mouse and modem into drawstring "stuff sacks" from a camping store and puts diskettes in a wallet with a Velcro closure (Allsop's Softpack Transportable is a great wallet that holds up to 16 3½-inch disks). Before you pack your laptop, pull the battery out a quarter of an inch because a bump during travel could accidentally turn on your computer and wear down your battery. (You should also bring an extra battery that's fully charged, as well as a recharging adapter.)

FIVE: PACK SYSTEMATICALLY

Betsy Kovacs starts by making a list that is divided into two parts: day and evening. She decides exactly what she is going to wear and which accessories will go with each outfit. She lays her accessories and clothes out on the bed before she packs them in her garment bag. (Her tote bag holds shoes and cosmetics.) She also has a permanent list of basics that she keeps in a pocket of her garment bag. Kovacs tries not to take too much but she also puts great emphasis on looking her best. When it comes to cosmetics and toiletries, Kovacs packs each item after she uses it the last time before the trip.

I keep many items in my suitcase all the time, in between trips. I have a cosmetic case that duplicates the cosmetics and toiletries I have at home. Packing time can be cut in half when you have an extra toiletry kit that is ready when you are. The ideal time to replenish any supplies that are low is when you unpack at the end of each trip. Dental, medical, body care and makeup supplies in travel-sized containers are convenient. For extra protection, fill containers three-quarters full and secure them in self-sealing plastic bags. I keep four small, zip-lock bags in my cosmetic case for four different types of toiletries—dental, facial, hair and eye care.

I also keep an extra hair dryer and several brushes in the bag, too, as well a couple of large plastic bags and a bathing suit (I'm a native Californian).

Pack your wallet systematically, too, or should I say, *unpack* it. Leave behind unnecessary credit cards, papers or accessories. Make a list of the credit cards you decide to take and their numbers and keep that list separate from your cards. Include any phone numbers you may need to call if your credit cards should become lost or stolen. For a Visa card, call 800/VISA-911 in the U.S. and outside the U.S., call 214/669-8888 collect. For MasterCard, call 800/999-0454 and if overseas, call 314/275-6690 collect. (By the way, you should already have a complete, up-to-date list of all your credit cards.) Don't keep all your money or traveler's checks in your wallet, or any one place for that matter; stash some of it in other places for reserve.

If you're going to travel with film, be sure to pack it separately and accessibly so that you can hand it to the security people at airport security or pack it in an lead-lined x-ray film bag. X-rays won't hurt computer disks but the magnetic security devices in walk-through scanners will.

Finally, pack as lightly as possible—it's better for your back and your body.

SIX: USE TRAVEL CHECKLISTS

It's always a good idea to maintain at least one travel checklist of items you always take on a trip. See Figure 12-6 for an example.

Figure 12-6. THE POSITIVELY ORGANIZED!
          TRAVELING OFFICE CHECKLIST

Here are some items to include in your traveling office. Check off the ones that you already have, circle the ones you want to get and add any others that would come in handy:

[] Briefcase
[] Attache case
[] Tote bag
[] Document case
[] Notebook—size:
[] Organizer
[] Calendar/appointment book
[] Telephone/address book
[] Paper—pads, loose sheets, personal or company stationery, business cards—underline any of these items or add what you'll need:

_____

[] Writing tools—pens, pencils, markers:

_____

[] Accessories: tape, scissors, stapler, clips, portable office kit

_____

[] Equipment: pocket calculator, dictaphone, small tape player, portable computer

_____

[] Labeled file folders, file pockets, expansion pockets, plastic folders

_____

[] Stamps, return envelopes, Jiffy envelopes, Express/Federal Express envelopes

_____

[] Work: schedule, agenda, files/info related to business trip, reading material, paperwork, project work

_____

[] Travel materials: itinerary, tickets, legal documents—driver's license, passport, visa, certificate of registration (from U.S. Customs for items such as cameras and watches made in a foreign country); travelers checks, cash, credit cards

_____

[] Any extra conveniences you can think of: _____

_____

In addition, you may want to keep sample packing lists for different types of trips that you will take again. If you have a computer, keep your lists there. Whether you prepare packing lists manually or on computer, group items by category. Some useful categories are:

clothing, personal care, business materials and recreation.

You can even buy a handy checklist that was created by veteran world travelers called Trip Mastr ($2.95) available from Champion Publications, 800/238-4809 or 310/260-5040.

You may want to develop your own special checklist of extra convenience items. For example, "Bill Butler's batch of things to carry" includes: the *OAG Pocket Flight Guide*, a small atlas, a name and address book, a list of restaurants in the major cities you'll be visiting, a digital alarm clock that keeps both current time and home-based time, a pocket calculator, extra shoelaces, a sewing kit and safety pins, aspirin, antacid tablets, foil-wrapped granola bars, a nasal decongestant in case you have to fly with a cold, cough drops, pleasure reading such as a John McDonald or Agatha Christie book and gifts wrapped with yarn instead of ribbon, which tends to become mashed in a suitcase.

Writer David Shaw takes Scotch tape, packing tape, extra glasses and contact lenses, a Swiss army knife, a spot remover, a laptop computer, rope, his own gourmet food (he refuses to eat airline fare), pre-addressed post card labels and a small pocket tool kit with pliers, chisel, hole punch, file, stapler, screwdrivers, measuring tape and scissors.

I bring along lots of dollar bills for tipping and change for phone calls. I also stash pre-moistened towelettes in my carry-on bag to freshen up. I also take along my sleeping pillow (which happens to be small and compact anyway).

Magellan's mail-order travel catalog features such handy items as nylon "hidden pocket" money pouches, inflatable neck pillows for long plane or train rides and emergency dental kits.

Have your doctor write up extra copies of prescriptions you may need while away or in case you lose any medication.

SEVEN: TAKE CARE OF YOURSELF WHEN YOU TRAVEL

To maintain your rhythm and your effectiveness throughout your trip, recognize that as you travel you are subjecting yourself to different demanding environments. Part of staying organized on the road is preparing in advance for the adjustments you and your body may need to make and then following through while on the trip.

Bill Butler says avoid unnecessary travel. "Make sure you need to ake the trip in the first place, that there is no other way you can ossibly accomplish your goal. See if they can come to you. raveling is mean to your body." With all the technology we have vailable, there should be less need to travel.

Butler suggests you avoid overeating and overdrinking. He also uggests drinking bottled water wherever you go. "Just the different hemicals in the water can have an adverse effect."

Don't forget to exercise. Betsy Kovacs suggests running or even imp roping. A jump rope is an easy item to pack, too.

Derrick Crandall keeps his body on Washington, D.C., time. He ever resets his watch (unless he's on an extended trip for a few eeks, several time zones away). "I like to maintain East Coast entality and body time," he says.

Take special care of your body when you fly. Most airlines are amped and uncomfortable, but fortunately, there are steps you can ike to help your body adjust.

Protect yourself against dehydration. When you're on board a etliner you will experience dehydration of body and skin because f the cabin's low humidity. Dehydration leads to weariness.

Be sure to drink enough liquid—one expert recommends one glass f water every hour. Apple juice, cranberry juice or fruit punch are so good. Avoid tea, coffee, alcohol and soft drinks, all of which can ave a diuretic effect.

Bring along lip balm and hand cream to combat cracked lips and ry skin, likely symptoms from exposure to cabin air. Don't forget a ibricant for your eyes, especially if you wear contact lenses.

Order your airline meals ahead of time, if possible. Most airlines ill allow you to order special meals such as fruit and cheese; egetarian plates; low-salt, low-fat, low-cholesterol fare; and special elections for frequent travelers. Ask each airline what kinds of ieals are available one or two days before you fly. Or better yet, lace your order at the time you book your reservation. Remember) avoid high-fat, salty foods, which cause body swelling and etention of fluid.

Keep your body limber and comfortable. There are four steps ou can take.

First, wear comfortable shoes you can slip on and off. Remove iem shortly after takeoff.

Second, to reduce swelling in feet and ankles, elevate your feet. (Body swelling and bloating occur because of an airplane's lower barometric pressure.) Elevating your feet even a few inches really helps; I place my feet on the carry-on case I stash under the seat in front of me.

Third, take short exercise breaks. Frequency of breaks is more important than time duration. Once every one to two hours is ideal. Take walks around the cabin and do simple stretches at your seat. Hold each stretch for 30 to 60 seconds. (You might want to tell your neighbors beforehand what you're doing.)

Fourth, help improve your posture by placing a pillow in the small of your back. The pillow provides extra support and helps you sit up straighter.

"You have to really pace yourself when you travel," says Kovacs. "If you have to wait," she advises, "find a comfortable place, know you're there for the duration and roll with it." If there's a delay at the airport, Kovacs like to go to the airport restaurant to read, work or relax.

In fact, much of pacing yourself is just learning to relax. "Don't get too excited, don't rant and rave," says Welch. "A lot of people create a crisis to be a hero. Don't let anything get to the crisis stage. The whole secret boils down to communication—up, down, sideways. Don't take anything for granted."

What do you do if, after all your planning, your airline cancels your flight? The best course of action, especially if you have a non-refundable fare, is to have the airline place you on the next available flight. If you try to make a new reservation or rebook yourself, you may lose out on your low fare.

If you miss a flight, be sure to call the airline immediately so that all of your other reservations aren't wiped out as well. By the way, if you don't board the plane at least 10 or 15 minutes before takeoff, you stand a chance of having your seat sold to a standby passenger.

There are always options, according to Bill Butler, even if you find yourself next to the little old lady from Des Moines who wants to talk your ear off. "I have a friend who speaks Spanish when she doesn't want to be disturbed. I'm tempted to learn a few words or something myself."

One final suggestion: Believe Murphy's Law next time you're on

e road. Or as Butler says, "You have to anticipate that things
on't be perfect, but most of the time you can organize and
repare."

RESOURCE GUIDE

ORTABLE OFFICE PRODUCTS

ompany addresses and phone numbers are provided unless products
re widely available through office supply dealers. Product prices are
pproximate and may vary.

uto Office Seat Desk by Rubbermaid provides a multi-purpose
ork organizer that combines the best elements of an office desk,
ling cabinet and briefcase and converts a passenger seat into a
esk. The system stores files for instant reference and also has small
orage compartments for office supplies, while oversized items such
s cellular phones, tape recorders, sales catalogs and samples are
oncealed under a secure latch.

More portable office accessories by Rubbermaid, shown in Figure
2-7, let you take your office with you. If you need to write while
n the road, consider the **Storage Clipboard** with a durable clip and
encil holder and a divided inside compartment that stores
otebooks, paper, pens and pencils and can hold a variety of
aperwork and supplies. The **Box Office** is a file/storage box that has
ides inside to accommodate hanging file folders and has a clear
ompartment in the lid to hold pens, pencils, calculator and other
nall office supplies.

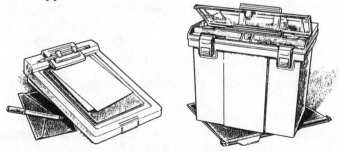

gure 12-7. Rubbermaid Storage Clipboard and Box Office

or a larger number of hanging files, Rubbermaid's **Trunk Tote File**

Box (not shown) is sturdy and lightweight and has a transparent li
for easier viewing of stored contents.

Fellowes Bankers Box Hang 'n' Stor Hanging Folder Storage Bc
is an ideal product for storing and transporting a large number c
letter-size hanging file folders. Plastic channels with a built-in trac
permit the files to glide smoothly. The file has a separate cover, tok
handles and a large labeling area.

Nu-dell Car Clip (Figure 12-8) unobtrusively attaches to car door
visors or dashboards to hold maps, directions, receipts or phon
numbers. Papers can be inserted or removed with one hand. $4.3
for aluminum; $3.18, black plastic. **708/803-4500.** Nu-de
Manufacturing Co., Inc., 2200 E. Devon, Des Plaines, IL 60018

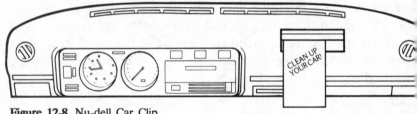

Figure 12-8. Nu-dell Car Clip

Oxford ToteFile is a compact, portable corrugated file that come
with a Pendaflex filing system—10 hanging folders in blue. The fil
box is white with a blue lid that matches the folder color. Also loo
for the **Oxford PortFile** portable file box, which comes in two size
and includes Pendaflex hanging folders, too.

Portable Desk Accessory Kit (Figure 12-9) is a zippered carry-a
that packs 15 tools, including stapler, staple remover, hole puncl
tape dispenser/pencil sharpener, tape, scissors, knife and notepac
$19.95. **800/225-5005** or 610/266-9313. Day-Timers, Inc., PO Bc
27000, Lehigh Valley, PA 18003-9859

Portfolio cases/notebooks are convenient tools to transport a note
taking pad and key documents. Some come equipped with a fla
pocket or special pocket folders, a business card holder, a calculatc
and a pen/pencil strap. Look for portfolios by Hazel and through th
Paper Direct catalog, 800/A-PAPERS. (These portfolios are not t
be confused with the art portfolios discussed in Chapter 5.)

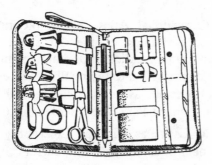

Figure 12-9. Portable Desk Accessory Kit by Day-Timers, Inc.

Rogers Auto Clipboard (Figure 12-10) is a handy note pad and pen for your car that attaches to any smooth, shiny surface (such as your windshield) by means of a suction cup. $5.95

Figure 12-10. Rogers Auto Clipboard

TRAVEL RESOURCE INFORMATION, PRODUCTS AND SERVICES

The Center for Disease Control (the Division of Quarantine in Traveler's Health Section) can provide information on immunization or vaccination when traveling overseas. 404/639-2572 (Atlanta) or visit its Web site: http://www.cdc.gov

Encore Marketing's Short Notice Club is a "last-minute travel club" that requires a charge card number to get information. $36 per year. 800/638-8976

Magellan's is my favorite travel mail-order catalog featuring hundreds of travel accessories. **800/962-4943** or 805/568-5400, PO Box 5485, Santa Barbara, CA 93150-5485

Moment's Notice is a "short-notice" discount travel club that acts as a clearing house for the travel industry's unsold space. Substantial discounts apply to cruises, tours and flights. Membership is $45 per year. 212/486-0500. 425 Madison Ave., New York, NY 10017

Rand McNally Commercial Atlas and Marketing Guide feature detailed and accurate maps of the 50 states, economic data transportation and communication information, population summarie and marketing statistics. Updated annually, each edition costs $395 or $295 if you sign up as a "subscriber." **800/627-2897**. Ran McNally, 8255 N. Central Park Ave., Skokie, IL 60076

State Department Overseas Citizens Emergency Center provide information on health conditions and current epidemics abroad 202/647-5225

State tourist offices for each of the 50 U.S. states are great source of information when you're planning a trip. Many of these office have 800 numbers. These offices are usually located in the capita city of each state and go by many a name. Key words to look for "Department of Commerce," "Convention and Visitors Bureau" an "Office of Travel and Tourism."

HIGH-TECH TRAVEL TOOLS, ACCESSORIES AND SERVICES

AmeriVox is a prepaid calling card providing long distance servic that is much less than telephone company cards, which cost mor per minute and add surcharges on top. You could save up to 5 percent using this card. World Telecom pioneered this prepai calling card technology. **800/784-2946**. 24542 Westhaven, Murrieta CA 92562

City Streets for Windows is a highly-rated electronic mappin program that helps you find locations quickly and easily. More tha 170 metropolitan areas are covered in extensive details, as well a the entire U.S. highway system. More than 50 European cities als are featured. **Win and OS/2** (soon). $99.95. **800/426-7623** or FAX 713/266-4525. Road Scholar Software, 2603 Augusta #100 Houston, TX 77057-5618

ClickBook is an award-winning printing utility that transforms you single-sided Windows or Macintosh files into double-sided booklet and brochures, saving you paper, space, time and money. **Win o Mac**. **800/766-8531** or 415/354-8161. Bookmaker Corp., 2470 E Camino Real, Ste. 108, Palo Alto, CA 94306

Hello Direct is an outstanding catalog of telephone productivity tool vith great service. **800/444-3556** or 408/972-1990. 5884 Eden Park ºl., San Jose, CA 95138-1859

The Magic of Cellular is a wonderful book best described by its ubtitle: "How the Magic of Cellular and Personal Communications Technology Can Help You Manage Your Business and Personal Time, Improve Your Bottom Line and Better Cope with the Stresses ind Strains of Everyday Life." Written by Stuart Crump, the author of several books on cellular phones and the portable office, the book is available for $19.95 (which includes shipping) from Creative Communications Inc., PO Box 1519, Herndon, VA 22070.

Map'n'Go is an award-winning travel planner that combines superb quality maps, unparalleled routing and an enormous database of oads, restaurants, hotels and points of interest throughout the U.S., Canada, Mexico and the Caribbean. It determines your best driving oute, lets you attach your choices for lodging and eating and allows ʼou to print out a detailed Travel Plan map with your highlighted oute, mileage and driving time. It includes a full-size, 128-page road itlas to take along. **CD-ROM for Win.** $49.95. **800/452-5931** or 207/865-1234. DeLorme, PO Box 298, Freeport, ME 04032

North American Official Cellular Users Guide includes maps, oaming usage costs and dialing patterns while traveling in over 350 najor cities in the U.S. and Canada. Annual updates. $20, includes hipping and handling. **313/561-3339.** Cellmark Publishing Company, ºO Box 2619, Dearborn, MI 48123

Pereos is an incredibly compact mass storage product that lets you have all of your information and software with you—no matter where ʼou are. Weighing about 10 ounces, Pereos stores more than a gigabyte of data on a cartridge that's the size of a postage stamp and ittaches to any parallel port on any PC. The base/deck/software is 649 and the cartridge is $28.95 each or two for $49.95. **Win or DOS. 800/328-2779** or 303/545-9500. Datasonix Corp., 5700 Flatiron ºarkway, Boulder, CO 80301

ProComm Plus for Windows is an award-winning program for ntegrated data and fax communications. **Win.** $179. **800/315-3282** or 314/443-3282. Datastorm Technologies, PO Box 1471, Columbia, MO 35205.

Rand McNally's TripMaker is highly-rated, easy-to-use trip planner software. $79.95. **CD-ROM.** 800/627-2897, Rand McNally, 8255 N Central Park Ave., Skokie, IL 60076

Same<>Same is a Windows file transfer utility that makes it eas to transfer files from PC to PC via floppy disks. It allows you t keep file and directories on different computers in sync. **Win.** $2: 619/693-4162. DPM Computer Solutions, 8430-D Summerdale Rd San Diego, CA 92126-5415

Street Atlas USA is a comprehensive award-winning street leve mapping program that offers extraordinary street and road detai You can search by place name, zip code or area code and exchange It's easy to use. (See also DeLorme's other mapping and geographi database products, such as Global Explorer, MapExpert and GP MapKit. **CD-ROM for Win or Mac.** 800/452-5931 or 207/865-1234. DeLorme, PO Box 298, Freeport, ME 04032

Streets on a Disk is road mapping software program that include complete map graphics, search capabilities and an editor. It ca generate travel directions and track moving vehicles. **Win and DO**$ $225 for the base package; County Map files are $95 each. **805/58**$ 1133. Klynas Engineering, PO Box 499, Simi Valley, CA 93062-049'

Voice Organizer is a key-pad-free, palm-size "office on the run" tha stores up to 400 voice-inputted phone numbers for 100 people an up to 99 voice reminders with time lags, so the Organizer beeps t remind you when they're due. It records up to 99 voice memos an sets up your calendar a year in advance. It has a locking securit code that you select. $219.95. **818/905-0950.** Voice Powere Technology, 15260 Ventura Blvd., Ste. 2200, Sherman Oaks, C 91403

WinBEEP Pro is highly-rated wireless messaging software fo transmitting and receiving of text from any Windows PC an supports both pagers and PCMCIA page receiving cards. WinBEE PRO provides extensive modem support with a list of over 30 modems to choose on setup. Features include: message sending t individuals, multiple individuals and user-defined groups; use signature and time stamp; message log with automatic purge; pre scripted messages; recurrent scheduled messages; spell checking; an customizable tool bar. **Win and Net.** $169. **(810) 362-2288.** Fourt Wave Software, Inc., 560 Kirts Blvd., Suite 105, Troy, MI 48084

13

TRAVELING
THE INFORMATION
SUPERHIGHWAY

Quick Scan: If you're interested in finding out more about the Information Superhighway, the Internet, the World Wide Web and getting on-line, this chapter will give you a very introductory look at whether you should explore "cyberspace" in the first place and which tips and tools could help you get started.

Exploring "cyberspace," a term that novelist William Gibson coined in 1982 for the Internet, may either open up a whole new world or a whole new can of worms. As an organizer, a consultant and a writer, I'm both excited and concerned about this new "opportunity" for myself as well as my clients.

If you have a choice, think very carefully before you plunge ahead. Carefully weigh the pros and cons. Let's explore some of them together right now.

On the negative side, get ready for an activity that's going to really gobble up your time and money. You may find it so entertaining that you let some of your higher priority activities slip or choose to communicate at times through cyberspace when it would be more time- or cost-effective to just pick up the phone. If you use the Internet carelessly, you could open yourself to all kinds of problems—from infecting your computer system with a virus that you happen to pick up to a hacker accessing sensitive company information.

On the plus side, you could use it for job listing or hunting, publicity and exposure, "networking" in the sense of expanding your business contacts (including those that are global), increasing your business, expanding customer service, collaboration, problem solving, research, product development and course work. You should have some very clear, compelling reasons to enter the Internet at the outset. Remember, making use of all the information you can tap can become a job in itself and can help you create another case of information overload for yourself.

ACCESSING THE INTERNET

Just in case you missed the definition of the **Internet** in Chapter 11, here it goes again with some amplification. It's a federation of 3.2 million computers in 48,000 networks around the world. It's unlike a network in a company, which feeds in to some central authority; there is no such authority for the Internet. It's an information free for-all that does, however, share, a common transmission language called **Transfer Control Protocol/Internet Protocol**, known as TCP/IP.

The fastest-growing part of the Internet is a subsection called the **World Wide Web** or simply the **Web**, which is a vast network of documents that combine text, images, sound and video, as well as various services, including news and file transfer. (The Web was invented by Tim Berners-Lee in the mid-80s.) Using a program called a **browser** and the **hyperlinks** that connect all the documents and services, you can navigate the Web. Mosaic has been a popular browser but others are replacing it; close to press time, *PC WORLD* selected their favorite "Best Buy" award: Netscape Navigator, which includes state-of-the-art security and excellent navigation tools and is available through Netscape Communications Corp. (415/528-2555).

Look, too, at Quarterdeck Office Systems' brand new Internet suite, Quarterdeck InternetSuite, which includes its own browser called Quarterdeck Mosaic and is a total front-end replacement (310/392-9851).

If you need a lot of access to the Internet, you'll probably need an **Internet provider**–a utility company that maintains hardware and software to connect a network of computers to the Internet.

An Internet provider is more difficult to use for novices or "newbies" than a commercial on-line service such as CompuServe or America Online. You may prefer an on-line service particularly since many are providing more and more access to the Internet.

ON-LINE TIPS AND TOOLS

When evaluating a commercial on-line service, you'll want to consider a number of criteria. If Internet access is vital, check how much access is provided. Select a service with a comfortable, user-friendly "interface." Look at the quality of content. Check out the reputation of a service; talk to users of the service and read reviews if you can. Finally, consider pricing.

If all of your criteria above check out but you're not thrilled with the interface, strongly consider using the service with an alternative **front end program** that you purchase. Look for a front end that has an "off-line reader," which will save you money. Here are some highly regarded front ends for CompuServe: NavCis Pro (Dvorak Development, 800/861-0345); CompuServe Information Manager for Windows, also known as WinCIM (CompuServe, 800/848-8199); CompuServe Information Manager for DOS (CompuServe, 800/848-8199) and CompuServe Information Manager for Macintosh (CompuServe, 800/848-8199). And for Dow Jones you may want the easy-to-use Cypress for Dow Jones News/Retrieval (Trax Software, 800/367-8729). (For more information about CompuServe and Dow Jones, which are considered to be the best on-line services for business users, see their descriptions in the Chapter 11 Resource Guide.)

Here are six ways to save time and money with your on-line service:

1. Find out in advance what services cost on line and what surcharges may apply and identify the most cost-effective times that are feasible for you in your work.
2. Track your monthly usage by the hour. Most front-end software programs will help you do this.
3. Print out directories or indexes from your service in advance to keep keywords, "jumpwords" and "gowords" close at hand to help you get around your service.
4. Avoid, if possible, large downloads, which are costly and tie up your system.
5. Find out what you can do off-line—reading, composing messages, etc.
6. Determine in advance, if you can, the most cost-effective way to get information and to communicate.

Using any on-line service today is still not as straightforward and integrated as it will be one day. Microsoft hopes to change that with its Microsoft Network (MSN), an on-line service that is planned to be part of Windows 95. The idea is to have a single interface that will let the service work seamlessly under the Windows 95 operating system. Also planned is Microsoft's Internet Explorer, which is expected to get you onto the Web quickly and easily. Stay tuned.

If you need someone's e-mail address there are a number of places you can look. If you're on a commercial service, you should be able to look up someone else on the same service—of course that's assuming you know they're on the service in the first place.

For an Internet address you can search The Four11 Online User Directory by e-mail or any Web browser. This is a database with more than 500,000 entries that's easy to use. Send e-mail to **info@four11.com**. Once you enter yourself in the directory, you in turn get unlimited searches via a password (there may be a fee in the future, though, for this service).

Another way to find Internet e-mail addresses is to use the Knowbot Information Service, known as the "knowbot." You e-mail **kis@cnri.reston.va.us** with: **query person's name**. If you're in a hurry you could telnet directly to **info.cnri.reston.va.us 185** and **query person's name**.

RESOURCE GUIDE

Accessing the Internet by E-Mail: Doctor Bob's Guide to Off-Line Internet Access is a 23-page free publication that shows you how to do almost everything in cyberspace using e-mail alone. Send a message to listserv@ubvm.cc.buffalo.edu. Leave the subject blank; the body should say only GET INTERNET BY E-MAIL NETTRAIN F=MAIL. Make a printout for easier use.

Doing Business on the Internet by Mary J. Cronin shows you how successful businesses are using the Internet, how you can track down important business information quickly and how to develop an Internet marketing plan. 350 pages. $29.95

The Instant Internet Guide by Brent Heslop and David Angell is a concise, plain English handbook that covers the basics. $14.95

The New Internet Navigator by Paul Gilster is a well-written and fun-to-read, comprehensive guide for Internet dial-up access. $24.95

The Internet Yellow Pages by Harley Hahn and Rick Stout lists dozens of resources in over 150 categories, a fully-annotated list of Usenet newsgroups and dozens of Internet access providers. 892 pages. $29.95. 800/227-0900.

Quarterdeck InternetSuite offers complete and easy access to the full range of global information and communications facilities through the Internet. **Win.** Below $80. **310/392-9851.** Quarterdeck Office Systems Inc. (California)

Quarterdeck Mosaic assists users in searching the Internet and exploring the Web for information on virtually any subject. You can track all locations visited and organize the information you obtain. You can view multiple Web documents simultaneously and easily store and quickly retrieve current documents. **Win.** Below $30. **310/392-9851.** Quarterdeck Office Systems Inc., 150 Pico Blvd., Santa Monica, CA 90405

VersaTerm is award-winning Internet connectivity software with a toolbar. **Mac.** $195. **800/876-8376.** Synergy Software

The Whole Internet User's Guide & Catalog by Ed Krol is the Internet bible. 574 pages. $24.95

World Wide Web Marketing by Jim Sterne is a brand new book. $25

14

POSITIVELY
ORGANIZED!
IN ACTION

Quick Scan: This is the companion chapter to any other chapters you've read. It's the most important chapter because this is where you commit to action. Discover how to dramatically increase your own level of organization easily and quickly. Learn how to focus on your key areas and goals for improvement in order to increase performance and achievement and become the best you can be.

If you want to be the best, it helps to be Positively Organized! But remember that's *Positively* Organized, not *perfectly* or *compulsively* organized.

I tell my clients, **"Be only as organized as you need to be."** Don't become compulsive or guilty about organization. This is a tool to help you *prevent* stress, not add to it. Organization is not another thing to feel guilty about.

AN ACTION ORIENTATION

Now's the time to act. While organization is a process that evolves over time, you can facilitate this process by taking action and using this book as a springboard for action.

DESIGNING EVOLVING ORGANIZATION SYSTEMS THAT WORK FOR YOU

As you organize, focus on this phrase: "evolving organization systems."

Just as you're working in a time of change, so, too, must your organization systems evolve and change. Be sure to involve anyone who will be affected by a new organization system. If you don't, you will probably encounter great resistance. As support operations manager Stan Morel once said, "People don't like change unless they had something to do with it."

Every organization system you and/or co-workers develop should be a flexible set of tools and work habits for managing one to three of the following resources:

1. Time—planning, scheduling, recording, completing and tracking current and future meetings, appointments, commitments, activities, projects and goals
2. Information—developing productive paperwork and work flow procedures; keeping manual and computerized information accessible and up to date
3. Space—creating a functional and pleasing physical working environment both in the office and on the road.

For many, organizational systems have evolved quite by chance over the years. Your own style and degree of organization will depend on a number of factors—your level of activity, whether you have any support staff, if you deal face to face with the public, how you like to work and the "corporate culture" where you work. It's up to you just how much and what kind of organization you need.

WHERE TO BEGIN

Start small but think big. If you've read more than one chapter, go back to the table of contents and look at the titles of chapters that you've read. Which chapter will make the biggest difference to you and/or others in your career or life?

Now go back to that chapter and skim the headings and subheads, as well as any underlines or notes you made. What jumps out? Find a small change you can make that will make a big difference. It might be changing a work habit or using a new system. Many clients find, for example, that setting aside five minutes a day to plan the next day is helpful. Some clients decide to set up and use a daily paperwork system. Others work together jointly to create or streamline an office system or procedure.

YOUR PLAN OF ACTION

Dare to put your intentions in writing. When you write something down, you're giving a message to your subconscious. Besides reinforcing your subconscious, writing also helps you clarify your thinking so that you're better prepared to take action. Many, if not most people, though, are afraid that if they write something down, they'll forget about it. These people need to combine the act of writing with *reading* and *doing* what has been written. If you make a daily to-do list, for example, *read* it over several times during the day and *do* the listed activities.

Don't be afraid of change. Tropophobia, the fear of change, is the biggest stumbling block to action for most people. Once you accept and *initiate* change in your life, you'll have more control over it.

I have my clients write a **plan of action** at the conclusion of a seminar or consultation. The plan can take a number of different formats—it can be a simple letter to yourself or a prepared form such as the one in Figure 14-1.

Commit to yourself, commit to a deadline. The plan of action is basically a *written commitment to yourself*. Ideally, your first plan should focus on an organizational habit, tool, project or system that can be put into action in a *one- to four-week maximum block of time*. Create an experience of success. Don't overwhelm yourself with a six-month project where you may become discouraged or disinterested.

Be specific. Instead of the general "improving my time management skills," for your project, select something more specific, such as "I will take five minutes to plan and write tomorrow's to-

Figure 14-1.   **PLAN OF ACTION**

Today's Date: _____

Organization Project or Activity:

_____

Benefits or

Results:_____

Ideas/Sketch/Brainstorm:

Action Steps   How long/often?   Calendared?

_____

_____

_____

_____

_____

_____

Rewards_____

_____

Completion Date _____

do list at the end of each day." Instead of cleaning out all your file
cabinets from the last 12 years, complete one file drawer in one
week.

What's in it for you? Besides some hard work, you better be able
to rattle off a whole list of benefits or results you hope to gain.
Better yet, pick the *most important benefit*. Underline and star that
benefit.

Plan step by step. If your project has more than two or three steps try "mind mapping" your steps before you put them in linear order. Mind Mapping is a way to pour out your thoughts and ideas in a visual, picture outline. Once you can "see" your ideas, then you can determine their sequential relationship to one another. (See also Chapter 9 for a discussion of Mind Mapping.)

Make appointments with yourself. Once you've charted out your steps, schedule blocks of time to complete these steps. Schedule appointments with yourself and don't break them! Have calls screened (or let your voice mail take them), go off by yourself where no one can find you or pick a time when you won't be disturbed. Your plan of action should indicate how long steps will take–total time or time per day/week. Then write appointments in your calendar or planner based upon your plan of action projections.

Reward yourself! Make your plan of action more enjoyable by providing any or all of the three main types of rewards–tangible, psychological and experiential. Tangible rewards include physical things you give yourself–new clothes, a deluxe appointment book, a car phone. Psychological rewards are positive messages you tell yourself–stating positive affirmations and giving yourself little "pats on the back." Experiential rewards are a cross between tangible and psychological–getting a massage, taking a trip, dining out in a special restaurant are examples.

Getting others involved in your organization project can be a rewarding process in and of itself. Whether you engage a "buddy" who will offer positive reinforcement or you actually share the work with another, you will more likely increase your accountability and success rate as well as lighten your load. Encourage others to support you in your goals and do the same for them.

HOW TO CHANGE HABITS

Getting more organized almost always involves habit-changing behavior. But don't worry, it doesn't take a lifetime to change a habit. Actually it takes 21 to 30 days, provided you do the following:

1. Decide what new habit or behavior you intend to practice.
2. Write it down on paper. List *how, when* and *why* you're going to do it.
3. Share your new habit with someone else.

4. Reward yourself. Psychological affirmations before, during and after you practice a behavior can be particularly helpful.

5. Practice, practice, practice. You need to repeat the behavior, preferably every day, to create the habit.

COMMITMENT TO BE THE BEST

You will succeed with your plan of action and habit changes only if you are truly committed to being the best.

But what does being the best mean? For some, it's beating out the competition. For others, it's "doing your best"–being in competition with yourself.

It's fine tuning what you're already good at. Award-winning athletes, such as world champion whitewater canoeist Jon Lugbill, are always fine tuning, looking for a better way. See if you can relate Lugbill's whitewater canoeing description to your work or life:

> I love the sport and I love being good at it. The challenge is that you constantly have to search out all the little advantages: techniques in the boat, types of boats, what you eat, how much sleep you get, everything down the line–you've got to learn to get the most out of everything you can. The combination of physical and mental goals, that's what's exciting about the sport for me.

How about being the best human being you can be? When all is said and done, isn't that what *really* counts?

Define it for yourself. After all, the way you live your life makes a statement about you–why not make the best statement?

According to Dr. David Viscott, author and psychiatrist, we each have at least one special gift to give the world. I agree that your gifts should extend beyond yourself in some way to make a better world. What are your gifts and how are you making the *best* of them?

Being Positively Organized! will help you *use* those gifts so you can indeed be the best.

A PERSONAL NOTE

FROM THE AUTHOR

I want to hear from you. Please write me in care of Adams-Hall Publishing with your results from this book as well as any comments or suggestions for future editions. You, too, could be in print! (There's a simple, quick 'n easy communication box on the next page.)

Upcoming editions of *Organized to be the Best!* will feature your contributions and keep you up to date on the latest organizational tools and techniques. You'll see how others are dealing with the challenges we all face. What's more, you'll be part of an ongoing process that's on the cutting edge of quality, performance and achievement.

You can also be a part of that process even more directly. Work with me through a personal consultation or a customized training program designed to produce positive results in a minimum amount of time. I work with individuals, offices, companies and professional organizations. My bio is on the next page.

AUTHOR BIO

Author **Susan Silver** is a nationally recognized author, speaker and organizing expert who directs the Los Angeles, California, firm **Positively Organized!** Susan helps clients enhance personal productivity, improve office management and streamline day-to-day business operations.

Susan designs and conducts training programs for corporations and other professional organizations. Her private practice includes individuals in a variety of fields and professions.

Susan blends more than a decade of experience as a management consultant, manager, educator, writer and entrepreneur. A recognized expert on organization, she frequently appears in the media. She is past president of the Los Angeles Chapter of NAPO—the National Association of Professional Organizers.

Susan shows professionals easy, effective ways to manage time, track projects and activities, use personal computers, organize work space, simplify paperwork, maximize filing and information systems, improve communications and teamwork and achieve goals.

Here's a simple, Positively Organized! way to communicate with Susan or to get your ideas in print for the fourth edition of her award-winning book. Make a photocopy of this page, complete the box and mail it to her c/o Adams-Hall Publishing, PO Box 491002, Los Angeles, CA 90049. (Their toll-free number is 1/800/888-4452.)

HERE'S WHAT I THINK, SUSAN.....

1. This is what I liked about the book:

2. Next time include:

3. I'm interested in (check all that apply):
   ☐ an individual consultation
   ☐ Positively Organized! consulting/training programs
   ☐ purchasing multiple copies of the book at a discount

PLEASE ATTACH YOUR BUSINESS CARD.

INDEX

*Quick Notes: Assume that all products listed in the index and the book are trademarks and/or registered trademarks of the companies manufacturing the products. Numbers in **boldface** indicate an illustration or chart. Names in parentheses are company names, which are included in that way if only one product from the company is listed in the index. Companies with two or more products in this book will have a separate listing by company.*

A

Order Form

(Photocopy this page)

Are you a baby boomer thinking of retiring some day?
Are you related to one? If so, order a copy of

BABY BOOMER RETIREMENT:
65 Simple Ways to Protect Your Future (224 pages)

	Qty.	Total
Softcover: $9.95 plus $1.05 s/h = **$11 per book**	___	$_____
Sales tax for **California residents** 82¢ per book		$_____

Planning for beyond retirement? Look at

A PARENT'S (AND GRANDPARENTS') GUIDE
TO WILLS & TRUSTS (256 pages)

	Qty.	Total
Softcover: $11.95 plus $1.05 s/h = **$13 per book**	___	$_____
Sales tax for **California residents** 99¢ per book		$_____
TOTAL order		$_____

(FOR QUANTITY DISCOUNTS, CALL 1/800-888-4452)

PAYMENT PREFERENCE:

By check, payable to Adams-Hall Publishing or

By credit card: Visa ___   MasterCard ___

ACCOUNT #:_____ EXPIRATION DATE:_____

NAME ON CARD:_____

(PLEASE PRINT CLEARLY)

SIGNATURE:_____

PLEASE PRINT MAILING INFORMATION:

YOUR NAME_____

MAILING ADDRESS_____

CITY/STATE/ZIP_____

DAYTIME TELEPHONE (___) _____

Mail to: Adams-Hall Publishing, PO Box 491002, Dept. OF, Los
Angeles, CA 90049 or call 1/800-888-4452 or 310/826-1851

Order Form
(Photocopy this page)

Are you a baby boomer thinking of retiring some day?
Are you related to one? If so, order a copy of

BABY BOOMER RETIREMENT:
65 Simple Ways to Protect Your Future (224 pages)

	Qty.	Total
Softcover: $9.95 plus $1.05 s/h = **$11 per book**	___	$____
Sales tax for **California residents** 82¢ per book		$____

Planning for beyond retirement? Look at

A PARENT'S (AND GRANDPARENTS') GUIDE
TO WILLS & TRUSTS (256 pages)

	Qty.	Total
Softcover: $11.95 plus $1.05 s/h = **$13 per book**	___	$____
Sales tax for **California residents** 99¢ per book		$____
TOTAL order		$____

(FOR QUANTITY DISCOUNTS, CALL 1/800-888-4452)

PAYMENT PREFERENCE:
By check, payable to Adams-Hall Publishing or
By credit card: Visa ___   MasterCard ___

ACCOUNT #:_____   EXPIRATION DATE:_____
NAME ON CARD:_____
(PLEASE PRINT CLEARLY)

SIGNATURE:_____

PLEASE PRINT MAILING INFORMATION:
YOUR NAME_____
MAILING ADDRESS_____
CITY/STATE/ZIP_____
DAYTIME TELEPHONE (___) _____

Mail to: Adams-Hall Publishing, PO Box 491002, Dept. OF, Los Angeles, CA 90049 or call 1/800-888-4452 or 310/826-1851